n*e*

Leeds Playhouse; A Tale of Two Theatres

Dave's love of theatre started as a child, being taken to the theatre by his parents. This love has continued ever since. Throughout his career as a teacher and youth worker, Dave organized countless theatre trips for children and young people, sharing his enthusiasm and inspiring the next generation of theatre lovers.

Dave started to regularly write articles for national youth work journals. Later as a human rights observer in Palestine/Israel he wrote extensively about his experiences there.

Dave combines his love for writing and theatre to craft a meticulously researched history of the Leeds Playhouse. Drawing from both thorough research and personal observations, he provides a comprehensive account of the theatre's evolution. This book is not just a valuable resource for theatre scholars but also an engaging narrative that will captivate anyone interested in the development of the arts in Leeds and West Yorkshire. Dave's engaging style ensures that this history is accessible and intriguing, offering a vivid portrayal of one of Yorkshire's most cherished cultural institutions.

Leeds Playhouse

A Tale of Two Theatres

Dave Stannard

Naked Eye Publishing

Book design, typesetting and front cover by Naked Eye

Cover photograph: Tim Smith

ISBN: 9781910981306

This book was produced with the assistance of
Leeds Philosophical and Literary Society.

nakedeyepublishing.co.uk

Credits

With thanks to Leeds City Council, Gordon Hodgson, Simon Warner, Donald Cooper, Photostage and Tim Smith for the photographs.

Thanks also to Leeds Philosophical and Literary Society for their support.

Contents

Act II

Act II

Photographs

Forward and Acknowledgements

My first memory of going to the theatre was when, as a boy, I queued up with my parents outside the New (now Noel Coward) Theatre in London's West End. We were there to see *Oliver!* – over sixty years before the recent Leeds Playhouse production. As a teenager, living just outside London, I regularly went 'up to town' to see plays at the Old Vic, which at the time was the home of the National Theatre. I bought tickets for one shilling and six pence (7½ pence today!) 'up in the gods' from where I saw plays performed by Laurence Olivier and many other theatrical giants. I never wanted to be an actor, but do remember playing the part of a Tower of London beefeater in a school play – alongside 'celebrity' Russell Grant!

After school, I worked, in the West Midlands, with young people, both as a teacher and a youth worker. On many occasions I organised trips to the Birmingham Rep. and elsewhere, perhaps trying to share my love of theatre. Amongst many memories, I remember one young woman's surprise, when going to see a play about women workers in the local munitions factories, during World War II. She was surprised that the play had songs and was funny, and also that audience members did not 'dress up posh' to be there.

As a youth worker, I regularly wrote articles for national youth work journals. After retirement, I spent time as a human rights observer in Palestine / Israel and wrote about my experiences there. Four years ago, I decided to combine my love of writing and theatre; if everybody has one book inside them, you are holding it.

Early on, I interviewed Doreen Newlyn, who, by then aged 96 years, remembered campaigning for a repertory theatre in Leeds as if it were yesterday. Later, I interviewed Bernard Atha, also so important in the Playhouse's history. Sadly, neither will see this book finally published.

Lots of other people gave of their time, and expressed enthusiasm for this book. In particular, I should like to thank

Kathy Webster for all her help. She became involved with Leeds Playhouse in July 1970, agreeing to be the Senior Receptionist just for a month or two. Twenty-five years later she took retirement, but continued as a volunteer at the Playhouse until 2018! As the book evolved, Kathy read each section with a magnifying glass – both metaphorically and literally! Her comments and corrections have been invaluable.

Kathy organised for all the Playhouse archives to be transferred to the Special Collections Research Centre at Leeds University Brotherton Library. Without this, the book would have been impossible to write. My thanks go to the staff there, who patiently satisfied my requests. I must also thank my friend Mel Marchant who, like Kathy, read and commented on every draft, and helped with the structure of the book.

Finally, a big thank you to Mike Kilyon and Sue Vickerman at Naked Eye Publishing for all their hard work and enthusiasm for this project.

Dave Stannard
April 2024

Leeds Playhouse
A Tale of Two Theatres

Cast of Directors

BILL HAYS

Bill Hays, aged 31 on appointment, was born in County Durham. He had previously worked as a director in both television (Z *Cars*, *The Wednesday Play* etc) and theatre. He had also established, in 1960, the Living Theatre in Leicester. This consisted of a group of actors, led by Bill but also including Ken Loach, who pooled their savings to create a theatre space within St. Nicholas School Rooms. They presented plays on a fortnightly basis until January 1963 when the building was demolished. Bill directed as well as acted in productions, which included Arnold Wesker's *Roots* and *Chips with Everything*, Anne Jellicoe's *The Knack*, all plays which either originated in or transferred to the Royal Court Theatre in London, a theatre which specialised in the work of new, often left-wing writers. In Alan Strachan's The Independent obituary (Bill died in 2006), he describes Living Theatre as "an adventurous radical group". Bill was appointed as artistic director at the Leeds Playhouse in 1970.

JOHN HARRISON

As a teenager John Harrison joined the Birmingham Rep Theatre School, but in 1944 was taken out of the School to become a member of the theatre company. At this time, Paul Scofield was also in the company, and Peter Brook, aged just 19, was brought in as a director. Two years later Barry Jackson, the Rep's director, was then appointed director of the Shakespeare Festival in Stratford, and took with him several members of the company including John, Paul and Peter. Donald Sinden was also a member of the company.

Deciding in 1951 to give up acting and become a director, John was appointed at the age of 27 as Director of Productions at the Nottingham Playhouse, where he stayed for more than five years. After Nottingham John did live television drama work, but was invited back to the Birmingham Rep to direct a production of Oliver Goldsmith's *She Stoops To Conquer*, the cast of which included Derek Jacobi. After two more productions and following the death of Sir Barry Jackson, in 1961 he was invited to become Artistic Director. His return to Birmingham lasted five years; then in 1972 John was appointed at the Leeds Playhouse.

JUDE KELLY

After graduating in 1975, Jude founded a touring company, Solent People's Theatre. Between 1980 and 1985, she was artistic director of the Battersea Arts Centre in London. She directed plays for the Royal Shakespeare Theatre both in Stratford and London. In 1988 she was the Director for York Festival & Mystery Plays. She began work at the Playhouse in 1989, a year prior to the opening of the West Yorkshire Playhouse.

IAN BROWN

Between 1984 and 1988 Ian had been the Artistic Director of the TAG Theatre Company (Theatre About Glasgow). He was then the artistic and executive director at the Traverse Theatre in Edinburgh from 1988 to 1996. He was an associate director at the West Yorkshire Playhouse, prior to his 2002 appointment as Artistic Director.

JAMES BRINING

James was born and grew up in Leeds. He attended Leeds Grammar School before leaving for Cambridge University – just as the West Yorkshire Playhouse opened. It was at Cambridge that he got involved in theatre, and after graduating moved to Newcastle to set up a theatre company, taking plays to working men's clubs in the city. After this, he worked at the Orange Tree Theatre in Richmond, London, as a trainee director. Then, like Ian Brown, he became Artistic Director with TAG Theatre Company in Glasgow, touring productions for young people. Staying in Scotland, James was appointed as the Artistic Director at the Dundee Repertory Theatre in 2003, where he stayed for over nine years before returning to Leeds and the Playhouse.

Act I

Scenario

THE SOMEWHAT UNLIKELY SETTING FOR ACT I is a building, externally identical to the adjacent sports hall, at the edge of Leeds University campus on Calverley Street, a mile or so north of the Town Hall. This is the first Leeds Playhouse, which opens on 17th September 1970.

But the tale really begins in 1964 when a group of idealists start a campaign for "a new theatre, architecturally exciting, administered on a non-profit distributing basis, with a residential professional company of the highest quality, and a first-class director. We want to see, the year round, a varied repertory of plays, available at prices that are within the means of all sections of the community."[1]

First, a site has to be found, and this alone takes three years. The newly formed Theatre Planning Committee considers two possibilities: a piece of land to build on, or an existing building suitable for conversion. Many of the disused cinemas in the city are considered, along with religious buildings, factories and warehouses. Formal negotiations are started with the owners of two cinemas: the Shaftesbury on York Road and the Dominion in Chapel Allerton. The possibility of the Shaftesbury is taken very seriously, with plans being drawn up and costs estimated, but it comes to nothing when the leaseholder withdraws their offer. Similarly, no progress is made with the Dominion – which is eventually sold to MECCA for a bingo hall. At one point the committee even considers a new developer-owned and unused theatre in Bradford as a temporary home until a building in

Leeds materialises. Time is also wasted in pursuit of a possibility raised in 1965 by the City Council, of building a concert hall to which a theatre could be added, creating more of an arts centre. But many months of meetings about this idea get the Theatre Planning Committee nowhere. Indeed, to this day the city of Leeds does not have a concert hall.

At the end of November 1967 a real possibility is at last found. Leeds University has planned two sports halls, using their land on Calverley Street, and housing has been demolished for this purpose. However, funding difficulties have meant that only one of the sports halls has been built. The University's proposal is that the Playhouse can have rent-free use of the land if they pay the cost of building a shell similar to that of the existing sports hall, which they will then sell to the University after ten years. For this period, the Committee may install a temporary theatre, the internal structure of which can eventually move elsewhere.

Regarding this structure, the Planning Committee has already thrashed out its decisions about the most appropriate design for the auditorium, and top priority is an open stage:

"The city already has an outstanding example of the traditional stage and auditorium in the Grand Theatre. There is no point in duplicating the Grand on a smaller scale.

"To combine in a high degree the advantages of an open stage with the possibility of meeting effectively the needs of plays written for a proscenium theatre, we are satisfied that the primary need for good sight lines, good conditions for hearing, and a comfortable seating-space, could be met for an audience of about six hundred and fifty to eight hundred people. A good relationship of actors and audience would be assured by the disposition of the seating and by the fact that the furthest seats would be within approximately fifty feet of the stage. Audience and actors would be under a common ceiling ... without the disadvantages inherent in an oblong auditorium. There would be no pillars and no balcony."[2]

This particular auditorium design has evolved due to visits made to repertory theatres in England, but also owing to visits to theatres in Canada, USA, Australia and South Africa made by one of the Committee members, John Wood. Specifically, the design is adapted from a small theatre in Western Springs, a Chicago suburb.

Attracting grants from national and local government funds, as well as trust organisations, will be crucial to the success of the campaign. The Arts Council demonstrates their commitment to the Leeds Playhouse by promising a grant of £45,000, and other grants come in from the Calouste Gulbenkian Foundation (£17,400), The Pilgrim Trust (£5,000) and the Yorkshire Arts Association (£1,050). Less successful are attempts at attracting grants and donations from local business and industry; furthermore, the campaign group continues to experience a reluctance by the City Council to support the project. In the Leeds University Review in June 1968, Barbara Barber writes:

"We have been made painfully aware that the City Council is, to say the least, not working enthusiastically to promote this joint project. Two thousand citizens paying to become campaign supporters and over twenty thousand people signing the Theatre Campaign petition have produced as yet little sign of the goodwill of the Council beyond the writing of 'Concert and Theatre' on the redevelopment plan – in pencil!"[3]

The estimated cost of this temporary theatre is £150,000. Much fundraising takes place, but it is only when Leeds City Council, early in 1969, announces a promise of £25,000 in capital funding, as well as an annual revenue commitment of £5,000, that the dream of a Leeds Playhouse starts to become a reality.

By way of comparison, when the decision is made to build a new theatre in Sheffield in 1966, the total cost is estimated at £5-600,000. Sheffield Corporation agrees to fund half of the cost, and the Arts Council one third – leaving public fund-raising to find the remaining sixteen and a half percent. (When the

Crucible Theatre opens a year after the Playhouse, in late 1971, the total cost is £884,000.)[4]

The newly formed 'Leeds Theatre Trust' now needs to take some bold actions. First is to sign the contract with Leeds University, which needs proof that, at the very least, the shell of the building can be afforded – only possible once the City Council grant has been received. Next, following invitations to tender, is the signing of the building contract on the 20th September 1969 The contract has been given to Robert R. Roberts, a local company. Just five days later, a stone laying ceremony is held, performed by the Lord Mayor. This is seen by the Planning group as a symbol of their partnership with the City. The interior plans for the theatre have been drawn up by Bill Houghton-Evans, a local architect with twenty years of experience in public building design who has been a member of the Theatre Planning Committee for several years. Because of the requirements of the University in respect of the building's shell, Bill describes it as "rather like being presented with a packing crate and asked to design the contents to suit". Nevertheless the agreed design for the auditorium, with its steep rake, helps considerably: it provides space underneath for the foyer at ground level, and for the bar and restaurant on the first floor. Theatregoers will be able to enter the auditorium either at ground level or from the first floor. One arguably positive consequence of this design is that it does not allow for a stage door. Consequently, actors and audiences will enter in the same way, meaning, after the performance, they may well come together socially in the bar.

The limitations of the building's shell do, however, restrict space for all the aspects of the Playhouse's work. Consequently when the theatre opens, it immediately becomes necessary to rent parts of the disused Gaumont Cinema building (formerly the Coliseum Theatre) on Cookridge Street, to use as office and rehearsal space, for storage, as a second box office, and for Theatre In Education workshops.

In the ensuing years the work of the Playhouse spreads over six buildings, also using the Grand Theatre's workshop space for scenery construction. This is far from ideal because everything built has to be of a size that will fit into that theatre's lifts. Elsewhere, the wardrobe hire department is at Stansfield Chambers, and offices are in cabins on the car park. Additionally, the Theatre In Education team moves, in 1975, from the Gaumont to Quarry Hill School.

The other limitation of the building concerns its location. The distance from the city centre is one problem, so early on, a transfer service from the central bus station is introduced, leaving about thirty minutes before the performance time and returning five minutes after the end of the play. The cost is just three pence each way.

Another limitation is the size of the auditorium. The space is too big for smaller, more intimate productions, and for lunchtime and late evening ones. To overcome this problem, from 1976 the Artistic Director devises a method of occasionally converting the seven hundred and fifty-seater space into a 'studio' with a capacity of two hundred and thirty-five, by means of large screens placed along the first horizontal gangway, hiding the seats behind.

ACT I

ACT ONE, SCENE ONE

When the Leeds Playhouse reopened after refurbishment in 2019, a display board announced:

> *"The new Playhouse building belongs to the people of Leeds and beyond. Every brick, every tile, every nail is yours."*

To what extent can local people and communities be involved in the planning and building of a new theatre? Can their involvement be more than consultation? Is it really possible for it to belong to them; can there really be a sense of ownership?

THE COURTROOM TRIAL
5th May 1968

THIS OPENING SCENE TAKES PLACE not in the Leeds Playhouse but two years earlier at Leeds Town Hall. The Sunday afternoon event was cleverly promoted as a Courtroom Trial:

"The Leeds Theatre Campaign will answer to a mock public indictment. That (it), contrary to public interest has, over the past four years, conducted a conspiracy, which threatens to succeed, for the purpose of establishing a professional repertory theatre in Leeds."[5]

Even cleverer, the speakers for the defence were an all-star line-up, including actor Peter O'Toole, the academic Richard Hoggart, and playwright Keith Waterhouse, who all grew up in the Hunslet area of Leeds. Also speaking was John Neville who had until recently been Artistic Director of the Nottingham Playhouse. Also present was playwright Henry Livings. A report in the next day's Guardian newspaper included a photograph: a full house in a venue that can seat 1550 people!

Doreen Newlyn, in her book *Theatre Connections*, includes a wonderful account, particularly enthusing about the speech by Keith Waterhouse, who had stated with passion at a previous supporters' meeting back in 1965 that "a city without a theatre is a city without a heart". This time his rage was directed at the negativity of Yorkshire Post's drama critic Desmond Pratt, accusing Pratt of holding the view that Leeds's people are 'too thick and stupid' to warrant having a theatre built for them, and that they had too recently 'crawled out of the clay' to be ready for the same things as the people of other towns and cities. Waterhouse's retort was, "It isn't really essential that Leeds should have anything more than a gigantic factory site: provided, of course, that you happen to own one of the factories."[6] His subsequent tongue-in-cheek listing of other 'non-essentials' – libraries, art galleries, and museums – brought the house down.

Doreen Newlyn and her husband Walter had in fact been the instigators of a meeting back in March 1964, held in their living room, to talk about the idea of a playhouse in Leeds. Several of the city's theatres had closed down, leaving just two professional ones: the Grand and the City Varieties. There was also the Civic Theatre, but this was a venue for amateur productions, while the Grand was a 'receiving' venue for productions touring the country. The City Varieties concentrated on, as its full name suggests, Music Hall, variety (plus a Christmas panto).

The Newlyns were passionate about theatre, often taking their young daughters on Saturday trips to venues elsewhere in the north of England, all of which had one thing in common: they were repertory ones. The playhouses in Sheffield and Nottingham, the Library Theatre in Manchester and the Royal in York all had resident companies of actors performing seasons of several plays. This is exactly the kind of theatre that the Newlyns and the others at that meeting wanted for Leeds. Most of the thirteen attendees had connections with the university: four students, four lecturers, the rest being mostly teachers elsewhere, and all had some involvement in amateur dramatics. The four students were members of the Student Theatre Group; others were involved in the University Staff Dramatic Society.

Those at that meeting felt that the next move should be to put pressure on the City Council to establish such a theatre, given that other repertory ones in the north were council-established. The first decision, therefore, was to formalise themselves as a committee with a chairman and secretary (Doreen – the only one with a typewriter – becoming the latter) and they decided to attract supporters by way of a letter for publication in the Yorkshire Post.

Events moved more quickly than expected when a Post reporter decided to run the story and requested further information. A hurriedly written policy statement was produced, and an exaggerated number of existing supporters was given (150, not 13!). Thus the committee members set about recruitment. Luckily, the newspaper coverage attracted some significant and influential local people. Duly encouraged, a more formal meeting was arranged a month later at the Swarthmore Education Centre, not far from the city centre.

In between meetings, it became apparent to committee members that Leeds City Council was not particularly interested. Consequently the committee became less of a pressure group, more a campaign proper. So the next stage was the formation of a Theatre Planning Committee. The following years were mostly spent trying to find a site for such a theatre. This took three years to achieve, but remember that this was not the work of the local authority, it was that of a group of volunteers, mostly working full-time and supporting young families.

Once the site on Calverley Street became a possibility, the next move was a petition urging the City Council to help in establishing this professional repertory theatre in Leeds. The target was 10,000 signatures but by the time of its submission to the Council in March 1968 this number had reached 21,568. Another public meeting quickly followed, appropriately held in the existing sports hall on the university site, the guest speaker being none other than West Yorkshire playwright Stan Barstow.

Clearly, the Planning Committee members were well-equipped with the necessary knowledge and campaigning skills, as well as a belief that they could make the theatre happen. As one wrote later (1968), "We are not really a bunch of starry-eyed amateurs, but a team of experts covering many fields and united by a common enthusiasm and purpose."[7] They were also well able to attract the support of actors, writers and directors: nationally known names who would play a significant part in the rest of the campaign – and thus the Courtroom Trial came about.

Buoyed by the success of the Town Hall event, the priority over the next two years was fund-raising. In this time, several high-profile events were organised, making use of actors, writers and directors already committed to supporting the Leeds Playhouse. These included, in 1968, *A Choice of Valentines* devised by Patrick Garland and performed by Diana Rigg and Paul Hardwick, held at Leeds Grammar School, and a 'champagne evening' with Keith Waterhouse. The following year's events included an evening of excerpts from *The Northern Drift*, a programme of new northern writing, with Alex Glasgow and Henry Livings; also, *Michael Hordern Entertains*, held at the Civic Centre.

The harder work, however, involved campaign supporters speaking to local groups or organising fund-raising coffee mornings and parties in their own homes. These events were a chance, for example, to 'sell' bricks and seats in the future Leeds Playhouse. Other similar work was organised through the formation of a Playhouse Club. The first Annual General Meeting was held in September 1968, its initial constitutional priority being "To assist in raising funds for the building of the theatre". A further strand of fund-raising took place in local schools.

But it was only when Leeds City Council did commit to capital and revenue funding (as mentioned earlier) that plans for the Playhouse could go ahead. At this point, £110,000 had been raised in gifts or promises, leaving £40,000 still to be found. So, when building work began, fund-raising was even more crucial. Perhaps because the Playhouse building was becoming a physical reality, the newly formed Leeds Theatre Trust was more successful in attracting the support of local businesses. A consortium of firms was established with each member donating at least £1,000. With still not enough raised to cover the cost of the work already begun, the consortium member The Yorkshire Bank thankfully came to the rescue, offering overdraft facilities. The work could now be completed in time for the planned September 1970 opening.

And so it was that the first Leeds Playhouse opened on September 17th 1970, over six years after that first meeting in Doreen and Walter Newlyn's living room. Fifty years later Doreen recalled with delight an event at the theatre prior to the official opening:

"To see that place filled with children from all over Leeds, it was just unbelievable, it was everything I'd dreamed of".[8]

Of the many messages sent by northern writers on the official opening day, perhaps the wittiest was from Keith Waterhouse:

"As the bitchy actress cabled to her friend who'd just emerged from one of the longest pregnancies on record – 'Congratulations. Knew you had it in you!' The infant has been christened and is about to be baptised. May its lusty cries keep us all awake, and may its half-million godparents watch it grow to maturity with the same concern and devotion as Yours Sincerely, Keith Waterhouse."

And among the messages of support from actors was one from Michael Horden:

"Many happy returns of the day. May you speedily grow. May you delight, disturb, provoke, please, shock and entertain but never, never, never bore".

And Michael's P.S. – "May you offer me a job some day."

ACT ONE, SCENE TWO

For every artistic director, the choice for their first production can be seen as a statement of intent. When the theatre is also new, the opening production assumes even more importance. Will their choice indicate the kind of audience the theatre hopes to attract?

SIMON SAYS! by Alan Plater
17th September 1970

AT THE GALA OPENING OF THE LEEDS PLAYHOUSE, the very first actor to set foot on the stage was Tony Robinson. Over fifty years later he still remembers that day:

"[I] walked on stage to be greeted by a deafening round of applause – something that has never happened to me with that degree of excitement at any time since! And, of course, at first I thought it was for me. Then I realised it was down to the absolute sense of relief that all these people had, because a show was finally open in their theatre".[9]Tony Robinson was playing the title role in *Simon Says!*, a new play specially written for the Leeds Playhouse by Alan Plater. The production was directed by the theatre's first artistic director, Bill Hays. This post had been advertised nationally in The Stage, Guardian, and Daily Telegraph. Astonishingly sixty-five applications were received, with six being shortlisted. After two rounds of interviews Bill Hays was appointed, his annual salary for the first year £2,500, commencing on 1 June 1970. To involve him as early as possible he was additionally appointed on half-salary for the prior four months.

The appointment of Bill Hays reflected the kind of theatre envisaged by the original campaign group and in turn the Theatre Planning Committee. Remembering him over fifty years later, Doreen Newlyn says:

"Bill Hays was utterly wonderful. He took on board the whole feeling that we all had of what we wanted the theatre to be: a people's theatre."[10]

After his work at the Living Theatre and prior to his appointment at the Playhouse, Bill Hays had engaged in some freelance theatre directing. Contact with Alan Plater (who like Bill had worked as a writer for *Z Cars*) resulted in a meeting, also attended by songwriter Alex Glasgow, which in turn led to

Bill directing Alan Plater's perhaps most successful play for theatre, *Close the Coalhouse Door*.

This play tells the story of one particular family living near the pithead of a disused coal-mine, as a way of recording the history of the mining industry over the previous hundred years. The play uses comedy, satire and music, at times in a music-hall style. Always, the history is told from the point of view of workers: their fight for better pay and safety conditions, and the reality for them of nationalisation. Plater accepted the one-sidedness of the play:

"We set off with inbuilt attitudes towards the subject and the stated aim of creating 'an unqualified hymn of praise to the miners who created a revolutionary weapon without having revolutionary intention'. We selected those areas of history which confirmed our attitudes…".[11]

Close the Coalhouse Door was written for the Newcastle Playhouse, where it opened on 9th April 1968. It was a big success and was revived the next year before touring to Nottingham, Glasgow, Liverpool and Birmingham. The production also transferred to the Fortune Theatre in London with less success, and before returning to Newcastle came to the Grand Theatre in Leeds (18th – 23rd March 1969).

The social significance and success of *Close the Coalhouse Door* perhaps explains why Bill Hays approached Alan Plater and Alex Glasgow to write the opening production for the Leeds Playhouse. Initially titled *Simple Simon's Revenge*, *Simon Says!* is in many ways a companion piece. Both use music and comedy to tackle serious themes. However, *Simon Says!* uses a broader range of comedic styles: pantomime (Cinderella makes an appearance, and there is the equivalent of a 'he's behind you' routine); farce (trouser-dropping); running gags, and music-hall songs, with which the audience are invited to join in.

Perhaps the major difference between the two plays relates to their focus. *Close the Coalhouse Door* was specifically about governmental betrayal of the mining industry, *Simon Says!* was more generally an attack on the Establishment. The story may be mainly about the M.C.C. (Marylebone Cricket Club, then the governing body of the national team) but here its members simply represent the ruling classes. This was made clear in Alan Plater's notes to Bill Hays:

"The play is about the growth of revolution, the attempt at revolution, the outcome of revolution, in the context of the English Establishment".[12]

If this makes the play sound heavy-going, it is anything but: Alan Plater was clear that "the whole show should be played continuous with bags of 'go' ... It's got to be fluid and fast-moving, wild and anarchic"[13] – and the script is indeed riotous and funny.

So what went wrong? This should have been the perfect play to open the theatre. It certainly fitted with Bill Hays' intention to "leave intimate drama to the little box and kick his audience in the stomach – politically and emotionally – with big, colourful, amazing theatre."[14] But the day after the opening night, *Simon Says!* hit the headlines for all the wrong reasons. The Conservative MP for Pudsey, Joseph Hiley, must indeed have felt kicked in the stomach, because he walked out of the performance, explaining later, "I could not stand any more of it. As well as being utterly boring, it was vulgar ... it is a disgrace to the city. It is a dreadful start for something that has been hailed as a great achievement. I have never seen anything so dreadful before".[15]

Simon Says! was never published or produced by any other theatre, so it is useful here to summarize what the play is about. It follows the journey of Simon from his village, presumably somewhere in the north of England, to London, where the setting is the Long Room at Lords Cricket Ground, the home of the M.C.C. The main character in these scenes is 'Lord Thing', the Chairman of the Board (who, in his eighties, is also the cricket captain!), a target of ridicule throughout the play. Through events along the way, Simon develops from being 'simple' to politically aware and active. Ultimately he is on a mission (an Alan Plater note: "Simon is dressed as Fidel Whittington"):

"It's my destiny to cleanse the world of evil, to take up the banner and the sword so that we can build a new land where men can be free ... And in this land, every baby that's born gets a chance, not just them born in Richmond or Harrogate or Windsor ... but them born in Dewsbury or the Rhondda Valley or Consett ... equal chances all round".[16]

On arrival at Lords and meeting Lord Thing, Simon announces his takeover as England captain and introduces his own team (Alan Plater also notes, "the team should contain many contrasting elements – sort of a cross between Che's guerrillas and Robin Hood's merry men. But there must be real, identifiable elements within the group ... a miner or ship worker, for example..."). Simon explains that his team has already taken over clubs of privilege, the police, the House of Lords.

What follows is the scene which caused much controversy. Lord Thing, now wheelchair-bound, is blindfolded with his M.C.C. tie, placed against a screen painted as a brick wall and in front of a swivel-mounted machine gun. Simon tells him, "You're not just the M.C.C. nor even the landlords and merchants and money-lenders, you are ..." and at this point lists the names of the last 44 prime ministers. The machine gun is fired, and Lord Thing falls to the ground.

Reviews of *Simon Says!* were not good. Yorkshire Post theatre critic Desmond Pratt saw the play (correctly) as "a Left-wing assault on the Establishment"[17] and objected to this. Patrick O'Neill in the Daily Mail described the play as "ill-conceived, ill-prepared, tuneless and long-winded".[18] John Raymond of the Sunday Times commented rather on the audience:

"Luckily for the occasion, Alex Glasgow's songs ... went with a sinister, gleeful punch that left the largely professional middle class audience ... longing for more. Delighted with the pace and skill of the production, above all with the cheering nature of the occasion itself, the audience was mostly prepared

THE LEEDS GRAPHIC

Vol. 19. No. 149   OCTOBER 1970   Three Shillings

STARS ATTEND FIRST NIGHT

Among the many personalities who attended the first night of the new Leeds Playhouse were Peter O'Toole and his wife, Sian Phillips and Michael Hordern. They, together with other members of a celebrity studded audience, witnessed the world premiere performance of Alan Plater's 'Simon says . . .'   Gordon Hodgson to overlook the show's lack of satiric substance, treating the whole affair with baffled good humour".[19]

But above and beyond comments on the quality of production, politicians and critics questioned the choice of *Simon Says!* as the opening play. In the view of Lord Mayor Alderman Arthur Brown, "the theatre is very good, but with plays like last night's, it will never get off the ground",[20] while Sir George Martin, a former mayor, commented that "the beautiful building was spoilt by this kitchen sink production. It was a disgrace to put the show on on any night. The language was not fit for any place near the University".[21]

All this controversy could have been avoided if Bill Hays had taken notice of the pleading by the theatre's administrator, Alex Baron, to open the theatre with the other play rehearsed for the opening season: Pirandello's *Henry IV*. But in response to all this criticism, the writer and director appeared unrepentant. Alan Plater defended the choice of his play to open the theatre:

"I do not think the new Leeds Playhouse should be showing conventional old-fashioned drawing room comedies and thrillers. The Playhouse has got to take chances with its productions – to put its head on the block ... Our duty is to challenge. This show challenges authority."[22]

Brazenly, after the opening night reviews the Playhouse promoted the play with a 'disgusted' quote from the MP for Pudsey under the banner of 'Controversial Opening Show'! However there was great disappointment over its poor reception among those who had spent years campaigning for a Playhouse in Leeds. Doreen Newlyn described it as "a terrible aberration". Equally disappointed were the actors: one of them, Jerome Willis, writing that "the critical reaction to *Simon Says!* and the poor attendance for the first month certainly lowered the company's morale and I believe this affected the rehearsal period of *The Merry Wives of Windsor*".[23]

So was *Simon Says!* the right choice of play to open the theatre? Presumably Bill Hays had hoped that, in inviting Alan Plater to write for the Playhouse, the result would be a play as successful for Leeds as *Close the Coalhouse Door* had been for Newcastle. But there was one big difference: *Close the Coalhouse Door* was both set in and about the area where the play was performed, whereas *Simon Says!* had no direct connection with Leeds. In spite of the play's poor reviews, Alan Plater was to reflect (years later) that Bill had remained "totally loyal and unrepentant. He saw it as his duty to take risks, and if they ended in tears before bedtime and angry letters in the local paper, that proved he was doing his job properly. It was almost as if he liked it better that way".[24]

This was also reflected in an interview with Bill at the time:

"*Simon* didn't do very well at all ... but when they came, the ordinary audiences liked it. Of course the first night audience didn't: there were lots of Lords in the audience and we shot one on stage".[25]

So was it a bad play, or the wrong play? Years later Alan Plater summed up, "We delivered a slap of in-your-face agitprop ... which remains the major catastrophe on my CV – 'like spending a couple of hours in a refrigerated meat warehouse', as I later reported. I still remember the names of the four people who liked it".[26]

Thankfully the play performed at the official opening – a Royal Gala Performance nearly three months later on Thursday 10th December 1970 – was a play with music, appropriately called *Oh Glorious Jubilee!*

As you might expect, in addition to the then HRH The Prince of Wales, just 22 years old at the time, special guests included the Lord Mayor and Lady Mayoress of Leeds. Other special guests were the Government Minister for the Arts, David Eccles, and his predecessor Jennie Lee; Lord Boyle, newly appointed as Vice Chancellor of Leeds University, and his predecessor Sir Roger Stevens – who had acted as President of the Leeds Theatre Trust.

Perhaps less expected, it was decided that fifty tickets would be distributed for free to "groups of school children, students, factory-floor workers, seniors and immigrant citizens". Another 68 tickets were raffled amongst people connected with the theatre as donors, advertisers, etc. If this was confirmation that the Playhouse might become the kind of theatre the campaign group had wanted, so was the after-show dinner, attended by the company and theatre staff. Newspapers eagerly reported the unusual choice of guests, which included an usherette and kitchen staff:

"Chirpy, 77 years-old washer up Mr. Dave Parker will desert his dishes at the Leeds Playhouse restaurant on December 10 to enjoy a turkey salad with Prince Charles ... His name was drawn from a hat along with those of other behind-the-scenes employees at the Playhouse!"[27]

Oh Glorious Jubilee! was a new play, this time not written specifically for the Playhouse, by Cliff Hanley from Glasgow, with music by his fellow Scotsman Ian Gourlay. They were best known for popular comedy songs, and this is reflected in the play's style, as is its original title: *Oh Glorious Jubilee or the Merited Triumph of Zebidiah Grimpot Esq., a nice family play with music and a moral!* Set in London at the time of Queen Victoria's Jubilee in 1897, the play was a light-hearted send-up of the upper middle-classes. The director was again Bill Hays, who also acted the part of Sergeant Biff, a Warwickshire policeman. In the story, Zebidiah is near to gaining a peerage but is beset by family problems, including questions about his own parents. Meanwhile his daughter Alexandra worries she's pregnant because of being kissed by the coachman in the conservatory. A send-up indeed!

Local and national newspaper critics were kind, even though the performance they attended on the evening prior to the Royal Gala was delayed by thirty minutes due to a power cut: "...glorious and jubilant... a witty, irreverent, entirely unmalicious swipe at the foibles of Victorianism".[28]

Although The Guardian described the production as "splendid fun"[29], other national critics were less generous:

"*Oh Glorious Jubilee!* can cause offence to nobody except such as believe that the opening of a new theatre should be marked with an important play."[30] Or as the Daily Telegraph's critic commented, "There is, no doubt, plenty still to be said against the (Victorian) era, and presumably something to be said for it. The trouble is that Mr Hanley chooses to say nothing".[31]

Might it have been better to open the theatre with *Oh Glorious Jubilee!* instead of saving this for the Royal Gala Performance? The case for having opened with *Simon Says!* is that this play was much more obviously an 'announcement' of what people could expect from the Leeds Playhouse, and was targeted at the kind of audience the theatre hoped to attract. But the (arguable) fundamental flaw of this decision was articulated by Financial Times reviewer B.A. Young:

"Even if it had been much better than it is, it would have been the wrong play to open the Leeds Playhouse with. Leeds, for so long a theatrical wilderness, has got to be persuaded to support a serious theatre. You don't persuade the bourgeois audience on whom, like it or not, you will rely for the foreseeable future, by offering them an attack on (their) principles".[32]

The retort of the Playhouse's idealists was that the intended audience was *not* bourgeois. In this respect, by the end of the year, Bill Hays was recognising that the Playhouse still had to successfully reach that 'other' audience:

"The Playhouse hasn't yet broken through to people who don't usually go to the Theatre. I hope in the next year to break down the idea that the theatre's only there for people who can afford a mink stole. We're fighting the tradition that the theatre's not for ordinary working people".[33]

ACT I

ACT ONE, SCENE THREE

Artistic directors often have to make the unenviable choice between productions that are daring and challenging, and ones which are safe and comfortable for audiences. The latter is more likely to get people coming back for more. What happens if the former alienates audiences, who then look elsewhere for entertainment?

PICTURES IN A BATH OF ACID
by Colin Wilson
15th September 1971

AFTER THE INITIAL, MOSTLY HOSTILE, press reaction to *Simon Says!*, the productions which followed in the first year, in particular Arthur Miller's *The Crucible*, attracted many good reviews. The 1971-2 season opened with a 'safe' choice of production: a Noel Coward double-bill. However, this was followed by a new play, one which attracted almost as much controversy as *Simon Says!*: *Pictures in a Bath of Acid*, by Colin Wilson – better known as a writer of novels and non-fiction with themes of mysticism and the paranormal.

Pictures in a Bath of Acid concerns the life of the Swedish playwright, writer and painter August Strindberg. The action takes place in his Stockholm apartment during one night, somewhere at the start of the 20th Century. Much of the play is in the mind of Strindberg as he fantasises and dreams. The first act is essentially a monologue (which in Leeds lasted for over one hour) as he 'talks' to his psychiatrist, mostly about the troubled relationships with his three wives. The second act is something of a courtroom scene, but again is essentially all in his mind. It is not completely clear as to what are the charges against him, but they relate to his plays. The chief witness for the prosecution is a literary critic, who argues that his plays are the product of a deranged mind. The title of the play refers to a supposed incident, mentioned in another long monologue, where Strindberg explains a coincidence whereby a landscape image he sees in an emptied zinc bath of acid is identical to one which months later he experiences in real life.

On this occasion the Yorkshire Post critic was more positive:

"It is directed with considerable understanding, sympathy and atmosphere by Bill Hays' riveting production and the extraordinary strength and weakness of Alfred Burke's study of this tormented man ... To attempt that production is a challenge which Mr. Hays has accomplished and to attempt the central role is even more terrifying for this must be the longest part in modern stage literature."[34]

Elsewhere Alfred Burke's performance was praised as "mind-stunning" and "magnificent", and critics praised the Playhouse for daring to produce the play. However, it was recognised as having a limited appeal:

"It is courageous to inflict on Leeds audiences a play that they may not flock to in such large numbers as, say, to *Alfie*."[35]

And Peter Holdsworth: "The play was a remarkable creation which would probably be appreciated immediately in Paris or Berlin, but must have seemed strange to the bluff and 'let's get to the point lad' West Riding".[36]

This must have been the mindset of the five City Council members who left at the interval, three of them creating headlines with their opinions, as expressed to the Yorkshire Evening Post:

"If this is the sort of play they are going to perform at the Playhouse, it having such limited interest, it is no wonder that they are in financial difficulties", said Alan Redmond. "...lacked the change and variations in dramatic quality needed to hold the attention", complained Dr. J.R.Sherwin, while John Hunt moaned that the play simply failed to hold his interest. The Mayor of Leeds, Alderman Trevor Watson, sat it out to the end but afterwards said he too had not enjoyed it: "It was interesting and there was a lot of profound thought in it, but it was not sufficiently interesting".[37]

Picture in a Bath of Acid does indeed seem an obscure choice, given the kind of audience the Playhouse wanted to attract. The opening lines of the play have Strindberg referring to women as whores, nymphomaniacs, bitches on heat, killers, vampires, and specifically his third wife as "you evil, sexy, cunning little bitch"! Strindberg himself was a lesser-known playwright: not a single one of his plays has so far been produced at the Playhouse. Although, following this production, Colin Wilson's play was published (1972) as *Strindberg* (with a dedication to actor Alfred Burke "who brought Strindberg to life"), there have been very few subsequent productions.

When Bill Hays was appointed as Artistic Director in May 1970 he made it clear that he felt it would take four years for the Playhouse to become a successful regional theatre. Unfortunately, Bill was not given another three years to achieve that success.

Perhaps because of *Pictures in a Bath of Acid*, just fourteen months after the theatre had opened, governors of the Theatre Trust controversially began holding meetings, not necessarily formally conducted or minuted, to discuss Bill's future. Certain governors, like some of the councillors, were objecting to the choice of plays, in particular those which had not attracted good audiences and therefore sufficient income. This ignored the fact that, when Bill Hays was appointed, it was made clear to all candidates that the artistic director would be solely responsible for the choice of productions:

"The planning of the programme will be entirely the concern of the Artistic Director. The Trust feels strongly that, within the proper operation of its responsibility to manage the general affairs of the Theatre, the artistic policy at the theatre should be determined and executed by the Artistic Director."[38]

The governors were aware of other theatres where the relationship between the governors and the artistic director had been problematic. (One example is the Nottingham Playhouse, where in 1967 John Neville had resigned, in part because of his refusal to remove an art exhibition from the theatre's foyer that the Board of Governors considered to be tasteless. Interestingly, in 1969 John was approached about the post at Leeds Playhouse, but declined.) Consequently, a statement by the Leeds Playhouse governors in the brochure published for its opening included the statement:

"We are not unaware of the difficulties implicit in the relationship between a Board of Governors with ultimate responsibility, and a Director to whom full artistic freedom must be given if he is to serve us all as we wish."

The policy of giving exclusive control of the programming to the Artistic Director was in keeping with the expectations of the Arts Council, which, in exactly the same year as the Playhouse opened, published a report, *The Theatre Today*, outlining the role of governors:

"The Board's jurisdiction covers the budget, the building, general policy, seat prices, negotiations with the Arts Council and Local Authorities, theatre amenities ... The Artistic Director's duties are to choose the plays, select the artists, and plan the productions"[39]

The Arts Council report concluded with what was almost a threat – that "in subsidized theatres the choice of plays should rest entirely with the artistic director and failure on the part of Theatre Boards to implement this principle should be a major factor in Arts Council considerations regarding financial support."[40]

So, when the Chairman of the Governors announced in the Yorkshire Evening Post that he himself had compiled a list of three hundred authors "who would make ideal fare for Leeds Playhouse"[41] he clearly was at odds with the Arts Council edict. In any case, a list as long as this would surely include most of the authors whose plays were produced in the first season.

Controversy raged, therefore, when the governors decided not to renew Bill Hays' contract after two years, of which Bill was notified in November 1971, allowing a notice period of six months. Certain governors and other parties were quick to give their views to local and national newspapers, and as a result, the decision became described as a 'sacking'. One newspaper story reported how three governors resigned because of the decision and the rushed way in which they felt it had been made. Consequently, the Chairman of the Board, Dr. Patrick Nuttgens, who had instigated what came to be described as 'caucus' governors' meetings, felt it necessary to explain his actions:

"(Mr. Hays) must be deaf and blind if he did not notice anything wrong. This was not sprung on him and there was no breaking of faith with him … If the Playhouse is to be viable we must have a more positive programme of plays which will attract a more local and regional audience."[42]

Other consequent events also hit the headlines. The company and staff of the Playhouse unanimously passed a motion of no confidence in the Chairman, the Board of Governors, and the Theatre Trust. Roger Chapman, the director of the Theatre In Education team, announced his resignation (although in the end remained in post) and the Press Officer, Roger Tomlinson, revealed that he was considering his position.

How could this sea-change have come about? Perhaps the main reason relates to the composition of the Board of Governors. When the Leeds Theatre Trust was established early in 1968, the first board was essentially seven people who had been involved for many years in the Theatre Campaign. However, they recognised that the Arts Council, in offering funding, required a broader membership, including theatre professionals, Playhouse Club representation, and local authority councillors. Additionally, because of an earlier change to the constitution requiring a rotating membership, when the governors met to consider whether or not to renew Bill Hays' contract, this was not the same body of people who had appointed him back in 1969. The original governors and others involved in the Theatre Campaign had a clear vision of the Playhouse they wanted for Leeds and had appointed Bill Hays to make this happen. Unfortunately no policy had been formally recorded regarding this vision which would have guided and validated the choice of plays performed.

By November 1971, another issue facing the Playhouse was its uncertain financial situation. When the theatre finally opened, £30,000 of the building costs had still to be raised, with loan interest being accrued. Additionally, the 1970-71 season had made a loss of £2,222. It is perhaps understandable that the governors were concerned about ticket sales and other income.

Could more have been done to make the governors aware of the first difficult years at other regional repertory theatres? Would it have been helpful to point out to them that the situation in Leeds was not comparable with, for example, the Nottingham Playhouse or the Sheffield Crucible? Both of these new theatres had built up loyal support at their previous venues, whereas the Playhouse needed to attract a completely new audience. Plus, one stark truth was, the Leeds Playhouse's location was far from ideal.

ACT ONE, SCENE FOUR

All regional theatres give people the opportunity to see new plays and new productions of classic plays. Receiving theatres bring these, and more frequently West End musicals, to the regions. To what extent should regional producing theatres concentrate on productions which specifically relate to the communities which they serve? Should they also give priority to opportunities to kickstart the careers of local writers and directors?

AND WAS JERUSALEM BUILDED HERE? by Barry Collins
24th May 1972

ALAN PLATER'S CLOSE THE COALHOUSE DOOR was a good example of a play which was successful perhaps mainly because a regional repertory theatre, in this instance, the Newcastle Playhouse, had enlisted a local author to write a play about a local issue. As another example at this time, the Victoria Theatre, Stoke-on-Trent, was well known for such work. Many of the plays related to events in The Potteries: the Primitive Methodist movement; the rise of Chartism in the nineteenth century; the North Staffordshire Railway. They often addressed current events, such as the fight to keep open the local steelworks, and plays were often in the form of verbatim theatre, based on interviews with local people.

By contrast, Alan Plater's *Simon Says!* did not relate specifically to Leeds. This was also true of the other new play in the 1970-71 season: *Tight at the Back*, by Leonard Barras. Barras was from Tyneside so understandably whilst the theme was football, the team supported by the main character was not Leeds United.

Astonishingly, having not renewed his contract, the governors asked Bill to stay on for another three months to finish the season. These final productions included his re-staging *of Close the Coalhouse Door* – a change to the published programme, replacing Bernard Shaw's *Saint Joan*. With the 1972 UK Miners' Strike the hottest contemporary news topic, the production opened on 15th March, just two weeks after the strike had ended. New material was added to the third act to incorporate references to the strike. This production was so successful that the run had to be extended by two weeks.

The only new play in 1971-72 apart from *Pictures in a Bath of Acid* was the final one of the season, and at last it was a play with a Yorkshire connection. *And Was Jerusalem Builded Here?* was the first play by Halifax writer Barry Collins who had previously worked for seven years as a reporter for the Halifax Courier. His play told of the nineteenth century West Riding Luddites and the punishments they suffered for opposing the introduction of machinery for their specialist craft work. Barry was particularly interested to show "the destructive strain placed on ordinary men by forces too vast for them to understand or control".[43] He was apparently inspired to write the play after seeing the touring production of *Close the Coalhouse Door* at the Grand Theatre, hence the production was similarly staged, using verse and songs. The set consisted of ten large revolving panels onto which were projected images, including pictures of the original Luddites. Also projected were Tarot cards foretelling the fate of the rebels. On one side of the panels were mirrors, reflecting the actors and the audience itself.

The play and the production, which opened in May 1972, received mostly positive reviews, and was welcomed as a genuine local drama, "a classic example of a regional theatre doing its duty".[44]

As an aside – it would be nearly ten years before the Playhouse saw another play by a local author about a local issue. This was *Going Native* by James Robson, which opened in November 1981. Set in a Yorkshire town, the play concerns the local council's refuse collection service, and the initiation of a young man, on vacation work, into one of the crews. James was writing from experience: he had been a dustman with Ryedale District Council before becoming a full-time writer. The Playhouse had previously produced, in 1978, what was the regional premiere of his earlier play *Factory Birds*.

Sadly, *And Was Jerusalem Builded Here?* was the last play to be directed by Bill. His production was highly successful, praised in the The Stage for being "as usual, clever and striking if not indeed brilliant".[45] The play was Bill's thirteenth production in just two years; an astonishing amount of work.

Lunchtime performances, free to attend, were the new trend. When the Playhouse first opened, new plays were getting airings in this way, alongside Bill's productions. They were first introduced by actor Andrew Dallmeyer who performed in eleven of the twelve company productions in the first season. As well as writing and directing some lunchtime performances he gave opportunities to local writers and directors: for example, a first play by a Leeds Polytechnic student. The productions were performed by actors in the company, and typically attracted audiences of two hundred, many of them local students.

Andrew continued at the Playhouse for Bill Hays's second season, and that year received an Arts Council trainee director's bursary. One of his lunchtime plays, about two mass murderers (not lunchtime light entertainment!), was subsequently performed in London and Edinburgh. Whilst in Leeds, he wrote his first full-length play.

Lunchtime productions continued when John Harrison followed Bill as Artistic Director at the Playhouse, and late-night performances were also introduced. In John's first season he commissioned a new play by David Edgar, *Baby Love*, sponsored by Yorkshire Television. Although he would go on to become one of the most important twentieth century English playwrights, David was relatively unknown in 1973, and had also pursued a career in journalism – having moved to Bradford in 1970 to work for the Telegraph & Argus. The play deals with the subject of baby snatching: it is about a young woman who takes a baby from a pram in a busy shopping centre, having just lost her own in a miscarriage. It focuses on the way she is treated by society as a consequence. Two months after the Leeds production, *Baby Love* went on to be produced at the at London's Soho Poly Theatre, and in 1974 was televised as a BBC Play for Today.

Another late-night production, from 1984, was a play called *Mab*. This was specially written by Martin Lewton to complement the Playhouse's production of *Romeo and Juliet* (inspired by Mercutio's speech about Queen Mab). The publicity described the play as follows:

"Leeds. Motorway City of the Future. Two streetwise young lads. A cop in pursuit of an old tramp ... Queen Mab, the architect of all dreams – but what dreams remain in a motorway city?"

The production was appropriately directed by the Playhouse's Assistant Stage Manager – appropriate because Martin had also been employed in this role at the theatre.

Before the production of *Going Native* in 1981 there had been other pieces of new writing, and although not with local settings or about local issues, they were locally based in the sense that the writers were connected with the Playhouse. Two of these plays were written by John Harrison himself. The first, *Knight in Four Acts*, was included in his second season at the Playhouse. A complicated plot, the story follows the same knight through four centuries from Elizabethan times to when he becomes an Edwardian prime minister. John had written the play in 1968 and had tried, unsuccessfully, to get it produced at the National Theatre and several regional theatres, as well as through commercial managements. John tells this story in his autobiography, finally explaining that "in 1973 ... my associate director David Carson begged me to let him do it. We opened during a newspaper strike. Very few people know there is such a play at all".[46]

The attendance was indeed poor, the worst of any production in his eighteen years at the Playhouse. His other play, *Pop Goes the Nightingale*, he directed himself. Described as a musical fantasy, this was a Christmas production based on Hans Christian Anderson's fairy tale. Attendance this time was excellent, as was usually the case with Christmas family productions. In John's time at the Playhouse, four other pieces of new writing were produced at this time of year.

In 1980 there was another Playhouse-connected premiere production. Alec Baron had been involved with the Playhouse since the very beginning, and had been Chair of the Theatre Planning Committee. He was employed as the theatre's first Administrator. He was heavily involved in amateur theatre, directing many Proscenium Players productions. He was equally involved in Leeds Film Society. In 1980 he directed his play *Groucho at Large*, which was 'based on Groucho Marx's letters, writings, and ad-libs'. This was part of a double-bill, the other play being Alec's adaptation, with others, of a play by William Gibson, *Golda, Portrait of a Woman*, about the Israeli prime minister, Golda Meir.

In the years after *Going Native*, the Playhouse did support three other locally-connected writers. First was Martin Lewton, whose play *Prisoners* received its world premiere at the theatre in 1983. Martin had first come to Leeds in 1972 to do research at the university. Developing an interest in writing and theatre, he returned to Leeds in 1978, working first of all as a van driver for the Playhouse, followed by two years, as explained above, as Assistant Stage Manager. He helped in directing some productions, and then directed his own short play, *All Clear*. His first play to be professionally performed was *Prisoners*, set in Dewsbury Prison.

Crystal Clear was another Playhouse Production in 1984. The writer, Phil Young, came to Leeds to study for an MA in Drama & Theatre Arts. As explained in more detail elsewhere, in 1977, he received an Arts Council Trainee Director's bursary for a one-year placement at the theatre. After this, he returned several times as a freelance director. *Crystal Clear* was Phil's first play, and prior to writing this, he had worked as assistant director to Mike Leigh on an experimental improvised project for the Royal Shakespeare Company. Presumably this influenced his decision to write the play for the original production of *Crystal Clear* through improvisation with the three actors. The play is about going and being blind, and the consequences for relationships. The original production was performed at the Old Red Lion Theatre in Islington, London, in 1982, then transferred to the Wyndham's Theatre. He later won the London Evening Standard Award for Most Promising Playwright. After the Playhouse production, Phil went on to direct a workshop production in New York. In 2019, the play was revived at the Old Red Lion to celebrate the theatre's fortieth anniversary.

Presumably because of the success of this production, and because of his experience of playwriting through improvisation, in 1987 Phil was invited back to the Playhouse to work on another premiere, again devised with the actors. The title somewhat improbably became *Torpedoes in the Jacuzzi* (following its working title of *Sweet Potato, Lime Pickle and Yorkshire Pud)* and wasn't exactly the theatre's 'finest hour'. Phil and the six actors had spent fourteen weeks of research and rehearsal in Leeds. During the first three weeks, Phil talked separately with the actors about people they knew, people who were the same age, race and gender as themselves, with no theatre connections. In a programme note, one of the actors, Joan Carol Williams, describes this process:

"I was asked to compile a list of Black women of the same age as myself who I knew in Leeds ... I was asked questions about all of these women after which the number was cut down to four. We decided on the woman upon whom my character is based mainly because she was wanting to make more of her life and was willing to try different things".[47]

Joan's character became "Bev" from Chapeltown, who worked as a beauty consultant. The characters of the other actors evolved in the same way. One of these actors was Kulvinder Ghir, also from Chapeltown. Following *Torpedoes in the Jacuzzi* his acting career took off, first of all in the film of *Rita, Sue and Bob Too* and then *Bend It Like Beckham*, *The Arbor* and most recently (2019) *Blinded By The Light*. He has worked extensively in television, but also back in the theatre – often playing in Bolton, Manchester, and at the National Theatre in London. In 1992, he returned to the Playhouse for the premiere of Trevor Griffiths' play, *The Gulf Between Us*.

Although *Torpedoes in the Jacuzzi* achieved 50% attendances, it did not impress. John Harrison concluded, "I think we must admit (it) was not a success. But if we didn't take risks and experiment occasionally the theatre would die of inertia ... Doubt has been thrown on the whole concept of the devised play, but I would defend the attempt as a bold one."[48]

1984 also saw a production of *Turning Over* by Brian Thompson. Brian had lived in Leeds since 1961 and had worked as the manager of the Swarthmore Adult Education Centre where the first formal meeting of the Theatre Campaign had been held back in 1964. Whilst at Swarthmore he had started writing and left in 1973 to do this full-time. By 1984 he had already experienced success writing television plays and episodes for series. In the theatre he had plays commissioned and directed by Alan Ayckbourn for Scarborough, one of which transferred to the Wyndham's Theatre in London. Another play had been commissioned and performed at the Oldham Coliseum. Brian had also made several documentary films, and this was the inspiration for *Turning Over*. The play is a satire concerning how such documentaries are made. It had previously been performed at the Bush Theatre in London, with a cast including Charles Dance, receiving good reviews. In Leeds, where the cast included Terence Booth and Imelda Staunton, reviews were disappointing. Most praised the production: the direction, the acting and the set – but not the play itself:

"The play's message is about as shallow as a bowl of dishwater – and probably less interesting. None of this was the fault of the cast or the direction. They did what they could. The set too was very good. But why, oh why, does the Playhouse choose material such as this?".[49]

ACT I

ACT ONE, SCENE FIVE

In programming a season of productions, an artistic director will usually have to make certain decisions. Should they include a Shakespeare play, and should it be one that features in school examination syllabuses? They will have to carefully decide on a Christmas production: the rest of the season might financially depend on this choice. Should they also attempt to attract 'star' names for these productions?

THE CAUCASIAN CHALK CIRCLE
by Bertolt Brecht
27th September 1972

THIS WAS THE FIRST PRODUCTION directed by the Leeds Playhouse's second Artistic Director who had been appointed in the summer of 1972. John Harrison was forty-eight, whereas Bill Hays had been thirty-two when the Playhouse opened in 1970. There was also a big difference in terms of their repertory theatre experience. John's years at the Nottingham Playhouse saw considerable success. His seasons included plays considered standard classics, but also less well-known authors and new plays. In 1955 he directed the English premiere of Jean Anouilh's *The Ermine*. In John Bailey's record of the Nottingham Playhouse's first thirty years, he uses this production as an example of what John had achieved:

"The audience level of sixty-six percent for this production is interesting. Because of it being a premiere occasion there had been more publicity than usual and there were national reviews, but it was fairly testing dramatic material and the very reasonable attendance figure indicated that an enlightened and loyal audience had emerged."[50]

John resigned as director at the Nottingham Playhouse after the 1956-7 season, feeling in need of rest and change. Throughout his years, there had mostly been a new production every two weeks; this would be unthinkable today.

All this experience, as well at the Birmingham Rep, must have seemed very impressive to the Board of Governors at the Leeds Playhouse when looking to appoint their second Artistic Director. However, his experience of theatre boards of governors had not always been positive. In his autobiography, he says:

"Board meetings… The only appropriate comment seems a groan. Those terminally tedious gatherings of a city's amateur Great and Good to lord it over poor bloody professionals."[51]

In fact, he only accepted the job in Birmingham because he was promised by the administrator that he would hardly ever have to meet them. This only lasted until the administrator left, and reflecting on his experience afterwards, John says:

"I'm no good with boards. I don't tell them enough. I don't, as the saying goes, 'take them into my confidence'. I'm too busy running the place. In my view theatre does best as a dictatorship, preferably benevolent, but even maleficent will give you better theatre than any committee … it's a pain to drag this protesting collection of amateurs along with you."[52]

One can only assume that he kept these opinions to himself when interviewed in Leeds.

John says he was persuaded by the then Drama Director of the Arts Council, Dick Linklater, to apply for the post at the Leeds Playhouse, and that he had lots of doubt about taking it even if it were offered to him. He also records that he was offered the job after an interview with five Board members, not having even seen the theatre, and that "the salary offered was a joke after what I'd been getting at Rediffusion. I said I would need them to double it. They doubled it."[53]

His reluctance about the post diminished once he had seen the Playhouse and fallen in love with it. He was particularly attracted by the thrust stage. He claims the interview panel of five Board members agreed that he would work with them, and not the full Board, but this promise would never be fulfilled.

With Bertolt Brecht's *The Caucasian Chalk Circle,* John made a wiser choice than Bill Hays for his inaugural play. The production reflected his enthusiasm for working on a thrust stage and he used the opportunity to break down barriers between actors and audience. As the house opened, actors were positioned around the auditorium and chatted with audience members. He focused on the story-telling aspect of the play and used music and sounds to heighten the atmosphere.

The production was well-received by local and national critics, the Yorkshire Evening Post describing it as "an evening of spell-binding theatre".[54] The Yorkshire Post's Desmond Pratt said it was "the most imaginative and colourful picture of the intricate story I have ever seen",[55] and The Leeds Student Review concluded, "a powerful production of a powerful play".[56]

Several reviews commented positively about the young cast (which also included John's not-as-young wife Linda Gardner in the lead role of Grusha) working as a team:

"Free from false piety, Mr. Harrison and his young company offer a gay and unsentimentally moving performance."[57]

"What this amounted to in the ultimate was a vital expression of teamwork which resulted in a profound and poetic experience."[58]

The Guardian was less impressed, somewhat bizarrely concluding that "only one thing is disturbing about the new company – its youth. Many of the characters could have expanded with the irreplaceable experience of age. I only hope that the reason is low wages that hardly support an actor and family, not employment of old actors"[59]

For most critics, John Harrison's arrival represented a turning point for the Playhouse: "He has lit a fuse to explode a powder keg of talent",[60] and "if the Playhouse company can keep this standard up, then Leeds will certainly have a theatre to be proud of."[61]

Audience numbers increased during the run, and there were full houses during the last week. This success is reflected in the fact that the production was revived for a week at the end of the 1972-3 season. In his first months at the theatre, John also directed a production of *Macbeth*, wisely chosen because the play was a GCE O Level text. Attendance figures were excellent; the Christmas production which followed, *The Wizard of Oz*, was also great for the box office.

Nevertheless, John was to quickly learn that the Playhouse had not yet attracted a regular audience. In his first season he had also included two relatively new plays. One was the controversial *Saved* by Edward Bond, which had opened at the Royal Court Theatre in London in November 1965 but been censored due to its violence, including the stoning of a baby in a pram. The other was *Loot*, which had opened in London in the same year with limited initial success, but has been regularly revived, becoming a Joe Orton classic. Attendance at both productions was particularly poor.

So in programming his second season, John drew on his substantial experience of repertory theatres to make wise choices. He included musicals, knowing that these meant good box office sales. The musical version of *Canterbury Tales* by Martin Starkie and Nevill Coghill was a popular production, opening the season in September 1973. This was shown to be true again in the following season: *Joseph and the Amazing Technicolour Dreamcoat* achieved ninety-seven percent capacity, the best attended production at the Playhouse so far. Similarly, recognising the popularity of Christmas productions, his first season had successfully included an adaptation of *The Wizard of Oz* – set in Yorkshire! 1973 saw a production of *Beauty and the Beast*, with the story faithfully retold by Barry Collins (following his play *And Was Jerusalem Builded Here?*).

Looking to the successes of Bill Hays, John observed that his predecessor had taken opportunities to cast audience-attracting 'star' names. Thus Bill's production of *Alfie*, the best-known work by Lancashire's Bill Naughton, saw another Bill, Bill Simpson, in the cast – an actor widely known from the long-running BBC Television series *Doctor Finlay's Casebook* which had been broadcast since 1962, of which Bill Hays had directed some episodes. Bill's casting for *Alfie* also roped in Shirley Anne Field who had acted in the film version of the play four years earlier. Bill Simpson stayed on to play Polonius in *Hamlet*, but the title role was played by Robert Powell. At this early stage in Robert's career, his first success had come with another BBC Television series, *Doomwatch*. By the time he was killed off at the end of the first series, Robert had become a TV heartthrob.

Using the same audience attraction ploy, John Harrison ended his second season with a production of Colin Welland's play, *Say Goodnight to Grandma*. This play had previously run for four months at the St. Martin's Theatre in London, and Colin Welland acted in both productions. Colin Welland was already well-known for his role in the landmark television series *Z Cars* and also as the teacher in Ken Loach's film, *Kes*. (Interestingly, the cast of *Simon Says!*, back in 1970, also included Dai Bradley who played Billy Casper in this film.) The same year saw a production of Shakespeare's *The Tempest*. John Harrison's friendship with Paul Scofield had continued after their work together in Birmingham and Stratford thirty years before. Paul agreed to play Prospero when at this stage of his career he had already achieved much success on stage, particularly with the Royal Shakespeare Company. For example, in 1962 and although only forty at the time, he had played Lear in *King Lear* directed by Peter Brook, and two years earlier Sir Thomas Moore in *A Man for All Seasons*, both in London and New York. In 1966, he starred in the film version of this play, for which he won the Oscar for Best Male Actor.

This 'star' name clearly attracted the much-needed box office success. The production played to ninety-four percent capacity, also becoming the Playhouse's first West End transfer, where at the Wyndham's Theatre it achieved the record of the longest continuous run of a Shakespeare play in London.

How long does it take to successfully establish a new regional theatre? When the Playhouse opened in 1970, Bill Hays had suggested that it would take four to five years – and he was right. For the Leeds Playhouse, *The Tempest* was a turning point.

ACT ONE, SCENE SIX

Many regional theatres started as repertory ones, often with a company of actors performing three or more plays in the same week. Today, very few theatres are producing in this way, even if some, like the Birmingham Repertory Theatre, have retained the 'repertory' name. Ending producing in this way is an example of theatres having to make decisions other than for artistic reasons: for financial ones.

THE GOOD WOMAN OF SETZUAN
by Bertolt Brecht
30th January 1974

DEATH OF A SALESMAN
by Arthur Miller
28th February 1974

THE DAUGHTER-IN-LAW
by D.H. Lawrence
27th March 1974

ONE OF THE OBJECTIVES included in the very first policy statement for the Leeds Playhouse, written in 1964, was the necessity of a resident company, "because working permanently together, it could produce work of a consistent quality in a planned programme, and working permanently in the same city would be able to establish a close relationship with its audiences".[62]

This objective was achieved with the first productions at the Leeds Playhouse in 1970. Plays were presented in a true repertoire system so that three different productions could be seen during most weeks. *Henry IV* by Luigi Pirandello had opened just four days after *Simon Says!*; Shakespeare's *The Merry Wives of Windsor* opened three weeks later. The first two of these were rehearsed and performed in advance both at the Edinburgh Festival in August 1970, and in the case of the latter at the Nottingham Playhouse prior to Edinburgh. *The Merry Wives of Windsor* was rehearsed once these two had opened in Leeds. This was always hard work for the company of actors, since it necessitated rehearsing one or two plays in the daytime whilst performing a third in the evenings and for Saturday matinees. Nevertheless, most of that first company of actors remained at the Playhouse for the whole year, and some for much longer. The company mainly comprised of young actors starting out on their careers. A notable example was Malcolm Keith, born in Leeds, who had trained at the Webber-Douglas Academy in London. He had been involved in the campaign for a theatre in Leeds, and said at the time that "he was waiting for Leeds Playhouse to open" for his first job! With the exception of *Henry IV*, Malcolm appeared in all twelve productions during the opening season.

John Harrison's decision to accept the post of Artistic Director at the Playhouse was not only because he wanted to work on a thrust stage, but also because he was attracted by the idea of directing a permanent company offering plays in true repertoire: "a director's dream".

The significance of *The Good Woman of Setzuan*, *Death of a Salesman*, and *The Daughter-in-Law* is that these were the last productions at the Playhouse to play in true repertoire. They were promoted as a trilogy of plays with the theme of 'money is the root of all evil'.

The Good Woman of Setzuan opened first, with a cast of eighteen actors, eight of whom were playing two or more parts. Fifteen of these actors went on to play parts in one or both of the other two productions. Significantly the reviews for these productions singled out particular but mostly different actors. Elizabeth Bennett, playing the Good Woman herself, "brought a blend of strength and humanity to the role that was always moving, never soft-centred", while [63] Tim Barlow, as the Salesman, was "commanding, overbearing and at the same time intensely vulnerable".[64] The Yorkshire Evening Post review for *The Daughter-in-Law* described it as an "authentic and painstaking production" and singled out "the two typical Lawrentian sons in Philip Wilde's Joe and Christopher Crook's Luther, who simmer and boil alternately".[65] Both actors had played in all three productions in the repertoire season. In *Death of a Salesman*, Philip was also praised by Desmond Pratt, in the Yorkshire Post, for "an honest insight into American youth, troubled and intense, almost heartbroken with his father's dilemma". The same reviewer went on to describe the production as "the finest realisation of a great play that I have seen in the Playhouse since it opened".[66]

Fifty years later Phil Wilde still remembers his experience of working at the Playhouse in the 1973-74 season:

"This was only my second professional engagement since leaving drama school. The experience of being able to perform plays in repertoire was new to me and a huge challenge. Doing this with a sizeable company was not only inspiring but also glorious fun. It was certainly hard work. I recall the very long hours. Whilst doing at least two matinees and six evening performances a week, you would also be rehearsing the next shows to come into the repertoire. This had to be sustained six days a week for the entire season. Of course, you weren't playing a major role in every play so you did occasionally have a chance to take a breather."

Phil has a special memory of the production of *The Daughter-in-Law*:

"the cast and director spent the morning down a coal mine near Wakefield. The young men in the cast wore their stage costumes whilst down there. I remember feeling quite chuffed that I had actual coal dust from a real pit on my costume and boots. Obviously this helped my performance enormously!".[67]

David Carson was director of two of these three plays. David had worked alongside John Harrison since 1972, directing seven other plays, one being *Richard III*. Phil had again been in the cast, and David remembers how "*Richard III* was the scene of an amusing nightly experience which was caused by the fact that we did the production complete and unabridged. This meant that King Richard was still alive and kicking when it came time for a great section of the audience to depart in order to catch their last bus home. As far as I can recall the curtain didn't fall until at least 11.15pm so from 10.30 onwards the house got steadily thinner until there came a time when there were often more folk on stage than there were in the audience!".[68]

After Leeds, David Carson went on to produce work at other regional theatres, followed by television work in the 1980s. However, in 1989 he moved to the USA to direct for television and film. His first work was four episodes of *Star Trek: The Next Generation*. Perhaps his biggest claim to fame is two feature films: *Star Trek Generations* and *Carrie*.

But the repertoire system was doomed. The decision to end it at Leeds Playhouse was purely for financial reasons and John Harrison hoped that the theatre would one day return to repertoire, but this did not happen in his years at the Playhouse.

As well as ending performing productions in repertory, other decisions were made for financial rather than artistic reasons. The play which had preceded the three last plays in repertory was the Feydeau farce *Paradise Hotel*. This would be the last expensive stage show: future productions were to be simpler and cheaper. Other cutbacks became necessary. The company of actors was reduced to sixteen, instead of the preferred twenty to twenty-five. This, in turn, led to plays being chosen based on their having smaller casts. Where there were larger casts, as with *The Good Woman of Setzuan*, it became necessary for actors to double-up on parts.

Another central objective, emphasised in the theatre's first policy statement, had been to offer tickets at affordable prices. This was reflected in the pricing structure when the Playhouse opened. Tickets were sold at 6, 10, 12 and 14 shillings (equivalent of £4 to £9.50 in 2024) but with several concessionary prices. Children and pensioners could have tickets at half-price for matinees; students could save two shillings on the top three prices except for Saturday evenings. This pricing structure reflected a determination that the theatre be financially accessible to everyone in Leeds. By 1973 it became necessary to increase income through ticket sales; initially this was done in such a way that it was still possible to attend productions at a reasonable price. However, the number of the lowest price tickets was reduced, because when the theatre was only fifty percent full, too many people paid only this lowest price. Unfortunately, this coincided with the introduction of Value Added Tax, which meant ticket prices increasing by ten percent.

ACT I

ACT ONE, SCENE SEVEN

When a theatre depends for its very existence on local authority and national government income, this inevitably makes for a precarious situation. More specifically, where these grants are only decided from year to year, political changes can be disastrous. Increasingly, therefore, theatres have had to look for other ways to increase income, so as not to be dependent on grants and ticket sales.

HENRY V, by William Shakespeare
8th November 1979

Following the theatre's one-hundredth production of *Henry V* in November 1979, the new decade began with more successful productions. However, the first years of the 1980s saw continuing deficits. Already by the end of the 1980-1981 financial year this had reached £34,435; fortunately, one-off additional grants were given by both the Arts Council and the two local authorities to write off this sum. Nevertheless, more cost-cutting measures were necessary and staffing reductions were made. Additionally, cutbacks were made in respect of the number of productions and the length of each season. Because Christmas productions had always been costly to mount, there was no such home-grown one in 1981. More productions with small casts were put on, but this did not necessarily improve the situation: plays with small casts often attracted smaller audiences. For example, *Duet of One* by Tom Kempinski has a cast of just two but achieved only thirty-one percent attendances. Maybe plays with small casts are even more dependent on 'star' names.

Earlier decisions made for financial reasons had helped a little. For example, the ending of true repertoire did save money, and it also had the effect of increasing attendances. This suggested that theatregoers preferred more flexibility in deciding on which day of the week to attend. Increased income through ticket sales was obviously a positive development, but the future of the Leeds Playhouse always depended on the annual grants made by the Arts Council, Leeds City Council, and West Yorkshire County Council. Even in the successful 1974-75 season forty-eight percent of the theatre's income was from grants. And only because of additional grants from the first two of these was the initial capital costs of building the theatre finally covered.

The grants situation with regards to Leeds City Council first came to a head early in 1975 when the Council was asked to increase the 1975-76 grant from £20,000 to £23,000 in line with inflation. The Finance Committee not only rejected this but one councillor proposed a cut of £5000. As reported in the Yorkshire Post:

"Councillor Malcolm Davies (Con.) moving an amendment to cut the grant, alleged that the Playhouse had 'twisted our arms' for financial help in the past. As a result the council undertook to make a contribution for two years 'to get them off the ground'. "But they have come back year after year and got a grant. I think it is time we had called a halt" he added."[69]

Fortunately for the Playhouse, his amendment was defeated, but once again the purpose of the theatre was called into question. The Conservative group leader would only acknowledge that the Playhouse served a minority interest; on the other hand, the Labour party position was expressed forcefully:

"Coun. Bernard Atha suggested that if Coun. Davies had his way they would end up on a Philistine desert with no culture. 'A living theatre is extremely important to the cultural and social life of Leeds district", he said, and added that without the Council's grant, the theatre might have to close'."[70]

Ironically, the Yorkshire Post article was juxtaposed with another which reported that the committee had approved the doubling of the budget for councillors' expenses in the coming year. More seriously, it is relevant to note that the Grand Theatre was bought by the City Council in 1970, the same year as the opening of the Playhouse.

By early 1978, two years before the lease of the Playhouse was due to expire, things came to a head for the second time. At this point the City Council grant had remained at £20,000 whilst the Arts Council grant had increased from £72,000 to £110,000 since 1975. The Arts Council was essentially only prepared to match-fund local authority income. A meeting was held on 25 January, attended by representatives from the Playhouse Trust, Leeds

City Council, West Yorkshire County Council and the Arts Council. Both revenue funding and future capital funding were discussed, and the Arts Council representative stated that it was felt that the Playhouse had built up a high artistic reputation, was efficiently run, and had attracted a large and growing audience from Leeds and the surrounding area.

Countering this, the deputy leader of the Leeds City Council stated that the Conservative group of councillors mostly saw the Playhouse as the 'Theatre of the Left', referencing the production of *Simon Says!* (albeit eight years ago) and also that the theatre's Associate Director had been seconded to work on a Red Ladder Theatre production. Red Ladder were (and still are) a radical theatre company based in Leeds since 1976, and at that time also received Arts Council funding: £43,000 in 1978-79.

Following the meeting the Arts Council released a statement:

"The company will soon have to give up its present home and the Local Authority has been asked, as is normal in such cases, to take the initiative in planning a new theatre. All parties agree that this will have considerable financial consequences. If the disappointing first reaction from the Conservative group is confirmed by the City Council as a whole, the Arts Council will be forced to reconsider the whole position."[71]

On March 13th Councillor Peter Sparling confirmed in writing to the Chairman of the Playhouse Trust:

"I put to the Conservative Group last week the financial situation concerning a new Playhouse – both as to the capital amount needed and also the future revenue contribution. I regret to say that ... there was very little support for the Playhouse and I cannot see any chance of a majority of the Conservative group supporting even a considerably reduced commitment. I put it very clearly to the Group that if they said 'No' then that could well mean the end of the Playhouse – and they made it very obvious that this is preferable to putting up the sort of money asked for."[72]

He also suggested that the Labour Party's view would be the same as the Conservatives'.

But this storm was weathered, for the time being. The University offered an extension to the contract for the existing building, making the need to find a new home for the theatre less urgent, and as the new decade began, the theatre started to look for other ways to generate income. An attempt to increase audience size saw the introduction in 1982 of a subscription scheme, marketed as follows:

"Booking early means you save money and have all the benefits of being a Leeds Playhouse Subscriber. In return your support enables us to mount productions of the highest standard."

Benefits included priority booking with the best choice of seats, and 'your own seat' throughout the season as well as priority booking and a special discount for the children's Christmas show. The main incentive, however, was the possibility of seeing, for the first season of four plays in 1982-83, at a forty percent discount, which amounted to seeing all four for as little as £6. This scheme was immediately successful, attracting 2,560 subscriptions. The scheme continued throughout the 1980s, and the 1985 season saw a record figure of 5,514 subscribers.

The 1980s also saw specific productions being sponsored by local and national companies. *The Rocky Horror Show* was most appropriately sponsored by Kitchens of Leeds, the city's famous music store on Queen Victoria Street, which three years later celebrated its 100th anniversary. Other sponsors included Yorkshire Television, the Yorkshire Post, and British Telecom. 1982 saw a donation of £1000 by Sainsbury's, not for sponsoring a specific production, but for having the company name and logo printed on theatre tickets.

Without these initiatives, a future for the Playhouse might have been impossible, but because of them, the situation did improve in some of the 1980s' financial years. 1984-85, for example, saw a budget surplus, albeit just £585, as opposed to a deficit of £30,426 in the previous year. Nevertheless, the very existence of the Playhouse continued to depend on grants from the two local authorities and from the Arts Council. But by 1985 there was not only uncertainty about the future of West Yorkshire County Council, but also of the Arts Council. The Playhouse was informed by the latter that, because of national political changes, they might have to withdraw funding without giving a year's notice of doing so.

Consequently, despite the small budget surplus, 1985 saw the need for yet further cuts in the size of the company, production budgets, and technical staff overtime. One consequence was technical staff becoming dispirited due to the low levels of pay, particularly skilled workers in the carpentry and props departments. The theatre was aware that if these staff left, they would be difficult to replace.

Cuts continued to affect the choice of plays. Too many period plays would adversely affect costume costs, and musicals often incurred higher expenditure. Sometimes unforeseen costs arose: for example with the 1986 production of *Little Shop of Horrors*, the lighting board blew up just a few days before the opening night, incurring £2000 of hire and repair costs. Additionally a production day was lost, necessitating staff overtime. This example illustrates the precariousness of the financial situation in practical, day-to-day terms. Such events led to the theatre's administrator, Will Weston, who had been in post since 1980, to conclude, "The fact of the matter was that the theatre had been trying to produce large scale work on minimal funding".[73] Later in 1987 he commented further, and sadly, that:

"One of the basic facts about the Autumn season was that the plays chosen were not particularly popular but were economical, and the savings would be greater even though it was possible some business would be lost."[74]

ACT I

ACT ONE, SCENE EIGHT

If you look through recent programmes of the National Theatre, the Royal Shakespeare Company, or West End productions, the biographies of actors and directors will likely list the early years of their careers at regional repertory theatres. Ian McKellen, for example, talks proudly of the first four years of his professional career at theatres in Coventry, Ipswich, and Nottingham. Greg Doran, recently retired as artistic director of the Royal Shakespeare Company, began his professional career as an actor and then as a director at the Nottingham Playhouse.

THE IMPORTANCE OF BEING EARNEST by Oscar Wilde
12th February 1975

IN HIS AUTOBIOGRAPHY, John Harrison, remembering his time at the Leeds Playhouse, says:

"Much of my satisfaction over those years came from being able to give a bunk up to younger directors". [75]

Michael Attenborough was the first to have benefited from such a 'bunk up'. On arrival at the Playhouse early in 1975 he worked alongside John on the production of Bernard Shaw's *Saint Joan* "which gave him, very shrewdly, the opportunity to experience my work in the rehearsal room".[76] He must have been impressed, because through an Arts Council award, John appointed Michael as Associate Director. Thus, at the age of just twenty-five, Michael directed *The Importance of Being Earnest*. The critics were also impressed: "a rewarding and wholly enjoyable evening of theatre".[77]

Michael stayed at the Playhouse for four years, directing twenty-two plays across a wide range of work – not just plays by regional theatre 'regulars' such as Oscar Wilde. *The Merchant of Venice*, in 1975, was Michael's first attempt at a Shakespeare production. The following year he directed *Twelfth Night*, the second time this play was produced at the Playhouse. He directed recent plays by writers such as Tom Stoppard, Joe Orton, Harold Pinter, Alan Ayckbourn, Howard Barker, and Willy Russell, and at Christmas 1976 he directed a new children's play. Two Christmases later, he would direct *Crackers*, the premiere of a new play he had commissioned from Alan Bleasdale. This was his second production of Bleasdale's work, the other being *No More Sitting on the Old School Bench* earlier in 1978, and both of which he is particularly proud.

Kathy Webster, box office manager at the time, remembers *No More Sitting on the Old School Bench* very well:

"It was a very good play, and there was a lot in the news about education at the time, it was very topical. Because it was a newish play, nobody knew about it, so sales were a bit slow at the start. But word of mouth is the best advertising, so by the end of the run, the last two or three days, we had queues across the car park!".[78]

In 1977 Michael co-directed, with John Harrison, Arnold Wesker's, *The Wedding Feast*. Being the British premiere of the play it drew national attention. By 1977, Wesker was a key figure in British theatre, known for plays such as *Chicken Soup with Barley*, *Roots*, and *Chips with Everything*.

The Wedding Feast was reviewed in the national newspapers, and according to Wesker received his best reviews since *Chips with Everything*. Writing in the Sunday Times, Bernard Levin concluded:

"London's failure to show it reflects the deepest discredit to those responsible. And, correspondingly confers the highest honour on the Leeds Playhouse". [79]

There was, nevertheless, talk of a London transfer, and the National Theatre offered a two-week run in its Lyttleton Theatre. Unfortunately, five of the cast of sixteen were not available. Equally, this large cast perhaps explains why it was not attractive to commercial West End theatres.

Another significant Michael Attenborough production was *The Hollow Crown* (1977), a play originating in 1961, devised and directed by John Barton for the Royal Shakespeare Company. Being a celebration of England's monarchs, *The Hollow Crown* was revived in Leeds to mark the occasion of the Queen's Silver Jubilee. What was new about this production was that it toured to seventeen venues in Yorkshire, as far apart as Malton, Doncaster and Keighley, before opening at the Playhouse. This tour is an example of the way the Playhouse had started to attract additional grants for specific productions: in this case, from West Yorkshire County Council, the Yorkshire Arts Association, the University of Leeds, and the various district authorities the production toured in.

Looking back on his time in Leeds, Michael recognises it as an extraordinary opportunity:

"Once John Harrison believed in my work he was extremely generous in what he allowed me to do, and what he gave me to do. A lot of the plays I directed were my choice. He was wonderful at encouraging young writers, actors and directors. He let you get on with your work and didn't interfere. I owe him a huge debt for that".[80]

Michael also recognises that his time at the Playhouse was valuable in other ways:

"It was an important time for me. Not only had I cut my teeth on a lot of productions, I'd also cut my teeth on how to run a theatre".[81]

In this respect, he was involved with John in planning and producing a policy for the Playhouse in a new location. This experience of running a theatre was crucial to his next appointment as Artistic Director at the Watford Palace Theatre. After there, Michael took on the same role at the Hampstead Theatre. He was Principal Associate Director and Executive Producer with the Royal Shakespeare Company from 1990 to 2002, then from 2002-13 was Artistic Director at London's Almeida Theatre.

In 1977, Michael had observed a production at Leeds University directed by Phil Young, as part of his MA in Drama and Theatre Arts course. With Michael's encouragement Phil received an Arts Council Trainee Director's bursary for a placement at the Playhouse. Initially, he worked alongside John Harrison on the production of Alan Ayckbourn's *Absurd Person Singular*. He remembers this production well:

"The audience were rolling up and down with laughter; I'd never seen anything like it before – or since!".[82]

He then directed two lunchtime plays, and compiled a 'Playhouse Plus' workshop for schools, to accompany the production of *Twelfth Night* (in which he also acted).

Phil's 'big break' came when he was offered the chance to direct *Equus* by Peter Shaffer; a complex play, a modern story but in the non-realistic form of a Greek drama. The opportunity came about because Michael Attenborough had been seconded to direct a play for Red Ladder Theatre. This was a big challenge for Phil, and of all his work at the Playhouse the production of which he is most proud. After *Equus*, in his year as Trainee Director he was also responsible for another Ayckbourn play, *Just Between Ourselves*.

At this stage in his career, Phil recognises that the Playhouse gave him an insight into aspects of directing which were very new to him. For example, he learnt how to work with a designer. He also learnt the process of casting: negotiating with agents, auditioning actors, etc.

After his Trainee year, Phil returned to the Playhouse on several occasions on a freelance basis. Particularly successful was his production of *Once a Catholic*, by Mary O'Malley, which achieved ninety-one percent attendances, achieving the best financial return since *The Tempest* back in 1974. The cast included Lesley Manville; also Pam St. Clement (who went on to be one of the longest-serving cast members of the BBC soap opera *East Enders*). A year earlier he directed a production of a new play by Pete Morgan, *All the Voices Going Away*, based on the life and writings of R.C. Scriven – a project organised jointly with the Ilkley Literature Festival, where it opened. It then toured to three other West Yorkshire venues before performances at the Playhouse.

As well as an opportunity to learn new skills, Phil's time at the Playhouse allowed him to make contacts, which in turn led to work at other theatres, including three London ones: the Greenwich Theatre, the Old Red Lion Theatre, and the Hampstead Theatre. It also led, indirectly, to his appointment as an Associate Director at the Liverpool Everyman Theatre. And, as mentioned earlier, he was back at the Playhouse in 1987 to devise and direct *Torpedoes in the Jacuzzi*. Phil went on to have a successful freelance directing career in America and Germany, and a teaching career at RADA and elsewhere. He was also resident playwright at Essex University.

Who else was given a John Harrison 'bunk up'? Steven Pimlott and Nicholas Hytner, whom John refers to as "the lads from the opera", were beneficiaries. Prior to the Playhouse, both worked for Opera North, and both "welcomed the opportunity for crossover to the drama".[83] Steven and Nick had been friends since their days at Manchester Grammar School. Indeed they both had arrived in Leeds at the start of their careers to work with Opera North. Then, at the Playhouse, in September 1983, Steven directed Tom Stoppard's *On the Razzle*, followed by *A Patriot for Me* by John Osborne and *The Genius* by Howard Brenton in 1984 and 1985 respectively. After Leeds Steven continued to direct both opera and theatre, including at the Crucible Theatre in Sheffield. At the start of the 1990's he began working at the Royal Shakespeare Theatre in Stratford where he was an Associate Director from 1996 to 2002. Afterwards he worked as a joint Artistic Director at the Chichester Festival Theatre, followed by other freelance directing. Sadly Steven died of lung cancer in 2007 at the age of fifty-two while rehearsing a play for the National Theatre. Nick took over this work of his friend.

Nick Hytner first directed at the Playhouse in 1983, following the start of his theatre career at the Northcott Theatre, Exeter. Early that year he directed *Tom Jones*, an adaptation of the Henry Fielding novel, followed by *The Ruling* Class by Peter Barnes later in the year, and in 1984, a musical version of *Alice in Wonderland*. He returned in 1985 to direct Arnold Wesker's *Chips With Everything* and in that year was appointed as Artistic Director at the Royal Exchange Theatre in Manchester, where he stayed until 1989. He directed both the London and New York productions of the musical *Miss Saigon*. He is best known, of course, for his appointment, in 2001, as Artistic Director at the National Theatre, where he had been directing since 1989 and had been an Associate Director. He is also well-known for directing many of Alan Bennett's plays and films since 1990. Now Sir Nicholas Hytner, in 2017 he and Nick Starr, his colleague at the National Theatre, founded the London Theatre Company at the Bridge Theatre in London.

Thinking back to his time at the Playhouse, Nick commented:

"There could not have been a better place for a young director to learn the craft. John had created what I still consider to be the most committed and astute audience in the country – and if you missed what the audience was trying to tell you about your work, there was always John. I made some sort of leap, under John's guidance from being a smart undergraduate with ideas about a text to being a real director."[84]

And what of actors? Leeds Playhouse has boosted the careers of many who have gone on to dazzling success in theatre, some becoming household names and faces. In Bill Hays' time as Artistic Director the Playhouse helped the careers of Tony Robinson, Paul Copley and Zoë Wanamaker. Under John Harrison, Lesley Manville, Charles Dance, Nigel Planer, David Troughton, Hugh Ross and Ian Barritt all appeared on the Playhouse stage. Art Malik, prior to his successful career in television (starting in 1984 with *The Jewel in the Crown*) and cinema, acted at the Playhouse. Imelda Staunton, soon after graduating from RADA, appeared in *The Gingerbread Man* at Christmas in 1989.

In 1983 Natasha Richardson, daughter of Vanessa Redgrave and film director Tony Richardson, made her professional stage debut at the Playhouse in a production of Tom Stoppard's *On the Razzle*. She also performed in the next two productions, *Top Girls* by Caryl Churchill and by contrast the classic farce, *Charley's Aunt*. After Leeds Natasha achieved a substantial career in film and television, as well as theatre in London and on Broadway. Tragically Natasha died in 2009 at the age of just forty-five.

ACT ONE, SCENE NINE

Provision for children and young people has always been an important part of the work of most regional theatres. Today, many have youth theatre companies. However, in the 1970s and 1980s Theatre In Education was the more typical provision.

RAJ by Leeds Playhouse Theatre In Education Company 3rd February 1982

THIS SCENE TAKES PLACE NOT AT THE PLAYHOUSE but at Thornhill Middle School in the Wortley area of Leeds. It is the first performance of a play, one which went on to become one of the biggest successes for the Theatre In Education company.

Raj is set in 1940s India. It follows the life of an Indian woman, Nandita, from childhood. Her parents having died, she is brought up by a British circuit judge. In adulthood she works as a nanny for Colonel Gower, a British officer in the Indian army. Her uncle also works for Gower, and his son joins the Colonel's regiment. The story then focuses on these characters' loyalties, including the Colonel's wife and children, whilst he and her nephew are away with their regiment. With the rise of nationalism in the country, Nandita's loyalty is divided, as an Indian woman working for, and having been brought up by, a white family. *Raj* is "about imperialism, about power and where it lies, about divided loyalties: loyalties born, nurtured, and handed down over generations of British rule".[85]

After Thornhill School, Raj was performed over the following three months at other middle schools in Leeds: sixty-eight performances to 2,839 children. At the end of the year, and in early 1983, *Raj* also toured to the city's secondary schools.

From the start, Leeds Playhouse saw provision for children and young people as essential. An early policy document presented this as a way of increasing the theatre-going population, but more than that, "It is hoped that a close relationship will be set up with the Local and County Education Authorities in the promoting of interest in drama among young people".[86]

This was the reason for the visit made by those early Planning Committee members to the Octagon Theatre in Bolton – where they persuaded Roger Chapman, in charge of their

Theatre In Education programme (TIE) to come and work at the Playhouse. He brought with him three of his team of actor-teachers (the term used for TIE staff). Two further appointments were made, so a team of six workers was in post as the Playhouse opened.

The concept and name of TIE had originated at the Belgrade Theatre in Coventry in 1962 where Roger Chapman had worked prior to Bolton. When the Playhouse opened in 1970, other TIE staff from Coventry had also moved on to set up companies elsewhere. This 'explosion' of TIE perhaps explains why "neither funders nor main house establishments knew quite what to expect from setting up a TIE company, but there seemed to be money for it and there was kudos to be gained. The issue for actor/teachers and TIE directors was, managing erroneous expectations."[87]

By the time TIE was happening in Leeds, eight years had passed since that pioneering work in Coventry. Roger Chapman and his team were able to learn from the successes and the mistakes made at other regional theatres, as well as drawing on their own experience of working elsewhere. This applied not only to the work itself, but also the relationships with Theatre Boards, the Local Education Authority, and its teachers.

Whilst the themes and content of Leeds Playhouse TIE clearly evolved and developed over the years, the structure of the work was established at the start. The actor/teachers provided programmes of work for schools, usually working with just one class at a time. The pupils were participants rather than audiences. The teachers were expected to be directly involved: as well as attendance at pre-programme briefings, this might involve preparatory work in lessons before the arrival of the TIE company, and follow-up work afterwards. The TIE team would often be at a school for the whole day, and their performance would be just one part of that day.

Also from the start, a crucial aspect of the work was that it be provided free to schools. In Leeds, at least initially, it was decided to work only in schools within a three-mile radius of the Playhouse. Because the work was with five-year-olds through to sixth formers, already in 1971 the team was working in seventy schools in Leeds.

Typically TIE would tour three programmes each year, varying the targeted age-range. The performance aspect of the programme would be devised and written by the Leeds team, although occasionally they would use a programme developed by another TIE company. In terms of content this was seen as a 'springboard', enabling pupils to understand and reflect on the world they live in, and sometimes to challenge the 'facts' they are given. As such, by promoting and developing critical thinking amongst children and young people, it could be seen as very much ahead of its time.

Sometimes the programme's theme would relate specifically to Leeds. For example, *No. 30* for six-year-olds, was about buses in Leeds: the people who work on them and the people who travel on them. *No. 30* toured in the Autumn of 1979; it was presented thirty-eight times, reaching a total of 1,140 children. Another programme with a local theme was *Away From Home* which toured in 1980 and 1981. This programme, for eight to nine year-olds, concerned the experiences of children evacuated during World War II, specifically from schools in Leeds to the east coast of Yorkshire.

Some programmes focused on issues not covered in the school curriculum. *Snap Out of It*, from 1971, concerned aspects of mental health. The programme aimed to present the facts about this issue, to emphasise the commonplace nature of mental illness, and the thoughtlessness often displayed towards people experiencing mental health problems. At other times programmes would focus on national issues and events. For example *Priorities*, a 1980 programme for 12-13 year-olds, concerned the National Health Service. Although programmes like *Raj* concerned global issues, the plays focused on individuals, sometimes real, sometimes fictional. Another example is *Flags and Bandages*, first performed in 1986. The spark for this programme was an article about Mary Seacole, a Jamaican physician in the Crimean War. She is a character in the play, as is Lord Cardigan, but the story concerns Matilda, a paid nurse, and Joe, a wounded soldier. *Raj* and *Flags and Bandages* are also examples of programmes which, whilst concerned with events in the past, raise issues – in this instance inequality and racism – relevant to today.

Certain programmes were intended for specific groups of pupils. *In the Bag*, from 1977, was one of a number of programmes specifically intended for pupils at special schools. *Doris, Boris and Morris* (1979) was for pupils learning English as a second language. The actor-teachers performed a number of everyday situations using simple language and making use of rhythm and repetition. Props were also important, so that understanding was not solely reliant on language. For example, the performance culminated in a conjuring trick, taught to the pupils for them to perform.

The teaching of a conjuring trick is one simple example of how pupils were much more involved in the action than is the case when attending a theatre performance. This might also be through preparation before the TIE team arrived at the school. For *No. 30*, the teacher and the class involved were expected to create the environment of a bus in the classroom where the play was to be performed. In other programmes pupils were drawn into the action of the play performed. In *Away From Home* pupils were treated as evacuees, experienced being in an air-raid shelter, and had to make a decision on whether or not to help a German prisoner of war who was trying to escape. In *Snap Out of It*, part of the programme involved pupils being blindfolded before listening to readings and completing exercises. The purpose of the blindfolding was to give pupils a sense of isolation and confusion as an analogy for mental illness.

Whilst programmes such as these were the core work of TIE at Leeds Playhouse, the team's involvement in other work was very different to that of many TIE companies. This is partly explained by the excellent working relationship that evolved between the first Artistic Director, Bill Hays, and TIE Director Roger Chapman. Also relevant is Roger's experience prior to

TIE, which included acting at the National Theatre; he also had an interest in directing plays.

As a consequence, once a year the company performed a play in the Leeds Playhouse auditorium, typically at the end of the schools' summer term. This aspect of the work was essentially children's theatre. Roger Chapman also got involved in Playhouse Christmas productions, directing *Old King Cole* by Ken Campbell in 1970 and *Toad of Toad Hall* the following year, plus *Dracula* in 1971. Even more unusual for TIE actor-teachers was that they also acted at the Playhouse: one of the team in Brendan Behan's *The Hostage*, and all of the team in *Hamlet*. They played 'the players', a touring company of actors who perform at Hamlet's request, a play within the play. Annalyn Bhanji remembers it well:

"We played the players; the feeling was that the whole other world (to Hamlet's) had come in here as the players. How appropriate this is, because the TIE company is a whole other world that thinks differently from the world of the play."[88]

Later, team members also performed in *Lulu*, *Waiting for Godot*, and *Close the Coalhouse Door*.

Some TIE companies had a less than positive relationship with their repertory theatres, possibly because the latter were more interested in the funding than the work itself. Perhaps because of the TIE team's involvement in Playhouse work, the relationship was much better in Leeds. This relationship also benefited from the TIE Director's regular written reports and attendance at Board Meetings. Furthermore the governors were regularly invited to observe TIE programmes in schools. Another significant way in which the Playhouse was kept informed of the work was through performances specifically for Playhouse Club members.

Like most TIE companies, Leeds received funding from the Arts Council. This was included in the annual Playhouse grant but intended specifically for TIE, thus in 1973 the theatre received an Arts Council grant of £48,500, with £8,000 earmarked for TIE. This part of the grant was dependent on

Leeds City Council match-funding (£4,000 from Education Department funds in 1973). The TIE programme operated with a separate account. This was one way in which the TIE company was able to remain independent of the Playhouse.

The team's location is also relevant in this respect: fortuitously, the lack of space at the theatre building meant that their base and some of their work needed to be elsewhere. Initially the team was based at the old Gaumont Cinema, a short distance away on Cookridge Street. In 1975, they moved to Quarry Mount School in the Woodhouse area of the city.

The TIE company was also accountable to the City Council's Education Department because of the support and funding they provided. Furthermore, the TIE sub-committee of the Playhouse Trust was chaired by the Director of Education, and one committee member would be a local head-teacher.

Paul Swift, who joined the Leeds team in 1981, saw the joint funding and accountability as a major factor which enabled TIE to survive. Talking about TIE work more generally, he said this meant that "people in the theatre thought, 'this is Education, we don't quite understand it' and people in Education thought, 'this is theatre, we don't quite understand it'. So the companies had a lot of autonomy. Joint funding meant that if the main house wanted to appropriate the funds, they would lose the education authority funding. Similarly if the education department wanted to pull it, they would lose the Arts Council money. It gave the companies a degree of independence."[89]

TIE teams did not typically get involved with what today would be called 'youth theatre'; in Leeds, however, the provision of young people's leisure activities was a regular part of the work. By 1971, weekly sessions were being offered on Tuesday and Thursday evenings at the Gaumont, and on Saturday mornings at the Playhouse. The 1971-72 school year saw 105 sessions taking place, with an average attendance of thirty.

As well as performing at the Playhouse, the TIE team occasionally toured to other venues in Yorkshire and beyond.

This might be the same play as performed at the Playhouse each summer; it might also be a play devised as part of the work in Leeds schools. One aim of this touring work was to take productions to industrial areas of the region where very little children's theatre was seen. Tours also generated income, which helped fund the core work of the team.

The reputation of Leeds Playhouse Theatre In Education grew, and they received invitations to perform internationally. As early as 1974 the team was chosen and funded by the British Council to spend nine weeks touring in the Far East, including visits to Malaysia, Thailand and Singapore. Obviously productions needed to be devised specifically for audiences in these countries, and the programme included a play about food, *A Feast of Fun*, for audiences with no English.

Flags and Bandages, mentioned earlier, was another particularly successful schools programme. This success culminated with a substantial tour of Canada in the summer of 1986. In Vancouver there were ten performances at the city's Festival, as well as six at high schools. There were ten performances at the Vernon Children's Festival. Finally, *Flags and Bandages* was performed eight times at Toronto's International Children's Theatre Festival.

Although tours such as the one in Canada were primarily about performances for children, they were also a way of promoting the concept of TIE. For the Playhouse team this was an important aspect of their work, more usually achieved through workshops and courses for teachers and in Further Education. The majority of (mostly half-day) workshops for teachers took place in Leeds, initially either at the Gaumont base or at the Teachers' Centre. Additionally, however, workshops were provided in places as far apart as Lincoln, Hull, Durham, London and Belfast. In Leeds the workshop might specifically relate to a programme currently touring local schools; alternatively, the content might be broader, for example an in-service day on TIE techniques for infant teachers.

In Further Education settings, Playhouse TIE Directors occasionally contributed to courses such as the M.A. in Theatre Arts at Leeds University. More common were sessions for students on Teacher Training courses, most frequently at the City of Leeds and Carnegie College / Leeds Polytechnic (now Leeds Beckett University). The team also contributed to Further Education courses elsewhere in Yorkshire and further afield, including one in Berlin.

More informally, TIE was promoted through welcoming visitors from abroad. For example, 1978-79 saw over one hundred visitors from Africa, Australia and America. The following year saw visitors from India, Sri Lanka, and Belize. By 1984 the list had also included China, Israel, and European countries such as France and Denmark, visitors from the latter being students teaching drama and theatre studies.

The Playhouse TIE team was also active in the Standing Conference on Young People's Theatre, sometimes giving workshop demonstrations at this annual event. In 1978 they hosted this conference over five days with events being held at the Playhouse and the University. This was attended by two hundred people representing thirty-five TIE and Young People's Theatre companies. At conferences elsewhere they performed plays, for example *Raj* at Manchester in 1982. In the same year, they also performed *Raj* at the Newham International Festival of TIE, where there were representatives from Europe, America, Australia and Canada.

A further dimension of Leeds TIE's incredible record of achievements was the publication of some of its plays. *Snap Out of It* was included in the Eyre Methuen Young Drama series. The value of publishing plays is that it enables productions by other TIE companies, thus *Snap Out of It* went on to be performed in New Zealand, Australia and Canada. Closer to home, the publication of *Raj* by Amber Lane Press in 1984 resulted in performances by other TIE and Young People's Theatre companies based at theatres in Sheffield (Crucible), London (Half Moon), Ringwood (Forest Forge), Watford

(Palace) and Derby (Playhouse). The play was also performed by the Theatre Foundry company in Walsall and the M6 Theatre Company in Rochdale.

It is hard to imagine how Leeds TIE could have been more successful; however there was indeed a further dimension to their achievements, namely, the filming of some of the plays. A 1975 project with pupils at Cardinal Square special school in Beeston was filmed, delightfully capturing the spontaneous reactions of children with severe learning difficulties to the four actor-teachers involved. The British Film Institute asked for a copy for the National Film Archive. Then in the autumn of 1977 *Changes* was adapted and recorded for the BBC Schools Radio Drama Workshop series.

The TIE team was, in short, a powerful dynamo carrying out phenomenal work alongside whatever was going on in the main house. With its global and multi-media reach, the impact of Leeds Playhouse's Theatre in Education programme has been inestimable.

ACT I

ACT ONE, SCENE TEN

One major difference between regional producing theatres and commercial ones concerns when buildings are open to the public. The latter tend to open an hour or so before 'curtain up'. Most producing theatres are open all day, because much more is going on besides the matinee and evening performances.

WHEN THE WHALES CAME
10th December 1989

A TYPICAL COMMENT MADE about the Leeds Playhouse was, "there's always something going on". The theatre was open all day. The restaurant was open from half past nine in the morning until eleven in the evening. The bar was open during normal licensing hours. People might call in to see one of the regular art exhibitions. The foyer and the staircases were used for this purpose, and exhibitions changed every three weeks. The first of these was organised by the group called 'Printmakers from Yorkshire', and the regional emphasis continued with exhibitions of paintings and sculptures by Leeds-based artists.

All this was in line with the objectives included in the very first policy statement for the Leeds Playhouse, written in 1964. It was intended that there should be "good all round facilities, because an exciting theatre building could be a focal point for many other activities and should be used not only for plays, but for concerts, jazz recitals, talks and demonstrations, and should offer amenities such as a coffee bar and restaurant, a bar, a club room for exhibitions and many other activities".[90]

One very important activity was film screenings. As the Playhouse opened, the British Film Institute (BFI) approached the Trust about establishing the Playhouse as a Regional Film Theatre, guaranteeing a minimum of fifty-two performances a year. Films were to be shown on Sunday evenings as well as late-night Saturday showings, billed as 'The Best of World Cinema'. A membership system operated, and the programme was the responsibility of Leeds Film Society.

There was a Gala Opening on 27th September 1970, and the special guest, something of a scoop, was Harold Lloyd, the American actor and comedian, who appeared in many silent comedy films. A week later the first film to be shown, a members-only event, was *My Night With Maud*, the French New Wave film directed by Éric Rohmer, released the previous year.

The Society continued to use the Playhouse even when the BFI ended their commitment. In April 1973 the Playhouse assumed responsibility for the operation. Films continued with late-night and Sunday showings, but there were also daytime showings for school children, as well as summer seasons. Occasional special events linked the Playhouse productions with Film Theatre screenings; for example in 1979, Mike Leigh came to talk about his films during the period when *Abigail's Party* was being performed in the theatre. The Film Theatre was seen as an integral part of the Playhouse's work, always reporting to governors' meetings.

Films were often organised in seasons: in 1980 there was a season of New Soviet Cinema; also a season of German films. Prior to these there had been a season of late night sci-fi films including two 3-D ones (on each occasion, people had to be turned away). One very special event in 1983 was a rare showing of the 1927 silent French film, *Napoléon*, an epic historical film originally lasting over five hours. The Leeds audience got to see a new restored version by Kevin Brownlow and the National Film Archive; they had pieced together almost all of the original film by accessing archives across the world. The Playhouse Sunday showing, with intervals, began at 3 p.m. and finished at 9.45 p.m. There was piano accompaniment by Andrew Youdell who had previously performed at the Playhouse for other silent film showings. Other special film events included an afternoon of archive cricket films, a silent film evening, and an all-nighter Suspense film show.

This latter event attracted an audience of more than three hundred, and occasionally audiences reached above five hundred. Average attendances increased over the years, but from the start were typically around 200 (for example, 1975/76 saw 113 public performances and 25,756 attendances). 1986 saw the introduction of Saturday afternoon children's films, when there was not a play matinee, achieving 100+ attendances.

Today, any 'art house' cinema would be overjoyed to achieve such numbers.

It is amusing now that in March 1980 the Governors were informed there had been occasions when "punks" threatened to cause trouble during late night performances, but this had not "developed into serious disturbances".

As well as showing films the Playhouse also became a venue for live music. There was much variety: for example during three months in 1974 there were concerts by Leeds singer-songwriter Jake Thackray, Liverpool's The Scaffold, as well as Chris Barber and His Jazz Band and The Fitzwilliam String Quartet. During this same period, there was also a booking of the American punk band Iggy Pop And The Stooges, but sadly this got cancelled: the group disbanded in February 1974, and apparently their last concert ended in a fight between the band and a group of bikers. Over the years, jazz became particularly popular, especially late-night performances on Fridays at 11.15 p.m. There was also Sunday lunchtime jazz. During the periods when theatre productions were not programmed for Mondays, this evening was used for other visiting musicians including The Albion Band, Roy Bailey, Richard Stilgoe, George Chisholm, Boys of the Lough, Alan Price, Ralph McTell, Fascinating Aïda, and Barbara Thompson's Paraphernalia.

A major event never before attempted in the UK, took place in Leeds in the summer of 1971; namely an International Children's Festival. Thus the end of the Playhouse's first season was busy with festival events. For two weeks, children's theatre companies visited Leeds from as far apart as San Francisco and Leningrad, with events also held at the Grand Theatre, City Varieties, the Civic Theatre and the Gaumont building. Most popular were puppet theatre productions. Although a Children's Festival, some events were pitched at young people aged up to twenty-five.

Other special events were occasionally organised, such as *A Funny Kind of Evening* by well-known actor and story-teller

David Kossoff, and in 1983, *An Evening with Alan Bennett* (a fund-raiser for the NSPCC). 1984 saw a sold-out lunchtime poetry event with Seamus Heaney and Craig Raine. Furthermore, for several years the Playhouse hosted Carifesta, Leeds's festival of Caribbean arts and entertainment. The first, in 1978, lasted eight days; in the later years, until 1983, it became a two-day event.

In 1984 the Playhouse produced the play *Masterpieces* by Sarah Daniels, tackling issues relating to pornography, misogyny, and violence against women. To accompany the production, the play was sometimes followed with the screening of a 'witty, colourful and challenging' short film, *Give Us A Smile*, produced by Leeds Animation Workshop, a women's collective. A combination of animation and live action, the film showed "the effect of the constant harassment which women live with every day – from 'street humour' and stereotyped media images to actual physical violence".

After this showing, which took place on Friday and Saturday evenings during the run of the play, audience members were invited to stay and discuss the issues raised with members of the cast. Even more impressive, a programme note stated that "if any women want to talk about the play and the issues raised, there will be an opportunity to have a personal discussion with female members of the cast on Thursday evenings after the show".

Given the amount of work filling the stage for most of the year, it is not surprising that there was little space for visiting productions. Nevertheless, in the first years, there was a small number of visits by national touring companies, including Prospect, 7:89, and Temba. The very first visitors – Germany's Dortmund Theatre Company in May 1971 – proved controversial, achieving the front page in the Yorkshire Evening Post:

"The Playhouse appears to have had no warning that the play *Wildwechsel*, by Franz Kroetz contained full frontal nudity."[91]

Less controversial were regular visits by Polka, bringing children's theatre with actors and puppets, performances usually being daytime ones alongside Playhouse productions, or during the schools' summer holidays when other companies, as well as the theatre's own TIE team, would also provide children's theatre. For several years, the last week of the academic summer term was given over to Leeds Educational Drama Association, with productions by local schools. There were also occasional visits by dance companies such as Ballet Rambert, and 1983 and 1984 saw the National Theatre on Tour, but these were entertainments rather than plays, with one performed at 11:15pm on a Friday evening.

But these successful diversifications of the Playhouse's use as a multi-media venue were not always lasting. The film screenings were to end. The newly released *When the Whales Came* was part of the Playhouse's last ever screen-show at the 1989 Gala Evening, along with the 1921 silent film *Never Weaken* with Harold Lloyd, plus archive footage of Lloyd from the 1970 Gala Opening. The choice of *When the Whales Came* was appropriate given that the film starred Paul Scofield (Prospero in *The Tempest* back in 1974).

Despite there being every possibility of showing films at the new Playhouse, the decision was made not to do so, which was contentious at the time, and even in retrospect continues to be surprising. It was a great blow for Leeds's film buffs, whose only hope after 1990 was that a permanent Film Theatre would be established one day in the future, somewhere else in Leeds.

ACT I

ACT ONE, SCENE ELEVEN

"If we take Box Office receipts as our sole guide to this important question (choice of play) we should not be sailing a true course. We should be forsaking an ideal for immediate gain – hugging the coast instead of venturing out across the ocean, braving unknown dangers in a voyage of discovery. For that is what every visit to the theatre should be – a voyage of discovery and revelation."

André Van Gyseghem, the first artistic director at the Nottingham Playhouse[92]

TWELFTH NIGHT by William Shakespeare
20th January 1990

THE FINAL PRODUCTION at the first Leeds Playhouse was Shakespeare's *Twelfth Night*. It took more at the box office than any previous production, selling out for the last two weeks, until the night of 20th January 1990 – the theatre's last performance. Then, almost twenty years after the 'temporary' Leeds Playhouse had opened (1970), the curtain came down on this much-loved building – and a new era of theatre in Leeds was about to begin.

The last performance formed part of a Gala Evening which also included the 'Green Room Disco', live foyer music and a cabaret. The eight hundred guests included Doreen and Walter Newlyn and Charles and Barbara Barber, four of the campaign group members from back in 1984. Interviewed by the Yorkshire Post, Doreen commented:

"Tonight is wonderful, although we are sad at it closing, it is like a birth, in a way, of a new theatre too. We saw this as the little man's struggle against insuperable odds."[93]

Also present was Kathy Webster who had agreed to being a temporary receptionist to help out for a few weeks in 1970 but had worked at the Playhouse ever since. Her memories of the building include the day the roof came off in strong winds, and the two times she arrived at work to find the place flooded. She said:

"It's been a friendly place and a lovely atmosphere and my second home for so long. I'm very excited about the new Playhouse, it's another challenge, we've reached our goal, we've got the theatre we've always wanted"[94]

The make-up of the cast of *Twelfth Night* demonstrated the love and loyalty shown by actors towards the Leeds Playhouse. Of the fifteen, only two had not played there before. Linda Gardner had regularly performed at the Playhouse since 1972;

two others had performed regularly since the 1970s. The printed programme included many goodwill messages, including one from playwright Tom Stoppard:

"... The plan for a new Playhouse in the centre of Leeds is very exciting and very welcome. Leeds deserves the best and the Playhouse company has proved many times that it can deliver the best. I can see that you are fairly set to become perhaps the most important regional theatre in the country, and a nicer thing couldn't happen to you or Leeds." [95]

So – what had the Playhouse proved to be best at delivering? Apart from anything else, it certainly had shown it was possible to produce an amazing amount of work. In its twenty years, there had been over two hundred productions.

What of the quality, though? Another of the objectives included in the very first (1964) policy statement for the Leeds Playhouse was the provision of "good drama, because the people of other cities in England and Europe have shown that [this], well presented, is what they want, but that the commercial theatre is limited to a narrow concept of box office possibilities". [96]

As regards the choices of these productions, the very first one, *Simon Says!*, started the debate about what plays a regional repertory theatre should be producing. The Artistic Director, the Administrator, the Theatre Trust and Board were, in a baptism of fire, facing the dilemma of every theatre: which is the priority – plays you believe should be staged, or plays that will fill the auditorium?

Bill's programme for his second season had a safe-rather-than-sorry air about it:

"Until you've got the audience there you've got to be a bit careful. You can only afford to do so much. When the magic 60 per cent capacity has been topped ... I'd like to be doing two new plays to one old one". [97]

However, the inclusion of *Pictures in a Bath of Acid* caused more upset, with one councillor concluding, "I think it is right that Leeds should support culture and have a theatre of this kind, but if people want to watch way-out plays with only limited public appeal, they must pay to watch them and not expect the ratepayers to subsidise them".[98]

The problem for the Playhouse was that, as with most other regional repertory theatres, it was partially dependent on Arts Council funding, and in contrast to the local authority, the Arts Council wanted to subsidise adventurous programming. So it must have been music to the local councillors' ears when John Harrison, taking over from Bill Hays, said, "we'll not push our luck with new writers just yet. We've got to realise that Leeds as a city without a tradition of repertory theatre has yet got to know the classics".[99]

Hence John's first season saw no premieres, although as well as Shakespeare and other classics he did include some new plays – even controversial ones: *Oh, What a Lovely War*, which had been staged nine years earlier; *Saved* and *Loot* from 1965. Unless theatregoers in Leeds had travelled to London to see these plays, this was probably their first opportunity.

Throughout his eighteen years at the Playhouse John programmed not only the classics but plays such as these – some having previously had little exposure. *The Old Order* by Stephen Bill had won the 1979 John Whiting Award given to younger British playwrights, and was produced in 1981 – its first main house production after its original production at Birmingham Rep's studio space. Similarly *Moving Pictures*, produced in 1984, was a new and retitled version of Stephen Lowe's play only seen at London's Royal Court Upstairs, another studio space, three years earlier. Furthermore, plays by more established writers such as Michael Frayn, Tom Stoppard and Stephen Poliakoff received their regional premieres at the Playhouse.

Another feature of John Harrison's programming was an emphasis on northern writers. The work of Alan Ayckbourn was regularly produced, as were plays by Willy Russell and Alan Bleasdale. Surprisingly, however, it was not until 1988 that an Alan Bennett play was chosen. Equally, no plays by another West Yorkshire writer, John Godber, were ever selected.

Not everyone was happy with John Harrison's programming. As early as autumn 1973 an article in Leeds Student challenged the work being produced, and argued that "the Playhouse was originally billed as a 'people's theatre' ... Popular social theatre; irreverence, not high art was to be the keynote".[100]

The writer, Paul Valleley, argued that because of financial problems, the Playhouse had resorted to popular classics, "bowdlerised and trivial productions".

"The Playhouse should provide a radical alternative to the kind of theatre we find at the Grand and the City Varieties. Instead it is trying to compete with them and over the past three years the choice of its plays and the standard of its productions has steadily declined as a result".[101]

However, the theatre's Administrator, Bill Johnson, defended the programming:

"The challenge which faces those who run the Playhouse, or any subsidised regional theatre, is attracting enough of the mass audience who seek 'light entertainment' to fill the coffers, while not disappointing the adventurous minority who welcome the 'radical alternative' ... Sadly, the support for [this] is not so great as we would hope".[102]

A year earlier, an article in the Leeds Weekly Citizen had argued almost the opposite in respect of who the theatre did or should attract:

"In my view it has proved to be anything but a 'people's theatre'. Perhaps (even with a grant from the Council) it was never intended to make it such? Experimental theatre – is that its aim? An appeal to the trendy types? An opportunity for 'way out' authors and producers to have a rare old time catering mainly for an already privileged minority?".[103]

These comments do indeed, somewhat controversially, raise the issue of who the Playhouse wanted to attract. Whilst disagreeing substantially, they would both likely also totally disagree with Dr. Patrick Nuttgens, the first Chairperson of the

Theatre Trust, who was quoted as saying that "the Playhouse's programme in its first year ... was not the sort of thing which would attract theatregoers who would be willing to write substantial cheques to clear the theatre's capital deficit".[104]

Five years later, Leeds Student would publish a further article, following an interview with the Playhouse's Associate Director, Michael Attenborough, arguing that the theatre did not, as claimed by its management, reach all sections of the community, but rather a predominantly young, student one. Michael had evidently agreed that whilst the theatre should be used by people of all backgrounds, it was too often a place for intellectuals:

"Not only is it a distance from the centre of town, I feel that people are put off by the proximity of the University. The closeness of the academic world can often discourage townsfolk from coming".[105]

Nevertheless, Michael considered *Factory Birds* by James Robson to be the production of which he was most proud. Again it was a regional premiere, having previously been produced by the Royal Shakespeare Company at their Warehouse Theatre in London (now the Donmar Warehouse), and having won the Evening Standard's Most Promising Playwright Award for 1977:

"It was a conspicuously working-class subject, set on a factory floor, and audiences were not the conventional Leeds Playhouse middle-class ones. A lot of people were coming because of the subject matter".[106]

The subject-matter was clearly important in terms of audience appeal, but this play involved a cast of eighteen actors. As it became necessary to produce plays with smaller casts, John Harrison found it difficult to find ones which would also attract good audiences – of any social class. He also found that plays which the Playhouse might have produced in the past were now touring productions and visiting the Grand Theatre. Similarly, new work was more likely being produced in London, or by the National Theatre and the Royal

Shakespeare Company who could afford plays written for large casts.

Despite everything, John continued at the Playhouse because he deeply appreciated those who supported the theatre:

"The audience here, the atmosphere here is the best in England. There's something very special about this building and the audience. I mean the fact that we are able to put together the group of plays we do, as a subscription package, and get five thousand subscribers, which is the upper bracket for English theatre, to be able to do that is quite remarkable".[107]

As John was often to point out, he came for one year but stayed for eighteen. Thus he was deeply disappointed not to be chosen as Artistic Director of the new West Yorkshire Playhouse..

Act II

Scenario

IN 1973 THE LOCATION OF THE LEEDS PLAYHOUSE is still on the edge of the University campus. But this has always been a temporary site: the intention from the outset has been for the shell of the theatre to be converted, after ten years, into a second sports hall. Once again the search is on for a city centre building.

Even before the existing Playhouse has successfully established itself, finding a new site has become a priority. After less than three years of operating, the strengths and limitations of the existing temporary site are apparent. Hence in March 1973 a questionnaire gets circulated to all members of the Playhouse Trust regarding planning for a permanent location. The responses to this highlight certain priorities.

Firstly it is considered essential that the new site should be central. A site near to the Grand Theatre, the Corn Exchange, or the Riverside would be ideal. It is hoped that the location will allow theatregoers to use the existing city centre car parks, rather than the Playhouse having to provide parking spaces.

Secondly it is felt that – presumably if only because of cost implications – the Playhouse will be an imaginatively conceived conversion of an existing building rather than a purpose-built theatre. Also important is that the building be big enough to house all aspects of the Playhouse's work: offices, rehearsal space, scenery workshops, and children's theatre, as well as a base for the Theatre In Education team.

Thirdly it is felt that whilst the design of the auditorium has been a big success, its size should be slightly smaller: ideally between six and seven hundred seats. On the other hand, there is substantial support for the provision of a second, smaller auditorium with between one hundred and twenty-five and two hundred seats, which is deemed a more suitable space for late-night or lunchtime performances. The continuation of the Film Theatre in one of these spaces is seen as essential.

In April 1974 the Playhouse Trust approaches Leeds City Council with a formal request for help in finding a permanent building for 1980. The Council suggests a consideration of the Playhouse becoming part of the Grand Theatre complex on New Briggate. The most relevant part of this complex was originally called the Grand Assembly Rooms, having a seating capacity of eleven hundred. By the beginning of the twentieth century this building had become a cinema. It was renovated in 1923, by which time the seating capacity had been reduced to nine hundred. After a series of management changes, in 1958 it became the Plaza Cinema.

The governors react positively to the suggestion of the Plaza, although there are doubts about the possibility of converting the auditorium into a space similar to the existing Playhouse auditorium. As the Playhouse's Administrator Bill Johnston explains:

"An important aspect of the Playhouse is that it has a thrust stage, with the audience sitting on three sides. If we were to try and convert the Plaza in any simple way, we could end up as a mini-Grand theatre, and not doing the job as well as the Grand."[108]

A feasibility study is hence commissioned from Theatre Projects Consultants Ltd. By now the Playhouse is already using the Grand Theatre's workshop space and equipment for scenery construction, space left unused since the Grand ceased creating its own productions. The study takes two years to complete, which is obviously of serious concern to the

Playhouse governors, given the requirement to move from the University site in 1980.

The proposed scheme is costed at £4 million, and at a meeting held in July 1976 with councillors and representatives from both theatres, Councillor Peter Sparling (chairman of the Board of Directors at the Grand) makes it clear that £4 million is out of the question. He recommends exploring alternative sites and proposals. Knocked on the head, after two years of work! Hence the search for a city centre site begins all over again.

An obvious possibility is the Gaumont Cinema on Cookridge Street, by now a listed building. By the end of 1976 the governors have agreed that the Gaumont is the right place for a permanent Playhouse. The permission of the Council is requested to carry out another feasibility study in consultation with their Department of Architecture. This is conducted by Bill Houghton-Evans who designed the original playhouse. His report confirms the possibility of creating a permanent playhouse within the shell of the Gaumont and its adjacent buildings. The initial costing is £500,000-£750,000, but by March 1977 this rises to as much as £1.25 million. The governors are quite optimistic that the Gaumont project will come to fruition, especially because the Council has refered to it in their District Plan for the development of leisure provision in the civic area.

The Gaumont project remains a possibility, but at the beginning of 1980 the Council decides to let the building to Norwood Film Studios; following this usage, the building is used for bingo and as a nightclub (using the building's original name – 'The Colosseum'). After other music and nightclub usage it is sold to the Academy group, becoming the 02 Academy Leeds.

The Council then suggests the Electric Press Building on the corner of Cookridge Street and Great George Street. This is the former printing works of the firm Chorley and Pickersgill. The suitability of this site is doubted, particularly because of the potentially insurmountable problems with site development and consequent costs. (Interestingly, this building will eventually be partly occupied by the Carriageworks Theatre, which faces onto Millennium Square.)

Years later, Councillor Bernard Atha will describe the search for a site, claiming that whenever he pestered the Conservative Council Leader on the matter, "he would, sometime later – often much later – suggest a site, which we would then visit and find totally unsuitable but have to hence prepare a long document showing its unsuitability. The process was designed to keep us busy without making any progress at all".[109]

Perhaps more out of desperation than preference, the governors begin to explore the possibility of remaining on the existing site. The University is approached with a request for a long-term lease and on-site development. By March 1981 plans are drawn up, again by Bill Houghton-Evans, which will extend the building in two directions. The plans include a studio theatre, a cinema, and workshops, thus combining all aspects of the Playhouse on one site. Its estimated cost is £1.5 to £2 million.

Later in the year the University agrees to this. It offers a fifty-year lease with a one-off payment of £70,000 followed by a 'peppercorn' rental. Also attractive from the point of view of the University, the City Council is offering the possibility of a site for a new sports complex, which might allow the Playhouse to take over the neighbouring sports hall building.

The hope is that work on the site will begin in the spring of 1983, completing in September 1985. To this end, yet another fund-raising campaign is organised, with the idea of completing the scheme in stages, as funds allow. However, towards the end of 1982 news comes of the possibility of a new site for the Playhouse as part of the development of the city's Quarry Hill area – previously the location of the Quarry Hill flats, the largest social housing estate in Britain, built in the 1930s to replace eighteenth and early nineteenth century housing and open spaces. In 1978 the whole estate was demolished, being of poor construction and unpopular. It has just been incorporated in the City Council's Central Business Area District Plan and allocated as a site for parks and gardens, 'regional functions', long-stay parking spaces, and potentially a hotel. The location of the Playhouse on this site has been approved in principle by councillors, who are also considering a large sports and exhibition complex on Quarry Hill.

The Playhouse Board of Governors meets in March 1983 to make a decision on the future location of the theatre. Somewhat surprisingly, a plan to remain on and expand the existing site is still being considered. However, the governors are aware that the Arts Council's 'Housing the Arts Committee' is much more supportive of the Quarry Hill proposal; this matters because they are a major funder. Governors think that a new theatre on Quarry Hill will be more likely to attract other funding than an expansion of the existing site. The Quarry Hill proposal is also seen as attractive in that it will allow the existing theatre to continue right up to the time of the new playhouse opening. The governors hence vote unanimously (with one abstention) to wholeheartedly support the proposal.

After many years of governing what has been a relatively small-scale and temporary theatre, it is perhaps inevitable that a new permanent theatre, even more dependent on outside funding, will mean losing some control. That this might be a problem for some is highlighted almost immediately: the Arts Council announces an 'absolute condition' of funding, namely, the design of the new theatre should be selected by means of an architectural competition.

There is resistance to this idea. Some governors feel the Playhouse already has its own architect: Bill Houghton-Evans, who designed the original building and also the plans for its possible extension. Consequently Alec Baron promptly resigns as chair of the Theatre Planning Committee, arguing that the competition will just incur needless expense. Doubts continue to be expressed, then at the end of 1983 a decision is made by a vote at the governors' meeting. Astonishingly, the idea of a competition is narrowly agreed (six votes for, five votes against), which might have gone differently if not for the stipulation that the governors themselves would set the architectural brief; also that Bill Houghton-Evans could enter the competition as long as he discontinues his involvement at governors' meetings. Any other outcome might have scuppered all prospects for a future Leeds Playhouse.

Now that the need for a competition has been accepted, the next 'problem', perhaps inevitably, is the issue of who will be appointed to assess the entries. The agreed panel is as follows: three professional architects to be appointed in consultation with the Royal Institute of British Architects; two Playhouse governors; and attendance by the theatre's Artistic Director and the Administrator, acting as technical advisors. Perhaps realising the implications of this imbalance, a third governor is added to the composition; nevertheless, the chairperson is to be one of the professional architects, who will have the casting vote. The governors are also promised that if they do not agree with the final choice, they will have the right to choose another architect.

The next essential stage is to produce the initial design aims. These are agreed as follows:

1.   To provide a new theatre for Leeds and the North East which will be the permanent home for the Leeds Playhouse Company.

2.   To provide facilities and a building which enables the company to operate as a professional producing repertory company with the proper technical back up necessary. It will be a theatre dedicated to drama.

3.   To house all the various departments of the Trust in the one building.

4.   To recreate the existing auditorium and to retain and develop the existing qualities of the old building especially its informal and approachable ambience.

5.   To develop a second aspect of the theatre's work through provision of a new second auditorium.

6.   To enhance the facilities for the general public.

7.   To provide fully equipped spacious workshops and backstage accommodation.

8.   To make a major contribution to the environment of Central Leeds.[110]

Obviously these general aims get developed into a more substantial brief for those entering the architectural competition. Much detail is provided in respect of what are initially called Auditorium 1 and Auditorium 2. Auditorium 1 is required to mirror the existing Playhouse, having a thrust stage and a steep seating rake. The capacity is to remain at seven hundred and fifty. Nevertheless, the backstage area is required to be much bigger and more substantially technically-equipped. Rear entry to the auditorium is seen as necessary for latecomers; attention is given to provision for disabled access: wheelchair space, facilities for the hard of hearing, etc.

The specifications for Auditorium 2 reflect a concept which was quite innovative at the time. This second space is not conceived as a 'studio theatre', if only because such spaces are often too small for the requirements of many touring companies. The seating capacity is to be three hundred and fifty, and further, "the overall objective is to avoid this space being seen as in any way the 'lesser' or the inferior space. Rather the spaces are equal, with one or other having particular advantage of form or speciality for a production".[111]

Auditorium 2 needs to have a very high degree of flexibility – for example seating that allows for in-the-round productions as well as end-on ones, and a flat floor that allows for other configurations such as cabaret-style performances.

Another specification relating to the auditoria is rehearsal space. This is specified as needing to be larger than the acting area of Auditorium 1.

Further, the brief includes very specific requirements in respect of the front-of-house areas. A buffet and restaurant are to share the same space in a way which recreates an informal atmosphere similar to that in the existing building, where "artists, staff, audience all rub shoulders together". This area is also envisaged as being used for concerts and semi-staged events, including cabaret-style ones, such that a performance space needs to be included. Elsewhere, a shop is needed, selling magazines, gifts, books, prints, sweets, etc. The specifications also included a Board room / function room, and a creche. Outside there should be a terrace where outdoor events can take place in the summer months – an area as visible as possible from the city centre so as to attract attention.

Those producing the competition brief are greatly encouraged by the receipt of a capital grant of £1.2 million from West Yorkshire County Council. However, initial costings predicted a cost of over £7 million. Consequently, even before the brief's completion, cuts are deemed necessary, after which the figure gets reduced to £4.5m. It is decided that both the Theatre In Education company and wardrobe hire provision will continue to be based elsewhere. These cuts obviously compromise the aim of housing all the various departments in one building. Additionally, it is decided not to provide for the continuation of Leeds Film Theatre.

The architectural competition is at last announced. Without conducting interviews, the panel of assessors select thirteen candidates from the one hundred and twenty-nine expressions of interest, but exclude some internationally respected architectural practices, presumably because of their limited experience in theatre design. This decision not to interview later gets criticised by one of the three architects on the selection panel, arguing that it mitigated against the possibility that the selection process could "produce fresh ideas, possibly a higher quality of architecture and sometimes discover new talent".[112]

The thirteen chosen candidates are sent the detailed competition brief towards the end of 1984. Crucially they are told that the rest of Quarry Hill will likely remain as urban parkland and surface car-parks in the future. Most of them end up expressing difficulty in including all the requirements within the estimated budget; consequently, this gets increased to £5.8 million.

The brief is very detailed. As John Harrison writes in his autobiography, "William [Weston] and I masterminded the most exhaustive brief in the history of theatre".[113]

But the brief is too restrictive for most of the thirteen architectural practices – arguably reflected in the fact that their entries are mostly remarkably similar and lacking in fresh ideas. However there are two notable exceptions. One of the architects is keen to integrate the new building with the only existing Quarry Hill architecture, so proposes that the Playhouse should incorporate the Victorian warehouse buildings on St. Peter's Square. The Playhouse is in fact already looking to lease these buildings: they could become space, for example, for workshops and rehearsal rooms. The design aims to merge the past and the present on Quarry Hill, because the architect is fundamentally opposed to the concept of a stand-alone, 'look at me' building.

The latter concept is (in absolute contrast) precisely what the other exceptional design intends to do. The architect proposes a building high up on Quarry Hill so as to be very prominent. The design incorporates a round, castle-like structure on the hill-top, which also has the look of a big top circus tent, intended "to reveal clearly its theatricality".

All of the entries struggle with the dilemma of the relationship between the Playhouse and the rest of Quarry Hill, and in turn with the city centre. In this respect a significant development occurs regarding plans for the rest of Quarry Hill. The competition brief says the site will remain as parkland and parking, but a new proposal is announced just days before the competition closing date of 7th March 1985 which contradicts this. No wonder that one architectural magazine, Building Design, reports that "the competition has been thrown into disarray". The proposal is a £60 million scheme by a Dutch company called MAB to redevelop the Kirkgate Market and Quarry Hill areas. The scheme is to include a hotel, an exhibition centre, and a concert hall, plus a high-level road linking the two areas as well as a footbridge crossing. The road and the footbridge therefore contradict the City Council's statement that vehicular access will be via a new road from St. Peter's Street.

The Building Design article reports that "several of the shortlisted thirteen practices have complained that the plans will change the whole context of the site, forcing a rethink of their designs. This development will certainly suit practices that have approached the problem with the future development of the site in mind, but will seriously undermine the chances of those competitors who have used a contextual design approach".[114]

Regardless of whether or not the final twelve submissions are compromised in any way because of the MAB scheme, perhaps the biggest difference between them relates to the proposed access to the Playhouse and the consequent direction in which the theatre 'faces'. One architectural practice wisely recognises that whilst theatre-going pedestrians will more likely be willing to walk further from the city centre to the Playhouse entrance, this might deter lunchtime trade in the bar, restaurant and shop. Another practice seeks to monopolise on the existing pedestrian footpath which will be alongside the theatre, as a way of drawing attention to the Playhouse. One of the other entries toys with the idea of re-routing this pedestrian path right through the building!

Once the twelve submissions are received, the six assessors, with the support of Playhouse and Council staff, meet over several days to make a decision, assessing submissions on the basis of the following criteria:

"...a solution which promise[s] a fine piece of architecture and which [is] well organised internally. Attractive and inviting front of house areas, an audience-stage relationship which [is] workable and similar to the present Playhouse, and well planned backstage requirements, and at a cost within the rather tight budget". [115]

The Appleton Partnership wins through, the assessors feeling that "this rather substantial building [is] the right solution for this corner site of Quarry Hill. The building uses traditional material but in a contemporary manner and should be easy to maintain. The scheme is well planned internally, especially in the front of house areas and meets most of the requirements of the brief. The restaurant is particularly attractive". [116]

The Appleton Partnership, a husband and wife team, Ian and Marjorie Appleton, is based in Edinburgh and is (in 1985) working on theatres at Edinburgh University and in the city's Wester Hailes district. Ian Appleton has previously worked for the practices responsible for the Barbican Centre in the City of London, the Nottingham Playhouse, and Hull's Gulbenkian Theatre. Another project with which he has been involved is the interior reconstruction of the Royal Opera House in London.

The Appletons' submission recognises that locating the theatre entrance is the most crucial decision. They work on the assumption that Quarry Hill will eventually become an urban park, and therefore propose that the public entrance and foyer should be in the north-east corner, which represents both the building's highest point, and the furthest from St. Peter's Street. Car-parking is to be located beyond the building. Another reason given is a purely practical one: St. Peter's Street is not seen as a safe place to incorporate a convenient drop-off area. The consequence of this layout means that the public will enter the park first, and then the theatre.

The internal plan which is so liked by the assessors means that once inside the building, theatre-goers will be on the same level as the box office and the foyer area. However, the bar-restaurant and the theatre entrances will be immediately visible, mostly on a half-level above. The location of the bar-restaurant area is intended to allow good views across to the city centre, and like all other public areas will maximise use of daylight.

The layout of the rest of the theatre is very practical, the stages of both auditoria, the scene-dock, workshops, rehearsal room and delivery access being at the same level. Because the theatre will cut into the side of Quarry Hill, these will be at the St. Peter's Street level. The rake of the larger auditorium will thus follow the hill's contours.

On 11ᵗʰ November 1987 the traditional ceremony for the 'first day of construction' takes place. Actor Donald Sinden 'turns the first sod' of the new Playhouse. Unfortunately, it has taken two years and eight months, following the outcome of the design competition, to get to this day.

Obviously it was always going to take some time for the Appleton Partnership to firm up their winning design, reworking it where necessary. Next, planning permission had to be obtained, and a construction company selected and given the contract. However, this process is subject to delays, and at one point in late 1985 the architects are asked to stop work: "all design work [to be] halted otherwise much of the work could possibly be abortive".[117]

There is no way that the Playhouse building will be completed, as planned, for December 1988. The main reason for the delay is the proposed MAB scheme for the area. The proposed road bridge between Quarry Hill and the two-thousand-space car-park above the new market complex has to run across the site designated for the Playhouse. The proposed pedestrian bridge will obstruct the design of the Playhouse: specifically it will block the view of – and the view out of – the restaurant. Fortunately Ian Appleton agrees for the site to be moved a little , further north, which will not necessitate substantial alterations to the plans.

Another reason for the delay concerns the concert hall which forms part of the MAB proposal. The governors are asked to consider the possibility of combining the Playhouse with this venue. Fortunately the governors decide that not only will this prove more expensive but it might also destroy the relaxed and informal atmosphere that they wish to recreate in the new Playhouse. Nevertheless, the governors are aware that the delays caused by the MAB proposal mean additional costs in terms of redesign work and the effects of inflation. There is also uncertainty about who will pay for the costs external to the building: access roads and so on. Additionally, any substantial delay could threaten their position with the Arts Council over grant aid.

Fortunately, capital funding does increase, in particular from the soon-to-be-abolished West Yorkshire County Council, which has already committed (in 1984) £1.2 million. Now, in March 1986, West Yorkshire agrees to put in a further phenomenal £2.7 million. Thus it is that the theatre's name changes to acknowledge its generous benefactor. The West Yorkshire Playhouse is born!

By July 1986, the estimated building cost has increased to £11,752,000, almost exactly double the competition budget of £5.8 million. In this period, a further cost of £130,000 has also been incurred for the purchase and renovation of the warehouse buildings in St. Peter's Square. Previously a clothing factory built in the 1930s, these buildings are intended to provide space for the facilities that have been taken out of the West Yorkshire Playhouse brief.

Even before these increasing costs, the Playhouse has been taking steps to raise funds in other ways. July 1985 sees the appointment of a Development Officer responsible for fund-raising, particularly within the business community. A target of £1 million is agreed, and a campaign launched in September 1985 called 'Get the Ball Rolling'. Good publicity is received when a seven-foot-sized football was 'kicked off' by Councillor Bernard Atha at the existing Playhouse and rolled all the way to the Quarry Hill site. There, it is received by the Mayor, Councillor Sydney Symmonds, the actress Stephanie Turner, and the Leeds United chairman Lesley Silver (who was also the chair of the Playhouse's Development Committee). Initially, fund-raising within the business community proves difficult, but it is felt that this would become easier once potential donors could see building activity on the Quarry Hill site.

A further delay is caused by difficulties in obtaining planning permission. This is at last granted in autumn 1986, but with certain provisos. Some of these relate to landscaping of the area immediately north of the theatre, and the provision of a footbridge (the estimated cost of £1.5 million to be met by Leeds

City Council). However, the required changes to features of the building will add another £600,000 to the building costs. These requirements include the following: a slate roof instead of tiles; red bricks alternating with the buff ones on exterior walls; stone sills; external bay windows in the bar-restaurant area; glass panels and floodlighting in the construction of the fly tower.

In June 1987, despite continuing negotiations with MAB, the contract for the building is put out to tender. Six firms are selected, and Fairclough Building is chosen. At this point the target for completion is revised to January-February 1990.

Since Quarry Hill was first proposed in 1982 as the site for the new Playhouse, the substantial administrative work necessary to get to the point where Fairclough Building could begin work was the responsibility of the Playhouse's Administrator, William Weston. Consequently, William is by now effectively doing two jobs: looking after both the existing Leeds Playhouse and the future West Yorkshire Playhouse (his dual responsibility will continue until January 1990 when the final performance at the Leeds Playhouse takes place).

Meanwhile, work is continuing on the West Yorkshire Playhouse, albeit now with a six-week delay. March 1989 sees a significant milestone event: Judi Dench lays the foundation stone – rather late in the day, considering the building is already one hundred feet high

It is now time to decide on names for the various spaces within the Playhouse. Auditorium 1 becomes the Quarry Theatre, reflecting both the design of the space and the site itself. Auditorium 2, again reflecting its design, becomes the Courtyard Theatre. Two other spaces are given the names of playwrights: the Priestley and Congreave suites. Alan Bennett declines to have a space named in his honour. Of those involved at the Leeds Playhouse from the start of the Theatre Campaign, Doreen and Walter Newlyn agree to the Newlyn Gallery, but Charles and Barbara Barber decline the offer.

The next milestone is the 'topping out ceremony', traditionally representing the completion of the building. This honour is given to the actor Albert Finney in September 1989. In doing so, he chooses "to bless the efforts of the artists, actors, directors, crafts people and technicians who will strive in this space, and bless their endeavours with imagination, inspiration and the glory of life".[118]

Finally, in January 1990, the theatre's completion is marked with a parade between the two theatres. Hearing that the West Yorkshire Playhouse is ready to open, Alan Bennett sends a highly cogent message:

"As a boy in Leeds in the forties I used to go every Saturday to the matinee at the Grand Theatre. It was always half empty (which is how I imagined all theatres to be) but it made no difference to me. I saw the original production of *The Cocktail Party*, Michael Redgrave in *Love's Labours Lost*, Flora Robson in *Black Chiffon*, Edith Evans in *Daphne Lauerola*, and Robertson Hare in *Will Any Gentleman*. Drama, comedy, high art, low farce... they were all the same to me. I hope the new West Yorkshire Playhouse will never be half empty. But I hope too there will be the same magic in the theatre that I found all those years ago and that somewhere in the audience there will be a boy or girl for whom it is a new world."

ACT II

ACT TWO, SCENE ONE

Typically, the larger regional producing theatres have two auditoria: a main house and a much smaller studio space. One consequence is that new writing tends to be produced in the studio; the main stage is mostly reserved for productions of classic plays. This makes financial sense, but has implications for the choice of new plays: only small-scale ones are possible. With no studio space, the West Yorkshire Playhouse was always going to be different.

WILD OATS by John O'Keefe
8th March 1990

THE OFFICIAL OPENING NIGHT of the newly-named West Yorkshire Playhouse was March 8th 1990. Prior to the performance and outside the theatre, the people of Leeds were treated to a firework display, while within the building speeches were made before a specially invited audience including actors Paul Scofield and Timothy West.

The theatre was officially opened from the stage of the Quarry Theatre (the Courtyard Theatre was still to be completed) by Diana Rigg, with the cutting of a large purple ribbon. In her speech she suggested that the Playhouse would likely be the last to be opened in Britain in the twentieth century. Describing it as the largest theatre complex outside London, she considered it as built to last:

"It seems to me that the quality of everything means that it will be here to stay for many years to come."[119]

Suggesting that it was unusual from her experience, she assured the audience that the backstage areas were of the same quality in decoration as the public spaces.

The choice of opening play was *Wild Oats*, written in 1791 by the Irishman John O'Keeffe and rediscovered in 1976 by the Royal Shakespeare Company. This was a most appropriate choice, given its content is a celebration of theatre itself. The main character, played in this production by Reece Dinsdale, is an itinerant actor whose everyday conversations are littered with extracts from Shakespeare plays. The somewhat complicated plot is full of twists and turns, often a result of mistaken identity.

The play is similar to *Simon Says!* which opened the Leeds Playhouse twenty years earlier, in the sense of being a comedy, full of verbal and visual gags. But unlike *Simon Says!*, *Wild Oats* is fairly harmless fun with no political message, albeit being a satire of eighteenth century social class and religious hypocrisy.

Most reviews praised the production for being a technical demonstration of what could be achieved in this new space. Claire Armitstead suggested in the Financial Times that it "accommodates every technical trick in the Quarry's book, from trapdoors which disgorge actors in rocking chairs, to pilasters which swoop down from the much-treasured fly towers to transform bucolic landscapes to Palladian halls".[120]

Consequently, some reviews suggested that the theatre itself was the hero of the evening:

"Robert Jones' magnificent set, the great walls of the open stage splashed with bold, glowing wash of sky-after-rain blue and luminous meadow green, dotted with sheep that appear to be grazing half-way up a wall when the location switches to an interior. Jones creates a magical fusion of pastoral quaintness and wonky perspectives, a Lewis Carroll dreamworld and a place of theatrical artifice – the set is framed by giant, precariously-leaning painted flats and gold-fringed drapes."[121]

Nevertheless, critics appreciated that the company was "spirited, happy enough to let camp enthusiasm stand-in for style."[122] Others found the acting over-the-top:

"One actor titters too often, another mugs too much, a third cannot enter except at the run and comically holding up her apron. Over-acting is a temptation when unsmiling dignitaries are present in numbers as they were on the opening night; but it especially needs resisting when the main character is an actor whose genial histrionics are supposed to distinguish him from everybody else."[123]

Presumably enough others in the audience were smiling, given that the performance ended with a two-minute ovation and five curtain calls. Michael Schmidt in the Weekend Telegraph finished his review by quoting the end of Diana Rigg's speech:

"'Let the heart of the West Yorkshire Playhouse begin to a beat'. It has, and strongly."[124]

Jude Kelly had begun in post as Artistic Director in January 1989 and had worked together with John Harrison for the old playhouse's final year. As detailed previously, the governors had controversially decided not to extend John Harrison's contract beyond August 1990, hence the post had been advertised, and of the forty-nine applications, six were shortlisted, with Jude Kelly ultimately being the appointee.

It had been necessary, if only for financial reasons, for John and Jude to direct almost all the final productions at the old site. Jude directed three, giving her the opportunity to work in a space like the future Quarry Theatre. The year of working together also allowed time to develop an artistic policy for the West Yorkshire Playhouse. Concerned that there should be unity of purpose at the new theatre, Jude and John had met with existing staff, in small groups, to discuss policy issues.

The opening play was hence under Jude Kelly's direction, and her choice of *Wild Oats* was not without controversy. Just as Bill Hays had experienced at the Leeds Playhouse with his choice for the Royal Gala Opening, *Wild Oats* was similarly criticised, in a letter published by the Yorkshire Evening Post:

"Good theatre is both intellectually and emotionally provocative. Is the Artistic Director of the West Yorkshire Playhouse aware of this? Are these present in *Wild Oats*? A play should enhance one's perception of the world in some way? Does *Wild Oats* do this? A romp is not enough in the later twentieth century. One hoped for artistic triumph. Instead one got the triumph of mediocrity".[125]

Another reader disagreed, because the following week saw this response:

"As one of those apparently inferior citizens who has, until recently, rarely gone to the theatre, I have to say that I have been persuaded to change my ways by the varied and interesting nature of the Playhouse's programme for the next few months. As a theatre for the people, surely the key is to entertain, not to be 'intellectually and emotionally provocative'".[126]

The question of which audiences the West Yorkshire Playhouse hoped to attract had been addressed by Jude Kelly earlier on the opening day of the theatre while she was giving critics a tour of the building. She aimed to achieve an eclectic programme with something for every age-group, regardless of class and social background. The Yorkshire Evening Post reported her as saying:

"'Popular does not mean populist... We will try to reach the people of West Yorkshire, of different age-groups, backgrounds and nationalities'. [Jude said] the Playhouse also had a duty to be educational and to encourage new writers – 'the lifeblood of future theatre'."[127]

The three productions in the Quarry Theatre which followed *Wild Oats* can be seen as Jude's desire for an eclectic programme. Next came *Glory!*, a play set in Trinidad, the birthplace of its writer, Felix Cross, telling the story of a young woman, abused by her father, who commits a terrible crime. It is set against the struggle for independence in her country. The play uses music and dance to create a carnival style. *Glory!* was significant in that it was the Playhouse's first visiting production, part of a tour by Temba, a Black theatre company. That it was performed in the larger space of the Quarry Theatre also demonstrated that new writing was not going to be confined to the safer Courtyard Theatre space. However, the Daily Telegraph reviewer did suggest that "the acting space is too large for the production."[128]

Other critics welcomed the production: "*Glory!* is not a cosy little entertainment. It is big, powerful exciting stuff",[129] and "*Glory!* is a complete experience and just what the West Yorkshire Playhouse needs. This type of work will help establish its reputation".[130]

The next production in the Quarry Theatre, *Carousel*, was arguably an example of 'popular' theatre. In an interview for The Stage, Jude explained that whereas *Wild Oats* was the kind of play that the old Playhouse did well, *Carousel* "is a family musical, one of the great works of Rodgers and Hammerstein, which was too big for the previous theatre, so we hope it will bring in a new audience who will be happy to see something with which they are partly familiar...".[131]

However, another interview showed that she had anticipated criticism of this choice. She stated that "this does not signify that artistic integrity has given way to commercial expediency. 'It's an artistic decision to do *Carousel*. It's a question of the way it's done – it's going to be quite surreal, not gingham frocks and petticoats'".[132]

Whether or not it was a surreal production it was indeed popular, attracting 86% attendances. Michael Billington, however, reported Jude Kelly as saying that she resisted the temptation to actually open the West Yorkshire Playhouse with *Carousel* "on the grounds that 'musicals are not our brief'". [133] This is somewhat ironic given that musicals were to be some of her most successful productions in her years as Artistic Director.

In keeping with the policy of encouraging new writing, *Carousel* was followed by the world premiere of *Safe In Our Hands*. This is a play by the writer, actor and stand-up comedian Andy de la Tour. The title is based on the Conservative Party's slogan about the National Health Service, and the play concerned the crisis in this service. The play had a classic farce structure. As Jude Kelly explained, "The plot includes missing bodies, porters impersonating doctors, doctors lying about patients, and feet being amputated by mistake. There are several hundred entrances, through doors, lifts and tunnels with trolleys, wheelchairs, bedpans and laundry bins, and the whole rehearsal period was a nightmare of building precision timing in order to ensure the laughs came on cue".

Nevertheless, she saw *Safe In Our Hands* as political satire, and said that, "behind the laughs and comic timing is an immense sense of the writer's own feelings of anger and outrage".[134] *Safe In Our Hands* won the West Yorkshire Playhouse's first award: The London Weekend Television Plays on Stage Award.

The first production in the Courtyard Theatre, *The Maple Tree Game*, was definitely not chosen as 'popular' theatre. It was a play by the Czech writer Pavel Kohout, described in the programme as sitting "firmly in the Czech tradition of politico/social satire". The production was one of two directed by John Harrison in the first season at the new Playhouse, where he was given the title of Artistic Director Emeritus. Interestingly the cast included several actors who had appeared at the Leeds Playhouse: for example, Ian Barritt had appeared in twenty-five of them, and Timothy Bateson was in the cast of *Simon Says!*. The Yorkshire Post critic Bob Keogh praised the "wit and ingenuity of John Harrison's direction". He also praised the choice of this play:

"But, a Czech political black comedy? Not, on the face of it, a bid for full houses. But if notices like this help to swell audiences, a critic can feel some satisfaction in, at once, supporting a worthy production and provoking theatregoers into a satisfying night out."[135]

Meanwhile, the Leeds International Young People's Theatre Festival – a ten-day event – had taken place, hosted by the Playhouse along with five local schools immediately prior to the opening of *The Maple Tree Game.* Along with a range of plays from other countries, the programme also included a Family Fun Weekend and a two-day conference for artists and teachers. As part of this Festival, the Theatre In Education company performed *The Doctor's Wife* in the Courtyard Theatre, a play which they had already toured around Leeds' secondary schools between October 1989 and February 1990. Strictly speaking, this had in fact been the Courtyard's opening play. Furthermore it is important to note that 1990 was not only the year of The West Yorkshire Playhouse's grand opening, but also the twentieth year of the Leeds Playhouse Theatre In Education company: certainly a double cause for celebration!

ACT II

ACT TWO, SCENE TWO

Producing theatres regularly receive unsolicited scripts: writers hope that in this way their work will be discovered, that they will get their big break. Should regional theatres be more proactive in nurturing new work? How can they encourage women and Black writers in this respect?

BACK STREET MAMMY by Trish Cooke 10th January 1991

Prior to the opening of the West Yorkshire Playhouse, Jude Kelly had met with local playwrights. This resulted in the formation of the Yorkshire Playwrights Group, demonstrating one of her priorities for the theatre: the encouragement of new writing. This commitment was further shown at the start of 1991 when, under the banner of *Lifelines: a season of contemporary plays*, six productions, overlapping in pairs, were presented in the Courtyard Theatre. Introducing the plays, Jude Kelly argued that this new writing "is something which should not be feared, but encouraged and delighted in. After all, it's interesting to see what is reflected back at us about our society when a living writer holds up his or her mirror to nature."[136] Like John Harrison, she also recognised the importance of regional theatres producing new plays which had often just had one previous production, usually in London.

The first of these *Lifelines* plays was *Back Street Mammy* by Black writer Trish Cooke, featuring a cast of Black actors. Born in Bradford, Trish completed a BA in Performing Arts at Leeds Polytechnic and started her career as an actor, but in 1988 was awarded a Thames Television bursary as writer-in-residence at the Liverpool Playhouse. *Back Street Mammy,* set in Bradford and concerning teenage pregnancy, received its premiere at the Lyric Hammersmith in 1989. Trish has gone on to achieve much success, not only as an actor, playwright and scriptwriter, but also as a television presenter and children's author.

With one exception, all the *Lifelines* plays had small casts of four or five actors. Half were set in the present day. Two were world premieres. Local writer Kay Mellor had been commissioned to write a play for the Playhouse, and *In All Innocence* was included in this season. This play concerns the subject of sexual abuse. Other plays in the season focused on equally serious issues: *Getting Attention* by Martin Crimp concerned child neglect; *Scrape off the Black* by Tunde Ikoli concerned bi-racial relationships. The season did end on a somewhat lighter note with *It's a Girl* by John Burrows, promoted as an antenatal musical comedy.

One of the plays, *My Mother Said I Never Should*, by Charlotte Keatley, was particularly successful and was revived for four weeks later in the year. All the actors were female, as was the writer and director. Like Trish and Kay, Charlotte had a local connection, having completed an MA in Theatre Arts at Leeds University. She says that whilst there, she attended "an impassioned public meeting in 1984 to discuss the future West Yorkshire Playhouse, [and] I remember standing up to ask for theatre space for new plays by women".[137] No wonder she was delighted that her play was produced at the Playhouse!

Jude Kelly had herself directed *Getting Attention*, and this play became the West Yorkshire Playhouse's first London transfer, playing at the Royal Court Theatre later in 1991. Reviewing all six productions for Plays International, Peter Hawkins made one particularly significant comment:

"I think the next step for the Courtyard is to make fuller use of its facilities. It is designed as a studio which can take any kind of staging and seating. Instead, every play so far has been watched from an unwelcoming, steeply raked block of seating all looking one way at an end-on stage". [138]

In fact the plays were to have been staged in the round, but the Courtyard was still missing the necessary complete banks of seating for this configuration.

Just after the *Lifelines* season took place, the Playhouse was involved in another project promoting new writing. *New Plays '91* was a competition organised by the Yorkshire Playwrights Group. The winning three plays were chosen from two hundred entries by Yorkshire-based writers. All of the entries were read by a team of professional readers, who were not looking for perfectly crafted plays: it was more about discovering new talent, writers who might blossom if given enough support. The three winners were each linked with a professional writer who gave support through the rehearsal process. In every case, it was the writer's first play. Finally, each play was given a rehearsed reading at the Playhouse, using professional actors (including Jean Ferguson, well-known for BBC television's *Last of the Summer Wine*). The hope was that these readings would attract playwrights, critics and theatrical agents, which might lead to full productions at other theatres.

The following year the Playhouse hosted another new writing event, the WHSmith Plays for Children National Awards. More than just a competition, this was seen as a way of promoting the writing of plays that would be produced in repertory theatres, not just as part of Theatre In Education tours. Eight hundred entries were received, and all were read twice by a panel of writers, educationalists and directors. The shortlisted plays were all read by a judging panel; four plays received joint first and second prizes (£5,000 and £4,000 respectively). One of the first prize winners was Adrian Flynn, and his play, *Burning Everest*, was produced in the Courtyard Theatre the following year. He also adapted the play for radio. Adrian has been successfully writing plays for children and young people ever since the WHSmith Award, as well as scripts for the BBC Radio 4's long running *The Archers*.

The final four years of the Leeds Playhouse had seen just three world or British premieres, whereas the same number had been achieved within a year of the West Yorkshire Playhouse opening, and in less than four years, by February 1994, the theatre was celebrating its twentieth world or British premiere, which was a production of *Postcards from Rome* by Adam Pernak – a play which observes five very different 'Brits' holidaying abroad. The production was significant in a number of other ways. Firstly, Adam was still a university student when he submitted a play to the Playhouse, his local producing theatre. Secondly, he was just twenty-three when *Postcard from Rome* opened. Thirdly, with the support of an Arts Council bursary, he had become the first writer-in-residence at the West Yorkshire Playhouse.

In fact it was a different play, *Killers*, that Adam had submitted. He had also submitted it to the Royal Court Theatre in London, and it was there that this play received a full-scale production, winning their Young Writers Festival award. With the help of the Playhouse, *Postcards from Rome* evolved from his script for a radio play.

Postcards from Rome was actually the third Playhouse production within a year which represented new work by local writers. July 1993 had seen *Father's Day*, also performed in the Courtyard Theatre, written by Maureen Lawrence, the choice of which was praised by Robin Thornber in The Guardian as "a new play commissioned from a local writer – another demonstration of how a producing theatre can connect intimately with its host community".

He described the play as being "deeply rooted in the Alan Bennett world of the aspiring working class of west Yorkshire – with authentically sniffy references to the Quarry Hill flats that once stood on the site now occupied by the theatre".[139]

Born in the Harehills area of Leeds, after university Maureen had followed a career in teaching and was already fifty-six when *Father's Day* opened at the West Yorkshire Playhouse in 1993. This play was based on her personal experience of working, in her student days, with geriatric patients at St. James's Hospital, and of her father's death in a nursing home after four years of suffering from Alzheimer's Disease. The play focuses on how a mother, Connie, copes with her husband's dementia, and the way their daughter is affected by their situation. *Father's Day* received glowing reviews in national newspapers. The Observer critic particularly praised the performance of seventy-two-year-old Richard Mayes, who "hits the heights in the part of his life".[140] The Times described Dilys Laye as giving "a searing, exquisite performance as Connie".[141] *Father's Day* is an early example of how the Courtyard Theatre could attract quality actors and more media attention than would be the case in a smaller studio space.

Earlier in 1993 another new play by Kay Mellor, *A Passionate Woman*, premiered at the Playhouse. Since *In All Innocence* in 1991, her career in writing for television had become very successful. *A Passionate Woman* concerns Betty (played in this first production by Anne Reid), an ordinary suburban housewife who is having a mid-life crisis just ninety minutes before her son's wedding. The play's setting has immediate appeal: in the first act, Betty has retreated to the attic of her house, from where she talks directly to the audience about her life, including memories of a now dead lover from her youth. By the second act she has climbed onto the roof. It is from this location that her son and her husband attempt to talk her into coming down, in time for the wedding. The rescue, in this respect, is something of a coup de théâtre.

The production was directed by Huddersfield-born David Liddement who was Director of Programmes at Granada Television. Kay had worked with him on television drama, but this was his first experience of theatre direction.

The Yorkshire Evening Post's Jim Greenfield declared that "*A Passionate Woman* is an extraordinary play which should run until every last person who wishes to has the chance to see it".[142] Whilst this might not have been possible in Leeds, after the Playhouse the play continued its success with a production opening at London's Comedy (now Harold Pinter) Theatre in November 1994. It ran for almost a year with Stephanie Cole playing the lead role.

Since then there have been many national and international productions, including amateur theatre ones. Two are particularly significant. In 2010 a new production by Hull Truck Theatre saw Kay Mellor herself playing Betty, her first stage-acting for twelve years. In 2017 a production with Liz Goddard opened at the Everyman Theatre in Cheltenham and then toured five other cities before arriving at the West Yorkshire Playhouse, this time being performed in the Quarry Theatre. *A Passionate Woman* was back at the Playhouse again in 2023; sadly Kay Mellor had died the previous year.

Other, and often local, writers continued to be given opportunities at the West Yorkshire Playhouse. For example, 1994 saw the world premiere of *Male Order Bride* by James Robson, two of whose earlier plays had been produced at the Leeds Playhouse. From Kirkbymoorside in North Yorkshire, his plays are often set in this area – *Mail Order Bride* in a Yorkshire Wolds farmhouse. Here, the farmer has 'ordered' a Filipino woman who visits for a trial period. Jude Kelly's production saw Timothy West play the lead, immediately following his role as Macbeth at Theatre Clwyd.

1995 saw Richard Cameron appointed as a Playhouse writer-in-residence, with a bursary from the Thames Television Writers' Scheme. Like James Robson he is also from Yorkshire and many of his plays are set in the Doncaster area where he was born. His earlier plays were often produced at the Bush Theatre in London, sometimes directed by Mike Bradwell who had founded Hull Truck Theatre in 1971. Mike directed

Richard's play, *With Every Beat*, which opened in the Courtyard Theatre in September 1995, about a young man attempting to beat the world non-stop drumming record whilst raising money for a local charity. It raises issues about unemployed life in a disadvantaged community. The cast included Paul Copley, now a familiar face through his film and television work, whose acting career started with the Leeds Playhouse Theatre In Education team back in 1970.

In the summer of 1997 Jude Kelly took the Playhouse's commitment to new writing a stage further. With a press launch in London as well as in Leeds, a festival was announced: *Sevenx7*. This consisted of seven new plays by seven new writers. Each play was both rehearsed and performed for just one week. This was effectively a fringe festival, one that would normally take place in a smaller studio theatre. It was a bold decision, therefore, to present these plays in the Courtyard Theatre. Nevertheless, the space was, as had been intended for the *Lifelines* plays, reconfigured for theatre-in-the-round, and the seating capacity was reduced to one hundred and fifty. The intention was to choose plays that would not be ones ready for a full Playhouse production with a longer run and a longer rehearsal period.

Whilst it was not particularly an aim to discover new writers, the intention was to nurture such writers. As Topher Campbell explained, "I think there's a manifest desire to try to programme work which would not automatically get the major go-ahead here. The risk is that you're looking at putting on work which is completely new – really new, not just a new piece of writing by Alan Bennett or Tom Stoppard. And they're pieces of work which won't be perfectly manicured plays or performances – they'll be very rough and ready, not in terms of their content but in terms of the energy with which they're put on".[143]

Topher was, with an Arts Council bursary, a trainee associate director at the Playhouse; he co-ordinated *Sevenx7* and was responsible for selecting the plays. The only commissioned play was from Richard Hope, another Playhouse writer-in-residence. The rest were chosen from the many unsolicited scripts which regularly arrived at the theatre. Topher and four others, mostly past or present trainee workers, directed the seven plays, two of which were presented as a double bill.

Welcoming *Sevenx7*, Lyn Gardner of The Guardian wrote: "The current boom in new writing has been almost entirely London orientated and almost exclusively white and male. Good then to see a new writing initiative that redefines the map and which is more geared to nurturing talent and not simply discovering."[144] The seven plays were all very different: characters included a Ghanaian man living in London; a drystone-waller in the Yorkshire Dales; a young offender; two immigrants from Jamaica in 1950s London; and a serial killer not dissimilar from the Yorkshire Ripper.

Inevitably some reviews were disappointing. Of *Precious* by Anna Reynolds, Kevin Berry in The Stage wrote, "It requires more time and thought, much more than the sixty minutes running time, and a few lessons in how to portray underclass characters other than by an over-reliance on swearing."[145]

On the other hand, about another of the seven plays, by Paul Boakye, he wrote, "It will be a pity if *Wicked Games* is neglected. It tackles new territory with freshness and authority and deserves a lengthy run somewhere, hopefully with some of this marvellous cast".[146]

Weathering the Storm, Dona Daley's very first play, was reviewed in the Caribbean Times:

"Anyone who enjoys the stories of how Britain's first generation of Caribbean migrants came to England will find *Weathering* both frank and funny as it saunters along and takes you on a roller coaster ride of emotions, from elation to horror, while expressing the savagery of romantic disappointment. *Weathering the Storm* is a must-see for people of all ages and creeds". [147]

The Yorkshire Post described Richard Hopes' play *Good Copy* as "very much a work in progress, not exactly rough but certainly not ready", but more positively as "an entertaining blueprint for a Black comedy which makes the opening play – Mick Martin's *The Life and Times of Young Bob Scallion* – now seem as finely finished as an Ayckbourn".[148]

Mick Martin's play did receive some of the best reviews; Kevin Berry felt that "it makes superb entertainment, never taking itself too seriously"[149], while Jim Greenfield in the Yorkshire Evening Post, in keeping with the young offender main character, concluded that "conspiracy to entertain is an intent four actors would readily hold their hands up to here. And the verdict passed by the public showed the case proven beyond doubt."[150] Kevin Berry also suggested that, "given five years or perhaps less, one of Mick Martin's plays will be on a school examination syllabus."[151]

High praise indeed, and even if this didn't happen, it was certainly the start of a successful career in theatre. *The Life and Times of Young Bob Scallion* is set in Mick's home city of Bradford. After studying a drama degree at Bretton Hall College, he started writing plays in 1990. Soon after *Bob Scallion*, Mick was back at the Playhouse, commissioned to write a play for the Schools Company, *Stepper Joe's Wicked Beat*, which toured Leeds schools in 1998. In 2003 a revised version of *Bob Scallion* was produced at the Northcott Theatre in Exeter, with Adrian Edmondson in the title role. The text of the play was published at this time, as was another of Mick's plays, *Once Upon a Time in Wigan*. Just as this latter play finished a run in Leeds, Mick, also at the Playhouse, undertook his first acting role for many years – in *Sunbeam Terrace* by Mark Catley.

Mick has written extensively for television, but in 2006 he co-founded Bradford's Bent Architect theatre company, established to explore 'issues of the voiceless, those who society feels uncomfortable with'. His plays for this company have included *England Arise!* about Huddersfield's socialist conscientious objectors. In 2011 his play about the creation of Rugby League opened at the Theatre Royal in Wakefield and toured other northern venues. He has also worked for Red Ladder Theatre.

Alongside the seven plays of the new writing festival, fringe events gave further opportunities to local writers. These included the reading of a play by Jonathan Hall, at that time a headteacher at a primary school in Bradford. *Behind the Aquarium at the Last Pizza Show* had been performed the previous year at the Edinburgh Fringe Festival. Another Leeds event was a performance by a company called Leikin Loppu, who specialised in out-of-the-ordinary dance works, using facial expressions as well as movement to entertain. Another reading was of a play by seventy-year-old Dinah Harris, former Lewis's curtain saleswoman and the mother of Kay Mellor. Kay directed the reading and Dinah's granddaughter read the main part.

One other of the *Sevenx7* writers, Richard Hope, had further success at the Playhouse. His play, *Odysseus Thump* opened the 1997-1998 season at the Courtyard. Jude Kelly directed the play, having chosen it for production because she was "'struck by what a lyrical piece it was and it is unusual that you see a play and think it is ready to be staged.' Hope penned the play following the death of his grandfather, and Jude felt it had a lot of relevance for northern men of a certain age. 'I think his grandfather had gone through the change from having absolute certainty about life to losing that'".[152]

Almost a monologue, the play's success was in part due to the Playhouse attracting David Threlfall to play the lead part. Jeffrey Wainwright, reviewing the play for The Independent, concluded that Richard "is fortunate to have an actor giving a performance of a scale, resonance and sensitivity unlikely to be bettered anywhere this season." Although Wainwright (and other critics) had reservations about the play itself, he concluded that "the writing showed enough heart, acuity and wit to make me eager for further work."[153]

Sadly this was not to be, as Richard died suddenly in May 1998.

Finally, mention must be made of Simon Armitage whose play *Mister Heracles* opened at the Playhouse early in 2001. 'New writing'? It was, at least, Simon's first major theatrical production, though he had previously written a play for the National Theatre's Connections youth theatre festival. However, Simon was already well-known for his poetry (becoming the country's Millennium poet in 2000). *Mister Heracles* is a modern version of the Euripides tragedy *Heracles*. It is modern both in terms of the present-day setting and in language, which nevertheless retains a classical poetic style. The Greek chorus is retained but, to quote the Yorkshire Post, is a "motley foursome, a cross between a gang of gossipy production line workers and a bunch of football fans".[154] Simon had worked on the play for three years, and originally submitted it to the Royal Shakespeare Company and the Royal Court Theatre in London. One big advantage of the Playhouse's decision to produce it was the chance for him to try out the text:

"When I had written about half of it, we had a two-week-long workshop involving seven or eight actors, and this was brilliant because I was able to change things; it was a great luxury, and the most important element in creating the play."[155]

Simon, of course, went on to be appointed Britain's Poet Laureate in 2019.

ACT TWO, SCENE THREE

In understanding the financial situation at the new West Yorkshire Playhouse, it is important to recognise that this was no different to many other regional theatres. In 1992-1993, the aggregate of regional theatres' accumulated surpluses and deficits was a deficit of £6.15 million. These same theatres were still carrying a combined deficit of £6 million, which was more than their collective annual subsidy.

PRATT OF THE ARGUS by Michael Birch 12ᵗʰ October 1991

PRATT OF THE ARGUS IS AN ADAPTATION of the novel by David Nobbs, known best for writing the 1970s television series *The Fall and Rise of Reginald Perrin*. Michael was an associate lecturer in drama at Leeds University and also involved in the theatre's community projects. The production, like the book, is a sequel to *Second to Last in the Sack-race*, included in the Playhouse's opening season. In *Pratt of the Argus*, the luckless character of Henry Pratt is now a reporter for a local Yorkshire newspaper. The play is full of Northern humour, but critics praised the production, directed by Jude Kelly, more than the script, as "a triumph of design, production and vigorous acting over a thin, rather clichéd and rather predictable script".[156]

Opening the 1991-1992 season with an almost full house, it was arguably a wise piece of programming:

"Yes those clever people at the West Yorkshire Playhouse know when they're on to a winner … The Playhouse's Autumn Season definitely has the bank manager in mind."[157]

As regards the theatre's finances, in the programme for *Pratt of the Argus* the 'welcome' page by Jude and Will Weston (Executive Director) suggested good news:

"At our AGM in September we were able to announce a threefold increase in earned income from box office receipts jumping from £342,000 to £1,143,000 in our first financial year in this new building … Gross turnover for the year was increased by 225% to just over £3 million from £1.3 million."[158]

Unfortunately the outcome of the 1990-1991 financial year was an operating deficit of £175,592. To give this figure a context, this represented 15% of box office takings for that financial year, or 13% of the Arts Council and local authority grants already allocated for the following year. It was a requirement of Arts Council funding that such a deficit be eradicated within three years.

An additional financial problem related to the capital costs of the new building. Although these costs had yet to be finalised, a potential shortfall resulted in the theatre negotiating a loan of £700,000 from Leeds City Council. This could not be interest free, so payment of £70,000 interest would be due at the end of the 1991-92 financial year. How did this come about? Well, as far back as 1984, a report had been commissioned by the Arts Council concerning the Leeds Playhouse development plans, including in respect of a proposed second auditorium. The report included a comment that "the present management have never run a double-headed building and may well find it more difficult than they presently think".[159]

In retrospect, whether or not this was a fair comment, it is certainly true that the West Yorkshire Playhouse evolved as something much grander than originally planned. Before the Quarry Hill site became a possibility, the hope was basically for a permanent home for a similar auditorium to the one at the Leeds Playhouse, with more office and rehearsal space and ideally a second auditorium. By the time the West Yorkshire Playhouse opened, it was being described as the 'National Theatre of the North'. It was the only regional theatre in England with two substantially sized auditoria (although both the Crucible Theatre in Sheffield and the Birmingham Repertory Theatre did have main spaces with more seating than the Quarry Theatre). In England it was soon to become the regional theatre with the largest public subsidy. And the programme for the opening production of *Wild Oats* lists a staff team of eighty-nine people!

Early in 1992, the Arts Council completed a substantial appraisal which suggested that the Playhouse's deficit at the end of the first year was because of higher than expected running costs, including staffing. It also highlighted the lack of financial control. It suggested that delays in programme planning hindered the work of the marketing department. The report recommended many managerial, financial and marketing changes. It nevertheless acknowledged that, in comparison with other regional producing theatres, for 1990-1991 the Playhouse had achieved the third highest total income and the lowest subsidy both per attendance and per performance, also achieving the highest number of performances. In respect of total attendances this was 198,802 for the year – second only to the Royal Exchange Theatre in Manchester (200,061) which of course had already been in existence since 1976.

By the end of the 1993/1994 financial year the situation had become very serious. The operating deficit had reached £236,123, even though the previous year had seen a small surplus. However, the bigger problem related to the continuing dispute over capital costs of the new building. Essentially, Faircloughs, by then AMEC Ltd., was claiming payment for an 'extension of time'. Delays had been caused for many reasons: in particular, adverse weather conditions; the discovery of a well underneath the site; difficulties with securing material and labour. Equally, there had been changes to the original design brief: relocation of the site and re-design requirements of the Council's Planning Department, amongst others. Certain other changes had been made to keep the project within the target budget but were reinstated after the work had started. There were also disputes about the quality of the electrical work, and the level of soundproofing between the two auditoria. In dispute was who was to blame for these delays. As early as December 1992, governors were warned that "if the claim made by AMEC Ltd. is more than £800,000, Leeds Theatre Trust is insolvent, and Directors are at risk of being held liable for wrongful trading".[160]

The dispute went to arbitration in October 1993, but in September of the following year governors agreed a settlement of £750,000, so arbitration proceedings were discontinued. It was agreed that this money would be paid over a period of nine years, with an initial payment of £200,000 by April 1995. The arbitration costs themselves were more than half a million pounds. If no additional grant funding could be found, these sums would have had to be paid from revenue income. The repayment of the loan by Leeds City Council was already a burden on this source of income.

Following a large revenue deficit of £383,000 for 1995/1996, the theatre's Finance Director reported that "the historical burden of the capital debt/deficit is such that in the absence of additional 'one off' funds and/or increased annual funding, we will be unable to continue to maintain our level of operation without increased and external bank finance".[161]

Governors were then presented with three options for the following year. One was to close both theatres for longer summer periods – between May and September/October. The second option was to close the Courtyard Theatre completely. The third option was the complete closure of the Quarry Theatre. Whichever option was chosen it was also deemed necessary to close the Literary Department and all budgets for commissioning and script-reading. It would also be necessary to reduce the work of the Community and Education Department in line with grant levels. The major savings of these options related to staffing: redundancies for 18, 34, or 46 full-time equivalent staff respectively.

With all three options, but particularly the ones involving the closing of one of the theatres, there would not only be a reduction in ticket sales, but other income would also suffer. For example, profit from catering would reduce; attracting income through sponsorship would be harder. Closing the Literary Department would adversely affect the theatre's commitment to new writing. If all capital expenditure was also stopped, then the absence of necessary upgrading could lead to health and safety issues. There was also an awareness that when other regional theatres had of necessity taken similar action, they had never returned to a full level of operation. Despite realising that closing one of the theatre spaces would lead to media reports of a crisis, Governors nevertheless chose to, if necessary, close the Courtyard Theatre.

In October 1996, Jude Kelly's 'welcome' page in the programme for *Popcorn* publicised the theatre's financial problems. After summarising all that had been achieved since the West Yorkshire Playhouse had opened, she explained:

"It is ironic that the Playhouse has built its success whilst plagued by financial uncertainty. A shortfall in funding for the original building requires us to generate an additional £200,000 each year to cover repayments and interest charges – to date we have paid a grand total of £932,000 out of our revenue income. Without outside help it will cost us £2.4m in total to settle the debts on this building, the repayment stretching over several more years."[162]

Earlier in the year the Yorkshire Evening Post had run a story about the theatre's dire finances. Under the headline of "Theatre begs for tax cash in legal wrangle", it unhelpfully spread the notion that, "Theatre bosses are asking Leeds council tax payers to bail West Yorkshire Playhouse out of a cash crisis caused by a fall in attendances and the cost of an expensive legal wrangle". Only in the smaller inside page editorial, did it comment that "even the airiest Thespians must eat and theatre like this has to be underwritten with public cash. Not in a carping, mealy-mouthed way, but in a generous spirit which recognises the intangible but priceless contribution theatre can make to all our lives".[163] But then a week later they opined that the Playhouse "is over-ambitious and over-trading with too many fancy productions".

Councillor Bernard Atha, chair of the Governors, responded by saying:

"After five years, the Playhouse is now one of the most famous theatres in Britain, with an international reputation. And if it really is going to be the National Theatre of the North, we must have increased funding."[164]

Despite its criticisms, in December 1996 the Yorkshire Evening Post launched its 'Save the Playhouse' campaign, reporting that it had gained support for its campaign from stars such as Sir Alec Guinness, Warren Mitchell, Bob Peck and Trevor Nunn.[165]

At this time, some help was achieved in the form of a new bank loan. This was for £600,000, to be paid back over a longer period, fifteen years, rather than the nine years that had been agreed with AMEC Ltd. This was possible because Leeds City Council had agreed to repay this money in full if the Theatre Trust became insolvent. As a result, in December 1996 the money owed to AMEC Ltd. was paid in full (but with no discount for early payment!).

However, it was in 1997 that real help was given. The Arts Council had established a Stabilisation Unit, attracting National Lottery funding. The Playhouse was awarded a grant of £2,645,000. Most of this was awarded in respect of underfunding of the new theatre complex, and included the costs of arbitration and interest charges on the capital debt. £595,000 was intended as working capital for the following four years, paid subject to the achievement of specific stabilisation requirements, one of which was to eliminate the trading deficit by 2001.

The next years continued to show how the Playhouse remained financially vulnerable. The 1998-1999 season could have been disastrous after two unsuccessful productions in the Quarry Theatre (one, *Picasso at the Lapin Agile* played to just 35% attendances) but was saved by the highly successful Courtyard Company plays with Ian McKellen, and the production of *Martin Guerre*. 1999-2000 ended with a deficit of £96,000, but mainly because Carnival Messiah Ltd (a company set up with National Lottery funding) agreed to put in £114,000 to co-produce *Carnival Messiah,* but never paid up the money.

Under the New Labour government, the Arts Council of England commissioned a review in 1999 of the 'Roles and Functions of the English Regional Producing Theatres' (ERPTs). The West Yorkshire Playhouse was one of the largest such theatres, of which at that time there were fifty in total (fifteen of which were in London). Councillor Bernard Atha, as Chair of the Board of Governors, Jude Kelly, Maggy Saxon (Executive

Director) and thirteen other Playhouse staff took part in the consultation carried out as part of the review. The consequent report, which became known as the Boyden Report, published in May 2000, argued for the development of a national policy for the ERPTs, but recognised that, because of inadequate public funding, many theatres were simply struggling to survive, with the fear of insolvency becoming a genuine threat. Consequently, the report argued:

"Many (if not most) companies began the deadly spiral of 'chasing the money' … On stage the work was often driven towards the chimerical pursuit of a 'safe' programme which could minimise box office risk on shrinking production budgets. The cost was frequently innovation, risk taking and relevance to young people. New audiences were not easily to be found; the old core audience frequently kept its distance. Chronic artistic and financial problems began to become acute."[166]

The Arts Council's response to the Boyden Report, 'The Next Stage', recognised the need for a framework for a National Policy for Theatre in England and accepted that additional funding would be required to make this possible. Consequently, the Arts Council allocated an extra £25 million for theatre from 2003-2004. Would this mean the West Yorkshire Playhouse was now out of the woods?

ACT II

ACT TWO, SCENE FOUR

Young directors usually start their careers with freelance work, grabbing opportunities to direct at regional producing theatres up and down the country. Obtaining a post as an assistant or associate director at a specific theatre is much more valuable, and not just because it means work for a longer period of time. It offers the opportunity to work more closely in the community which the theatre serves, and to acquire the broader skills essential if moving on to become an artistic director.

LIFE IS A DREAM by Pedro Calderón
1st June 1992

IN JUST A FEW YEARS the West Yorkshire Playhouse had demonstrated success in supporting the work of new, often young writers. At the same time the theatre was giving equal support to new directors. 1992 saw the appointment of the theatre's first resident director. This was Matthew Warchus, who joined the Playhouse at the age of twenty-five. Whilst a pupil at Selby High School he had been involved in Yorkshire youth theatre before studying Music and Drama at Bristol University. He made his professional directing debut in 1989 with a National Youth Theatre production. His potential was obvious, since this production gained him a Time Out award, and opened doors at both the Bristol Old Vic and the Royal Shakespeare Theatre in Stratford-upon-Avon. This was freelance work, so that becoming a resident director at the West Yorkshire Playhouse was attractive, as explained in an interview for the Northern Echo:

"He describes the post as 'fantastic' as it enables a director to get a feel of the value of his work in the community – 'having a body of work rather than a one-off. Freelancing is a bit of a hit-and-run thing'."[167]

This body of work was substantial both in terms of quantity and scale. His first five productions, within a space of two years, were all performed in the Quarry Theatre, and with one exception were big plays with big casts.

His first production was an indication of what could be expected. This was *Life is a Dream* by the Spanish writer Pedro Calderón, dating from 1635 and with only two previous productions in Britain. Matthew's production received high praise: for example, the Yorkshire Post described it as "a visually stunning spectacle of astonishing emotional depth".[168]

Reviews also praised Matthew's appointment at the Playhouse. Robin Thornber, in The Guardian, explained:

"Just when you begin to despair of British theatre – with all its bright young directors being sucked into opera or television and most reps trying to play safe – something like this happens to restore your faith in the future ... 25-year-old director Matthew Warchus clearly has vision, and here he's been given the resources to realise it. This is the sort of spell-binding theatre that matches inventive imagination, accomplished technique and powerful playing to a densely argued text, to bring a rare, musty old classic to vibrant life and keep you on the edge of your seat".[169]

And in The Independent:

"This is Warchus's debut at the Playhouse. His joining the team there looks bound to enhance what is now surely the best all-round repertory theatre in the north of England."[170]

Matthew used his time at the Playhouse to widen his experience. The Christmas 1992 production of *Fiddler on the Roof* was his first direction of a musical. He wanted to apply a freshness to the work, particularly possible because he had never seen a previous production.

Although his time at the Playhouse meant he missed out on more experimental work, he did demonstrate a similar fresh approach to mainstream plays. His 1994 production of Arthur Miller's *Death of a Salesman* used the wide-open stage of the Quarry Theatre to blur past and present rather than a style which emphasised realism. Reviews again wrote of Matthew's potential, the Daily Telegraph describing him as "a fast rising star among Britain's young directors".[171] (These reviews also praised Ken Stott's performance as Willy Loman, amongst a cast which also included a young Jude Law as Happy.)

Whilst at the Playhouse, Matthew nevertheless directed elsewhere. His 1993 West End production of *Much Ado About Nothing*, with Mark Rylance and Janet McTeer, earned him the Globe Theatre Award for Most Promising Newcomer. After the Playhouse his wide-ranging career continued, initially with Opera North and the Welsh National Opera, then further work with the Royal Shakespeare Company and at the National Theatre. He is well-known for the London production of *Art* by French writer Yasmina Reza, which ran in the West End for seven years, and which he also directed on Broadway. Another long-running success of his is *Matilda – The Musical*, which was produced by the RSC at Stratford in 2010 and in 2024 is still running in London's West End. He has received numerous Olivier and Tony Awards, and since 2015 he has been the Artistic Director of the Old Vic Theatre in London, succeeding Kevin Spacey. Matthew did just once return to the Playhouse, at Christmas 1995, to direct a very successful production of *Peter Pan*.

Prior to Matthew's appointment as resident director in 1991, the theatre also appointed Vicky Featherstone as an assistant director. This was possible because Vicky had won one of the four scholarships given by the ITV Association's Regional Theatre Young Directors' Scheme. Prior to the West Yorkshire Playhouse and following her degree in drama at Manchester University, Vicky had had limited experience of directing, so the Playhouse provided her with a much more substantial opportunity. In her year as assistant director she initially worked alongside Jude Kelly, and then with Michael Birch. She also assisted Trevor Griffiths in directing his 1992 play *The Gulf Between Us*.

In July 1992, at twenty-five and the same age as Matthew Warchus, she made her professional debut at the Playhouse, directing Steven Berkhoff's *Kvetch*. The play had originally been produced in Los Angeles in 1986, and then in London's West End, with Steven acting in it, in 1991. Vicky's production was described as a "vigorous, vital regional premiere". This reviewer also praised the choice of this play:

"So bravo Leeds for staging *Kvetch* … you will not see a show like it this year, unless other artistic directors suddenly follow Jude Kelly's lead."[172]

After her year at the Playhouse, Vicky's work included a period as resident director at the Octagon Theatre in Bolton. She also returned to the Playhouse to direct *Brighton Rock*. Her big break came in 1997 when she was appointed as Artistic Director of Paines Plough, the well-respected touring company which specialises in new writing. Whilst with Paines Plough, Vicky again returned to the Playhouse (2000), directing in *Ticket to Write:* short premieres by new writers. In 2004 she was appointed as the Artistic Director and chief executive of the National Theatre of Scotland, which was looking for "a genius ... somebody who has wide experience of theatre production, development and nurturing new writing as well as good administrative and financial skills".[173] Hopefully it was her experience at the Playhouse that helped her get the job! In 2023 Vicky completed ten years as Artistic Director at the Royal Court Theatre in London, another home of new writing.

Roxana Silbert was another trainee associate director who went on to work as an artistic director. She was appointed at the Playhouse in 1997, another Arts Council funded post. Her first work at the theatre was directing one of the *Sevenx7* plays. Prior to Leeds, like Vicky she had worked with Paines Plough; she returned there as Artistic Director and Chief Executive between 2005 and 2009. In 2012 she was appointed as Artistic Director at the Birmingham Rep. In 2019 she took over as Artistic Director at the Hampstead Theatre in London but resigned in 2023 when that theatre's Arts Council funding was cut completely.

Topher Campbell, coordinator of the *Sevenx7* programme and director of two of its plays, had been appointed by the Playhouse as a trainee associate director with an Arts Council Associate Directors' Bursary, his remit being to focus specifically on Black arts development projects. Later in his time at the Playhouse he directed *Jar the Floor*, the European premiere of a play by American writer Cheryl L. West, about four generations of African-American women. Since Leeds, Topher's varied career has included work in film, radio and television as well as theatre, plus he co-founded an arts collective promoting work by Black LGBTQ artists. In 2017 he became the first openly gay Black man to receive an honorary doctorate degree, from the University of Sussex.

The success stories of West Yorkshire Playhouse 'graduates' are countless. Natasha Betteridge, also involved in *Sevenx7*, was another associate director. In her time at the Playhouse she directed four other plays in the Courtyard Theatre and a very successful stage production of *Kes* in the Quarry Theatre. Since Leeds, Natasha has continued as a freelance director, working both in regional theatres and with touring companies. Jennie Darnel, a trainee associate director from 1996-97, continued to work in theatre then went on to become very successful in directing for television. Her CV includes *Eastenders* (ninety-five episodes!), *Holby City*, *Death in Paradise* and *Line of Duty*.

Perhaps uniquely as a northern regional theatre, the opportunities, training and experience offered by West Yorkshire Playhouse have made a massive contribution across the breadth of contemporary British theatre, television and the performing arts in general. The Playhouse debunks the myth that London is the only place where a director or an actor might forge a national reputation.

ACT II

ACT TWO, SCENE FIVE

Political changes, especially in relation to school budgets, at the start of the 1990s adversely affected the ability of local education authorities to continue funding Theatre In Education. For the work to survive, it needed to evolve differently and look for other sources of funding.

THE COST OF LIVING by Morris Panych
18th January 1994

WHEN THE WEST YORKSHIRE PLAYHOUSE opened in 1990, the Theatre In Education (TIE) team continued to tour schools as before. During the spring and summer terms of 1991 they toured Leeds primary schools with *The Poor School*, a programme that included a play set in mid-Victorian Leeds. By this time the team had moved from their base at Quarry Mount School and were housed in the Playhouse building.

In the days of the Leeds Playhouse the TIE team had had considerable autonomy: Arts Council funding separate from the main theatre grant; Education Department funding again separate from the main City Council grant; staff who were answerable to their own committee, rather than the governors. However, the West Yorkshire Playhouse management wanted TIE to be fully integrated into the community work programme. One consequence was that the Arts Council funding for TIE, from 1992, was subsumed into the main revenue grant; the Education Department funding was nevertheless maintained. Another consequence was that the theatre management disbanded the TIE committee, replacing it with the TIE Community and Education committee.

The most serious consequence of these changes was that the TIE team was now directly employed by the West Yorkshire Playhouse, at a time when the theatre faced a financial crisis. This perhaps explains why the TIE team was effectively abandoned and replaced with a 'Schools Company', managed by just one member of staff, with actors employed on a casual basis for each touring production. These productions were, at least initially, essentially a performance of a play rather than the kind of programme that the Leeds Playhouse team, in line with TIE nationally, had been offering to schools. Understandably, this team decided to continue independently of the Playhouse, becoming 'Leeds Theatre in Education', which celebrated its fiftieth anniversary in 2020.

Somewhat confusingly therefore, in May 1993 the West Yorkshire Playhouse issued a press release headlined "Expansion Announced of Leeds Theatre in Education", detailing a reorganisation and expansion of Leeds TIE provision and a commitment to doubling the number of performances in schools. The fact that this work was referred to as 'the educational theatre service' seemed to emphasise the concept of performing plays in schools. Teachers were understandably confused, expecting this expanded work to be provided by the team with whom they had built relationships over many years. On the other hand, the West Yorkshire Playhouse's continued use of the term Theatre In Education made it difficult for Leeds TIE to attract funding – on the basis that the Playhouse was already doing it.

The first production by the Schools Company was *The Cost of Living* by Morris Panych. The production was intended for fourteen-to-sixteen year olds. With just one actor who talks to the audience throughout the play, the production also included music and video projections. It is about a school pupil who decides to complete his social studies assignment on 'the cost of living,' by making a video rather than writing an essay. However, the title has another meaning: as he tells the audience, "I can't talk about the cost of living without talking about life". Through his monologues, he talks about growing up, working things out for himself, and finding his way in the world. The writer of the play is Canadian, but the director, William James, wanted to make the production local to Leeds, so the video work was filmed in places that audiences would recognise. The tour opened at John Smeaton High School (now John Smeaton Academy) and was performed at twenty-four other Leeds schools, and five elsewhere. Across eighty-three performances, attendance was estimated to be 3,495 young people.

As part of their appraisal of the West Yorkshire Playhouse in early 1992 the Arts Council had examined the work of the TIE team. One of their criticisms was, it had "become thematically repetitive and more entrenched in one particular approach".[174] The work of the Schools Company, by comparison, pursued a wider range of themes. In 1994-95 their four productions concerned four very different topics. *The Edible City*, by Jane Newton Chance, tackled conservation issues through the story of a boy who could take on the form of animals. *All the Helicopter Night* by Masitha Hoeane and Dave Kehman, concerns a community at war. *The Song From the Sea*, through the story of a young boy living in a noisy house with a busy family, tackles issues concerning growing up, relationships with adults, and a child's drive for independence. *The Waltz* is about the life of female sculptor Camille Claudel. The productions were for a wide range of age groups. The last two of these four plays were written by Mike Kenny who had previously been a member of the Leeds Playhouse TIE team and went on to write Christmas plays for the Playhouse. He has become a leading playwright of young people's theatre, including his very successful stage adaptation for the York Theatre Royal of *The Railway Children* film.

As with the Playhouse TIE programmes, all plays were provided free to schools in Leeds. The Schools Company director, Gail McIntyre, produced classroom resource packs to accompany each production. Often these were devised with the involvement of teachers, for example at workshops prior to touring. For specific productions, workshops were also offered to schools, either after the performance or elsewhere (for *The Waltz*, a workshop at Leeds Arts Gallery was possible). The work of the Schools Company benefited from having a teacher seconded to the Playhouse, as well as an advisory teacher in a post jointly funded by the theatre and the Council's Education Department.

One particularly successful Schools Company project was *Head On*, which first toured Leeds schools in Autumn 1998. It concerned drugs education and was targeted at eleven-to-fifteen year olds. The performance consisted of six plays, each fifteen-minute monologues. In advance, schools were provided with the play-scripts so that they could choose three plays which were considered most appropriate for their students. Each monologue gave a perspective on drug use from the point of view of a parent, a dealer, an addict, and a casual user.

Crucial to this project were follow-up workshops run by specially trained peer-educators. This was a team of young people aged between fourteen and twenty-two who had received training for their role over a six-month period. The team worked alongside the actors throughout the initial six-month tour. *The Head On* project was only possible because the Playhouse worked in partnership with other organisations, in particular: Base Ten, a drop-in drugs advice unit; the City Council's Attendance and Behaviour Project; and the Health Education Authority. The project also depended on additional funding from these agencies and from charities such as Comic Relief.

Typically the Schools Company mounted two or three plays every year. Those chosen for 2002-03 again illustrated the wide range of themes covered. *Sweetie,* by Gaynor Chilvers and Sara Allkins, was performed by Gaynor, a wheel-chair user affected by cerebral palsy, and was an insight into her own life as a person with disabilities. The play was targeted at eight-to-ten year olds and it visited nineteen primary schools. *Broken Angel* by Lin Coghlan was pitched at children in their last year of primary school, dealing with issues around a father's alcoholism and its impact on family life. For both *Sweetie* and *Broken Angel*, schools were given teachers' resource packs and offered workshop sessions. The third play was *Dr. Jekyll and Mr. Hyde* adapted by Mike Kenny. Stevenson's book was a GCSE text at the time, so this production and the accompanying workshop more obviously related to the secondary school curriculum and was targeted at fourteen-to-sixteen year olds.

Broken Angel and *Dr. Jekyll and Mr. Hyde* were also significant in that both of these plays were performed at the Playhouse, in the Courtyard Theatre, as well as touring to schools. A combination of daytime and evening performances meant that schools, who wanted their students to experience visiting a theatre, could bring parties, but also that adults could visit as for any other Playhouse production. And these, of course, were paying audiences.

Integrating the work of the Schools Company with the Playhouse programme of productions perhaps inevitably led to a change of name: plays began touring to schools under the banner of 'WYP Touring'. This integration is well illustrated by another play, *Crap Dad*, by Mark Catley. The play tells the story of a twenty-three-year-old young man, his earlier life, and his decision about whether or not to meet his children for the first time. The play unusually explored the issue of teenage pregnancy from a male perspective, having been developed through discussions with young fathers in Leeds. The production first of all toured to thirty-six secondary schools in Autumn 2003 and Spring 2004. Finally, the play was included in the Playhouse's *Northern Exposure* new writing festival in June 2004.

In the ensuing years, several more plays combined schools tours with Playhouse performances. *Runaway Diamonds* by Joe Williams was a play about the life of Frederick Douglass, a leader in the slavery abolitionist movement and the first Black citizen to hold high rank in the US government. This was essentially a piece of dance theatre, and in primary school settings the performance was followed with a dance workshop. In early 2005 the production also toured to community venues, followed by seven performances in the Courtyard Theatre. These public performances meant that the production reached a wider audience: *Runaway Diamonds* was seen by seven hundred and six children in schools, but by upwards of a thousand people at the Playhouse.

Not all plays, particularly those targeting the early years age-group, were appropriate for a wider audience in the Courtyard Theatre. Nevertheless, *Trouble*, another play by Mike Kenny in which children played a more participatory role, was performed for families in 2006 during a half-term week. *Trouble* was reminiscent of the work done at the Leeds Playhouse by the Theatre In Education team, as was *The Yellow Doctress*, by Marcia Lane, about the life of Mary Seacole, the British Jamaican nurse who worked with soldiers during the Crimean war. Performances of the play were followed by a session where children were able to talk to the actor 'in character' and ask questions about her experiences. Also reminiscent of TIE programmes was *Displace*, devised by John Barber, which told stories of children arriving in Leeds and elsewhere as asylum seekers or refugees. School pupils could participate in the action by interacting with an actor or, having been prepared by their teacher prior to the performance, could perform a poem by Benjamin Zephaniah as an integral part of the play. After the 2002-04 tour of *Displace*, it was then performed in China at an International Theatre Festival.

The partnership with China, specifically the Sichuan People's Arts Theatre, came about through Chinese Crackers, an organisation promoting creative exchanges between China and the UK. This partnership led to *The Dutch Daughter*, by Charles Way, inspired by the legend of Pericles. Touring schools in the summer of 2005, it was a highly visual production: projections, live music, costumes and puppetry. It was performed by both Chinese and British actors with both Mandarin and English dialogue. Performances were at secondary schools, to which children from their feeder primary schools were invited. The aim was to strengthen the links between these schools and support pupils in their transition from primary to secondary school. There were also six performances at the Playhouse, attended in total by nine hundred and fifty-five people.

A particularly ambitious project for schools began in 2009. Known as *Sharp*, this was a trilogy of plays about knife crime and its effect on individuals, families and communities. The project was developed in partnership with, and with funding from The Royal Armouries. Funding was also obtained via the Home Office Community Fund. *The Worm Collector* was particularly successful. Again, for schools this was more than just the performance of a play. Before the tour, teachers were involved in the development of resource packs, and on performance days they co-delivered a practical session, working with the actor in the play.

The Worm Collector also toured to Berlin where it was performed at Theater an der Parkaue. In partnering with this theatre, the Berlin company in turn visited the Playhouse, performing their production of *Die Kindertransporte* in the Courtyard Theatre alongside *The Worm Collector*.

Clearly the West Yorkshire Playhouse's 'Schools Company' and its successor, 'WYP Touring', were extremely accomplished in continuing the outreach work of the former Leeds Playhouse's highly successful Theatre in Education team, despite their shifting funding status and 'rebranding'. With its international reach – Europe, China, the USA and beyond – the West Yorkshire Playhouse has demonstrated to the world how theatre can be taken out into, and have an impact on, the community and society. Whilst being a regional theatre it has achieved the status of global role-model.

ACT II

ACT TWO, SCENE SIX

Many regional producing theatres actively encourage members of the community to get involved in their local theatre. Often there is a supporters' scheme, through which people can become involved as volunteers, or help with fund-raising events. For others, involvement might be onstage, for example as a member of a chorus in a production. Often there are community plays which are almost totally dependent on non-professional actors. There might also be ways in which theatres can move beyond the walls of their building and perform in other settings.

PILGERMANN *adapted by* Michael Birch
17th June 1995

BACK IN 1968, EVEN BEFORE THE FIRST THEATRE OPENED, a
'Playhouse Club' had been established, organising special
events for members such as an evening with the (by then very
famous) theatre director Sir Tyrone Guthrie. In supporting the
work of the theatre, members were involved as volunteers and
fund-raisers. They staffed the theatre bookstall. They provided
a refreshment service for the Green Room. They organised a
costume hire service – a successful fund-raising venture. In
1980, at the request of the theatre's new administrator, the name
was changed to 'Friends of the Playhouse'.

As the opening of the West Yorkshire Playhouse approached
there must have been a strong feeling of déjà vu amongst the
people who had been active in the fund-raising for the former
Playhouse back in the 1960s. The Friends embarked on fund-
raising events. Plans included a major sponsored cycle event, a
sponsored parachute jump, and a dinner with a theatre
celebrity present. The actor Peter Barkworth gave a one-man
show without a fee, a performance based on the life and work
of the World War I poet Siegfried Sassoon. Other famous names
donated items to a celebrity auction (including Terence Stamp's
trousers!) which raised over £2,000.

Members numbered four hundred people with the opening
of the West Yorkshire Playhouse and rose to seven hundred
over the first six years. Regular meetings took place before the
first Friday performance of a new production, enabling
members to spread the (hopefully good) word about the show.
Members paid a small membership fee; as members they
received regular newsletters and also had priority booking
access for shows.

Members were particularly keen to focus on specific
projects. They funded, for example, a grand piano for the bar-
restaurant area, a van for the Schools Company, and an audio
description unit for use by visually handicapped audience

members. Friends also funded the adaptation of the box office to enable disabled access. As needs arose, they continued to provide financial help. They purchased booster seats for children visiting the Courtyard Theatre; they spent £3,000 on new audio equipment for the Barber Studio. In 2004 they contributed £1,000 towards the refurbishment of the dressing rooms; the following year they contributed a similar sum to the refurbishment of the coffee bar area. In 2007, Friends were able to help in a substantial way with the First Floor project. The Biffa Award Grants Scheme offered £50,000, through the Landfill Communities Fund, on the condition of the Playhouse finding a third-party contributor providing 10% of this money. On this basis, Friends contributed £5,000, and the Biffa Award grant was made.

Friends also contributed towards events and productions. They paid for musicians to perform in the bar-restaurant area prior to performances, contributed £3,000 towards the theatre's twenty-first birthday celebrations, and effectively sponsored two Playhouse productions, *Carnival Messiah* and *Hijra*, donating £3,000 to each. All sorts of fund-raising events were organised, a particularly successful one being a regular second-hand book stall organised by Kathy Webster, which often raised £40 on each occasion. 'Friends of the Playhouse' also organised social events for its members: a theatre trip; a murder mystery event; a celebrity lunch (which would also be a fund-raiser). In 2008 Fraser Burchill, Chair of Friends at that time, recalls:

"We have Celebrity Lunches where famous cast members join us for a sit-down lunch, after which they answer questions. Last season Josie Lawrence [appearing in Tom Stoppard's *Hapgood* at the time] joined us and took the time to go round all the tables after the main question session, which was wonderful, it really made the event special."[175]

The first opportunity for people to take part in a Playhouse community production was in 1993 when the city of Leeds held an International Festival of Theatre for Young People, called *Pirates of the Imagination*. *Magnetic North* opened this event, which was effectively a culmination of all the school and community programmes and workshops organised by the Playhouse since its opening. *Magnetic North* brought together four hundred people for the production. The play was based on a story by Mike Kenny about the textile industry and what can go wrong when the departments within it stop co-operating. It was a kind of parable reflecting multi-cultural communities and celebrating the positive aspects of diversity. It must have been a logistical nightmare for Maureen Rooksby who co-ordinated it all. The two hundred and eighty students involved rehearsed at their schools during the day over a five-week period. The adults rehearsed in the evening. Other young people already involved at the Playhouse rehearsed there during evenings and at weekends. The play itself was divided into four sections, each with a different director. Finally everyone came together for dress rehearsals and then performances for three nights in the Quarry Theatre.

After this success, in the spring of 1995 a press release announced that the Playhouse hoped to attract five hundred volunteers to take part in *Pilgermann,* an adaptation of the cult fiction novel by Russell Hoban, written and to be directed by Michael Birch. Set in the eleventh century it was likened to the nightmarish content of a Hieronymus Bosch painting. The difference between this production and *Magnetic North* was that volunteers were involved not just as actors, but with the work of the various Playhouse departments contributing to the production: lighting, sound, design, scenery, costumes, stage management, and so on. As well as all the adult volunteer actors – including, as newspapers enjoyed reporting, a retired local police chief superintendent – the cast included students from three local high schools. There were two other significant differences. This production included one, but only one, professional actor. Secondly, *Pilgermann* had a two-week run in the Quarry Theatre.

Reviews in national newspapers acknowledged the scale of the undertaking: the Daily Telegraph critic commented that at times there seemed almost more people on the stage than in the audience.[176] If reviews were mixed, the reservations were largely about the play's 'heavy' content.. Many positive comments were made about the visual staging. And as with *Magnetic North*, one critic observed, "The cast may take the applause but the Playhouse takes the credit for its continued, far-reaching Community and Education policies – which in the current financial crisis are even more creditable".[177]

But not everyone who saw *Pilgermann* was happy. One audience member complained, "I have never sat through such a filthy, disgusting, offensive and blasphemous load of tripe in all my life. I actually did not sit through it but walked out in disgust after one hour … but what I saw in that one hour made me physically ill."

1999 saw another big production: *Carnival Messiah*, a Caribbean version of Handel's Messiah which was devised and directed by Geraldine Connor. It was described as 'an ambitious multi-cultural community theatre project'. Auditions took place to find one hundred or more people to take part. A number of these were students at Bretton Hall College near Wakefield, where Geraldine was now Head of Popular Music Studies. Those chosen were expected to attend rehearsals every weekend for twelve weeks, and then daily, nearer to the performance dates. In the end there was a fifty-strong community chorus, three separate twenty-strong children's choruses, twenty gospel singers and twenty members of a steel band. Writing in the programme, Jude Kelly said:

"*Carnival Messiah* is among other things a demonstration of our commitment to theatre as a participatory activity. Although the company and the creative team is comprised of a group of internationally renowned professionals, there are over a hundred local performers ... bringing their talent, energy, enthusiasm and commitment to the show,"[178]

Then in 2003, one hundred and fifty members of the Heydays community programme were involved in the production of a community drama, *The Phoenix of Leodis*, about the lives of the people who had lived on Quarry Hill. Research for the play had been carried out by Mavis Simpson, a retired teacher and local historian. Her fellow members of the Heydays creative writing group then wrote a series of scenes, recounting events on Quarry Hill, from the plague of 1645 to the present day – events including bull-baiting, witchcraft and body-snatching. The play recorded the fact that the low-cost back-to-back housing was popular with Russian and Polish Jews, and with Irish people escaping the Potato Famine in 1847. Overall, as Mavis Simpson explained, "what runs through the history of the area is a very cosmopolitan feel, a welcome to people from all parts of the world. We've tried to tell the story of that community and its spirit".[179]

Because the production needed young people in the cast, students from the City of Leeds High School and Notre Dame Catholic School Sixth Form College were invited to take part. Students from Leeds College of Music also helped with the production. The play ended with a loud rumbling explosion and darkness, signifying the demolition of the Quarry Hill flats – which of course enabled the building of the West Yorkshire Playhouse!

The Phoenix of Leodis was performed, appropriately, on the Quarry Theatre stage, for just two performances in July 2003. Reviewing the production for the Yorkshire Post, Sheena Hastings said the show was "a template for big-hearted community co-operation, and big ideas executed imaginatively in spite of a scarcity of resources".[180] Both she and another reviewer concluded. "it is a shame this was a one-night only production... but perhaps one day the Phoenix will rise again".[181]

The Phoenix did indeed rise again! Early in 2004 Richard Taylor was appointed as Music Creator-in-Residence, funded by the Performing Rights Society Foundation. Working with Heydays members who had been involved with *The Phoenix of Leodis*, they decided to rewrite the play and add original music. They also wanted to involve other community groups – and staff as well. The result was *Once Upon a Quarry Hill*, and three hundred people were involved in its creation. A cast of sixty appeared on stage, with ages ranging from four to eighty-five.

This version covers the same history of Quarry Hill as in *The Phoenix of Leodis* but focuses on particular people. One is Nellie, a seventeenth century single mother, who is publicly punished by ducking stool for her drunken behaviour. Another is a nineteenth century factory employee fighting for workers' rights. Finally, there is Slomo, a Jewish man who in the 1940s comes to Leeds after fleeing Nazi Germany. The real Slomo was a man who once lived on Quarry Hill, and regularly sat in the Playhouse looking out at the same view as from his now-demolished flat.

Reviews commented on the quality:
"*Once Upon a Quarry Hill* emerges as the Rolls Royce of community shows. As much care and attention has been

lavished on this ambitious musical … as any regular production."[182]

"The West Yorkshire Playhouse has always excelled at vast, egalitarian exercises in community theatre … It is the theatre's credit that it never sells its non-professional performers short; production standards remain as slick as for any main stage production."[183]

Several reviewers praised the performance of seventy-three year-old Dennis Butcher who played Slomo. A member of Heydays, he had been a professional tenor singer in the 1960s but hadn't sung in years. The cast also included Maureen Lillywhite, a local community health worker, who grew up near the Quarry Hill flats, and remembered them well. She had brought a group of people to the auditions, encouraging them to get active, and ended up performing herself. Another cast member was Maureen Kershaw, who had worked in the Playhouse box office for twelve years. Then there was fifteen year-old Clair Howarth, the daughter of a duty manager at the theatre, who had previously appeared in other community productions including *Carnival Messiah*:

"I'm pleased my mum got me into it. I really want to do something with my life and if I wasn't doing this I'd be at home doing nothing."[184]

As well as these specifically community plays, local people's involvement in Playhouse productions had occurred occasionally from the early years of the West Yorkshire Playhouse. The first happened in 1991 with the production of *Savages* by Christopher Hampton. A team of fifty, aged between nine and sixty-five, was recruited from the various Network programmes. They acted out and danced the Brazilian tribal rituals. Reviewing the production, Kevin Berry in the Times Educational Supplement commented:

"… their contribution is exciting and memorable. They fill the stage with vitality as they create Indian rites and ceremonies, all beautifully staged. I particularly enjoyed their stillness, and the way they crept around when other actors took centre stage; they looked so vulnerable and so very innocent."[185]

In 1993 the production of Eugene O'Neill's *All God's Chillun Got Wings* included a gospel choir, with sixty people drawn from community choirs across Leeds, led by Geraldine Connor, who "managed to perfectly recreate the heady atmosphere of jazz age New York, and the choir's rendition of *Amazing Grace* left the audience wanting more".[186] *All God's Chillun Got Wings* was directed by Burt Caeser who two years earlier had directed the first of the *Lifelines* plays, *Back Street Mammy*.

More ambitious still was the production of *Bollywood Jane* (2007) by Amanda Whittington, which involved two teams of dancers, Team Raj and Team Simran, each with twenty young people recruited from auditions held in both Leeds and Bradford. At least one had never danced before.

Since the first years of the West Yorkshire Playhouse, certain productions gave opportunities for local children to perform alongside the actors. This was regularly the case with Christmas productions: *The Lion, the Witch and the Wardrobe* (2007) had a Narnia Community Company; *The Wizard of Oz* (2006) and *A Christmas Carol* (2010) also involved community choruses. On some occasions children were essential members of the cast. In *Peter Pan* (2008) three boys shared the part of Michael Darling, two of whom had previously been involved at local youth theatre groups. The third, the oldest, had already been in *A Doll's House* and *The Wizard of Oz*, as well as in *Oliver!* at the Grand Theatre. All had to learn to fly. After interviewing the three children for the production programme, Sophie Barnes concluded:

"The boys' experience can be summed up when I asked them if they want to carry on treading the boards in the future, to which they unanimously reply, 'Yeah Definitely!' And who wouldn't. Flying nightly with your friends as a gob-smacked audience watches in delight makes for three very happy boys!"[187]

In 2016 another play concerning events in the history of Leeds had seen the involvement of adults from the local community. This was a new play by Alice Nutter: *Barnbow Canaries*. James Brining commissioned her to write this play, her third for the Playhouse, and insisted that the production would include a community chorus. The play concerns the Barnbow munitions factory in the Cross Gates area of Leeds during the First World War. 'Canaries' in the title refers to the nickname for the women who worked there: handling TNT every day caused their hair and skin to become yellow in colour. The major event in the play is the explosion which occurred there in 1916, killing thirty-five and injuring many more. The play also reflects on the way that the women, previously earning poor wages as domestic servants, were suddenly earning better money – men's wages. However, of course, after the war their circumstances reverted.

In advance of the production the theatre put out a casting call for sixty women aged sixteen upwards who "will act in scenes throughout the show, including several movement and dance sequences, and sing hymns and popular folk tunes". Auditions were held in three locations in the city. Alice herself was wary about this aspect of the production "but agreed on the proviso that by opening night the chorus would have to meet the same exacting standards as the main cast".[188] Some of the women who were chosen had connections with the Barnbow Canaries, either because they lived in the Cross Gates area or because their parents or grandparents had worked at the factory. Trish Burnley's father had worked there during the Second World War, and as a child she had taken part in the Barnbow talent competitions. The Yorkshire Evening Post reported that after one rehearsal she had a little cry:

"Partly it's because Trish, who is one of a forty-strong community chorus, has never acted before. It's partly because the rehearsal schedule has been gruelling. However, mostly it's because of the memories it has brought back."[189]

Then in 2017, *Queen of Chapeltown* was produced to mark the 50th anniversary of the Leeds West Indian Carnival. It was written by Colin Grant, based on first-hand accounts of the first Carnival in 1967. The story of how this came about is told through the lives of four recently arrived West Indians, determined to settle in Leeds. The play uses humour, particularly between the three male friends who organised the first Carnival. However, the play also shows the racism with which they and Beverley, who wants to be the Carnival Queen, have to contend. Beverley finds work in hairdressing, where she forms a friendship with Hilary, going dancing together. The community chorus members were involved in the play as salon and dance hall customers, and in:

"a rousing finale reminiscent of the glittering, pulsating and anarchic King and Queen shows which have graced the Quarry Theatre stage for the past four years". [190]

A very different production which brought together professionals and local community members was first performed as part of the Open Season in 2015. Billed as a Performance Ensemble and West Yorkshire Playhouse co-production, *Anniversary* combined five older professional dancers and five members of the Heydays programme to perform a piece of dance theatre. The following year there were six performances of *Anniversary* in the Courtyard Theatre. There was also a performance at the UK's first symposium on Older People's Theatre, organised by the Playhouse and attended by delegates from organisations across the UK. Describing *Anniversary*, Nicky Taylor, the Playhouse's Community Development Officer, explained that it "brings together an extraordinary group of performers. Some have 40 years' experience in world-leading dance companies, while other take their first steps in performance in their 60s, 70s and 80s. Members of the ensemble learn from each other, forming a supportive space to make art".[191]

The last production before the Playhouse closed for redevelopment in June 2018 perfectly reflected the theatre's aim to involve people of all ages in the work on the stages. On this occasion however, involvement was much more than as 'extras'.

This was another community production, a form of theatre which had started at the Playhouse back in 1995 with *Pilgermann*. Called *Searching for the Heart of Leeds*, it had six performances in the Quarry Theatre.

Four months before the production, open auditions were held, and applications invited from performers, musicians, and people wanting to work backstage. Seventy were selected from the more than three hundred who applied. Separately to this, the Playhouse's Creative Engagement team collected stories from local people about things which they felt made life in Leeds different and special. Alexander Ferris, who directed the production, summarised the findings as follows:

"No matter where we went we found that everyone had a different thing to say about the 'essence' of the city. But three distinctive messages came to the fore: Leeds is a caring city; it welcomes change and is constantly evolving; and above all the idea that if you embrace Leeds, it will embrace you."[192]

The next stage was to select some of the stories and to incorporate them into a play. This work was done by Mark Catley, whose writing career had effectively started at the Playhouse in 2003, with *Sunbeam Terrace*. He had last worked at the Playhouse in 2013, with his play *Sherlock Holmes – The Best Kept Secret*, a commercial co-production which went on to tour to other theatres in England. In selecting the stories, Mark explained:

"I chose those which I thought best represented Leeds but, also, those which suited the flow of the play. It was important that this wasn't an unrealistically positive portrayal of the city. I love this place and most of those we spoke to do as well, but it's the good and the bad elements mixed together, it's nostalgia and modern reality side by side and it's, hopefully, an honest reflection of where we are at now."[193]

He needed a framing device for the stories, so – as implied in the title – this is a young woman wandering the streets of Leeds, searching for its heart. Some of the people she meets tell their stories, sometimes these stories are acted out. And in some cases they really were the stories of the people acting on stage: for example, those in a scene set within Leeds's refugee community. Overall, those performing reflected the diversity of the people with whom the Playhouse worked:

"Those of a gammon mindset should look away now as Mark Catley's script ticks off an inventory of inclusivity featuring refugees, graffiti artists, wheelchair users, a gay boy from Bramley, Big Issue sellers, Carnival dancers and (of course) a female Vietnamese weightlifter all brought together by a sense of place – that place being Leeds. And it's a tribute to work over many seasons at the Playhouse that the involvement of a deaf character signing her performance live is now so commonplace on the Quarry stage as to pass without comment."[194]

A house band performed on stage during the production, playing music and songs by Leeds artists including Chumbawumba's *Tubthumping*. The Theatre of Sanctuary choir, Asmarina Voices, were also involved. There was also a 'World Anthem', the lyrics of which were written by Jaber Abdullah, again someone involved in the Playhouse's Theatre of Sanctuary programme. The production also included movement, choreographed by members of the Phoenix Dance Theatre.

The Playhouse itself engaged with the local community in other ways. For example, starting in 1993, the theatre organised *Rhythms of the City*, a summer festival of street theatre and entertainment. In its first year these free events formed part of the City Centenary celebrations. In preparation, and to recruit performers, a *Very Big Talent Show* was organised at the Playhouse, hosted by Niamh Cusack and other actors from the popular *Heartbeat* television series. *Rhythms of the City* became a regular summer event. In 1994 it took place over six Saturdays, each Saturday having a theme, such as a 'Wild West Day' which included square and line-dancing, for which Albion Place was turned into Dodge City, and an 'Art Day' which included a live dubbing performance by the sadly recently deceased Benjamin Zephaniah.

In 1995 Victoria Gardens was transformed into a seaside resort, complete with sandcastles and a Punch and Judy show. Victoria Gardens was also the venue for an outdoor tea dance. The programme for 1998 included a National Street Theatre Festival culminating in an aerial theatre display outside the Playhouse, performed by Leeds-based Exponential Aerial Theatre (who also performed indoors at night clubs and raves). By 1999 *Rhythms of the City* was very much an international event. The programme included a stilt-walking band playing swing, Latin and ska, also Cajun music, and a team of acrobats from Ethiopia. The Playhouse Heydays community programme gave a line-dancing demonstration, and dance also featured at the theatre: a Salsa night with free lessons; a performance by the Delphine Domingo Flamenco team.

Self-evidently, from its very beginnings the West Yorkshire Playhouse had, to repeat Jude Kelly's words, a "commitment to theatre as a participatory activity." Creative engagements with the local community were pursued through the diverse routes and methods detailed in this chapter: street theatre, festivals and more. This was another strong strand of activity alongside the highly successful outreach of the Theatre in Education team (reformulated as 'Schools Company' then 'WYP Touring'). Despite financial pressures and the gradual dwindling of state support, the Playhouse was continuing to demonstrate ideals and values in theatre that are social rather than commercial. As the Guardian's Alfred Hickling reflected in 1993 having attended Leeds's 'International Festival of Theatre for Young People':

"This is exactly what a major, regional dramatic centre ought to be doing – stretching a creative limb to embrace a broad sweep of the community. Theatre needs people ... and the most meaningful way to attract audiences through the door is to encourage them a step further onto the stage."[195]

ACT II

ACT TWO, SCENE SEVEN

The latter years of the twentieth century saw an increase in co-productions between regional producing theatres. The attraction of such arrangements is that production costs are shared. Co-productions between regional theatres and national touring companies also allow the latter a base and resources from which to develop their co-productions. However, do co-productions mitigate against the choice of plays particularly relevant to the communities which a regional producing theatre serves?

THE RIVALS by Richard Brinsley Sheridan 19ᵗʰ March 1992

THE BASIS OF A CO-PRODUCTION is that one theatre leads in terms of direction, scenery, costumes and all other production costs, but these costs are shared between one or more other theatres. Co-productions also mean longer runs in total, which are potentially more attractive for actors.

The Rivals was the West Yorkshire Playhouse's first co-production, with the Birmingham Repertory Theatre (Birmingham Rep), directed by John Adams, Birmingham's then Artistic Director. There would be three further co-productions with Birmingham over the following five years, directed by one of each theatre's associate directors. An advantage of co-productions with Birmingham was that the main space also had an open stage and was similar in size to the Quarry Theatre.

Sometimes co-productions with Birmingham were classics such as Arthur Miller's *A View from the Bridge* in 2003. Primarily a Birmingham Rep production, it was director Toby Frow's first big production, made possible because he was attached to the theatre on a bursary from the Esme Fairbairn Foundation. When transferred to Leeds it was given a local touch: the Playhouse recruited twelve people as extras to play the non-speaking roles of Italian-immigrant dockers and their families. In Leeds the production received excellent reviews from the local press: "utterly compulsive viewing"; "a spellbinding couple of hours"; "this production is everything that drama should be".

More often, co-productions with Birmingham were new productions of recent plays. So, *A View from the Bridge* exchanged with the Playhouse production of Alan Bennett's *The Madness of George III*, which prompted one reviewer to say, "There is now double cause to celebrate the new union between the West Yorkshire Playhouse and the Birmingham Repertory Theatre".[196] He particularly praised the director ("Rachel

Kavanaugh's magnificent new revival"). Other reviewers focused on the performance of Michael Pennington, who "excels as the sad and mad king",[197] his performance being "not just technically brilliant … but one from the heart".[198]

Other co-productions with Birmingham included revivals of recent plays such as, in 2008, Tom Stoppard's *Hapgood* and Peter Nichols' *Privates on Parade*. A production of *His Dark Materials* opened in Birmingham in 2009 and toured to five other theatres in England and Scotland before opening at the Playhouse two months later. The partnership also included Christmas productions: *The Wizard of Oz* played at the Birmingham Rep in 2005 and at the Playhouse a year later; *Alice in Wonderland* played at the Playhouse in 2005 and at the Birmingham Rep a year later. The same pattern continued with the Playhouse's revival of *The Lion, The Witch and The Wardrobe* and the Rep's production of *Peter Pan* in 2007-08.

Co-productions of Shakespeare plays with larger casts particularly benefit from shared costs, so *Romeo and Juliet* was jointly produced in 1995 with the Lyric Theatre Hammersmith. *Hamlet* and *As You Like It* followed, with the Greenwich Theatre and Bristol Old Vic respectively.

Similar plays were also mounted as co-productions with other regional theatres. Ibsen's *Hedda Gabler* (2006) and J.B. Priestley's *When We Are Married* (2009) were both co-productions with the Liverpool Playhouse and Everyman Theatre. Co-productions with other theatres also made possible new work at the Playhouse. *Fast Labour*, by Steve Waters, for example, was a co-production with the Hampstead Theatre in 2008. This play tackles the issue of migrant labour coming to Britain from Eastern Europe, focusing on one character, Victor, based on a true story. Some critics expressed reservations about the play's structure, but most praised it for being a more balanced view and a deeper discussion of immigration issues:

"It takes courage to tackle the topic of economic migrants in the UK without portraying illegal workers as one-dimensional characters. That's why Steve Water's *Fast Labour*, the tale of Ukrainian migrant Victor who worked his way from factory worker to exploitative gang master, is a success … it's an enjoyable piece of writing that tackles a complex subject with intelligence."[199]

There was also praise for director Ian Brown, whose approach "slowly draws out the politics of the piece, rather than bludgeoning you with the issues. Brown's direction also skilfully brings out the humour and he uses the comedic strength of the men playing the three immigrants well".[200] And several commented on the "ingenious video projections that whizz us up and down the M1"[201] which were created by Mic Pool, by then the Playhouse's Associate Director: Creation Technology, who had been working at the theatre, firstly as Head of Sound, since it opened in 1990.

As well as these co-productions, the Playhouse built partnerships with two Yorkshire theatre companies, the first being Hull Tuck Theatre, which was formed one year after the Leeds Playhouse opened, in 1971. John Godber became their Artistic Director in 1983; he is now considered the country's third most performed playwright (after Shakespeare and Ayckbourn). The Hull Truck's touring production of one of his most popular plays, *Bouncers*, was included in the first visitors' season at the West Yorkshire Playhouse in September 1990, and attracted 98% attendances. In 1992 John's play *Happy Families* received its professional world premiere at the Playhouse. Three further productions followed, two directed by John himself. In 1995, one of these, *Lucky Sods*, was performed in the Quarry Theatre, despite there being a cast of just four actors.

The other company which has had a long relationship with the Playhouse is Northern Broadsides, founded just after the West Yorkshire Playhouse had opened, in 1992. As with Hull Truck, the company's first play at the Playhouse was a touring production: *A Midsummer Night's Dream*, in November 1994. The week of performances had sold out two months in advance.

Northern Broadsides was founded by Barry Rutter who had previously worked with the Royal Shakespeare Company and at the National Theatre. At the latter, he worked substantially with the Yorkshire poet and playwright Tony Harrison. Barry was a member of the company which performed a three-part promenade production of the mystery plays; this was adapted by Bill Bryden mainly from the Wakefield cycle of these plays. Those who saw this production will recall the unforgettable performance by Brian Glover as God, perched on the top of a fork-lift truck.

The Mysteries was performed in Yorkshire dialect, and using northern voices is very much part of the philosophy behind Northern Broadsides. Initially their touring productions, mainly of classical plays, were taken to non-theatre spaces: factories, museums, castles, even to Skipton cattle market. Performances at theatres like the West Yorkshire Playhouse helped to fund those at other, less 'safe' venues.

The first co-production with Northern Broadsides was in early 1995. *The Cracked Pot* is a German comedy adapted by another Yorkshire writer, Blake Morrison. Barry Rutter both directed the play and took the lead part. Blake originally translated *Der Zerbrochene Krug* for the National Theatre, but when this was passed up, agreed a rewrite for Northern Broadsides, a specifically Yorkshire version, thus set in Skipton where Blake went to school. It was Blake's first play, and he was involved at the Playhouse throughout the rehearsal period. He tells a lovely story of how, after he had asked to proofread the programme, to which he had contributed, "my wife Kathy wonders whether I'm not exceeding my brief. Says, if the ice-cream lady cries off during the run, I'll no doubt be found in the aisles with a tray of vanilla tubs round my neck".[202]

The use of Yorkshire dialect was clearly the play's strength:

"From the opening scene in which Judge Adam complains of being 'tom-flogged by grenky dreams' we know to expect a vocabulary that takes its coat off, roles up its sleeves and sets about it with a passion."[203] Robin Thornber in The Guardian saw the play as "an uninhibited celebration of the Yorkshire tongue's talent for vivid phraseology packed with a poet's delight in the arcane and now obscure vocabulary of North

Riding farming folk. Bizzumhead, blathery, drabbletale, gowky, kittlish, rafflepack, scutters – archaic words which nevertheless are so powerful and richly coloured that, in context, they hardly need to be explained in the programme."[204]

Blake must have been impressed that his first play gained positive reviews in national newspapers. His production diary recalled how he had "suggest[ed] to one or two (London) friends, 'Why not come up to Leeds?' Gawping incomprehension. Might as well have said Latvia".[205]

Barry Rutter was back at the Playhouse in 1998 for another co-production – a revival of *The Trackers of Oxyrhynchus*, the play which had inspired him to establish Northern Broadsides. Tony Harrison had apparently written the lead part for Barry when it was performed, first of all, in the ancient stadium of Delphi in 1988 and then at the National Theatre in 1990. The title gives little indication as to what the play is about. It concerns two archaeologists in Egypt in 1907, who discover fragments of the text of a Sophocles play. This is a satyr play – a short tragicomedy featuring a chorus of characters with erect penises. The archaeologists then become part of the play as it is acted out. It finishes in the present day with a scene set amongst homeless people – a cardboard city – and it is written in rhyming couplets. Oh, and clog-dancing is central to the production.

Tony Harrison revised the play for the West Yorkshire Playhouse, removing references to the National Theatre's South Bank setting and replacing them with witty remarks about Opera North, Leeds Grammar School, and other local landmarks. In Leeds, publicity for the play included a warning: "The satyrs' excitement takes a highly visible and phallic form which though playful and celebratory, could cause offence".

Ironically, therefore, the production photographs used for publicity purposes were of this part of the play. Probably also for maximum publicity, local newspapers were fed a story about the posters being 'edited' to avoid causing embarrassment. The Yorkshire Post duly reported, under the headline 'Actor Cut Off to Spare Blushes', that "actor Barrie Rutter is furious at having his manhood chopped off in public. A poster showing the Northern Broadsides actor sporting a giant fake phallus… has been edited to save the public's blushes".[206]

Co-productions sometimes enabled productions which otherwise could never, for financial reasons, have been mounted. The best example of this is the 2006 *Wars of the Roses*, again with Northern Broadsides. This was a trilogy of plays. Barrie Rutter had combined *Henry VI Parts One, Two and Three* into two distinct plays: *Henry VI* and *Edward IV*. The third part of the trilogy was *Richard III*, the first play that Northern Broadsides had produced, exactly fifteen years previously. In an interview with the Yorkshire Post, Ian Brown, then Artistic Director, explained how the co-production came about:

"We [the Playhouse] were fifteen years old last year and Northern Broadsides, which has long been one of our key companies, is fifteen years old this year and it seemed to be a really good match. I just thought it was a wonderful idea really for both of us to do a project we wouldn't be able to do on our own."[207] He went on to explain the practicalities of a co-production:

"Basically, we are sharing the set up costs. So when it's out on tour Northern Broadsides take up the running of it, but we share the costs of the rehearsal period. It just makes the money go further because we are halving the costs of certain things to each organisation."[208] In the same interview, which was a week before opening, Barrie Rutter suggested another benefit of such a co-production:

"Ian's value to me will come next week in previews when I ask him as a colleague for help or observations or notes."[209]The three plays were very much a Northern Broadsides experience, both in respect of the northern accents and the company style ("*Henry VI* saved by a jazz band and clogs" reported Alfred Hickling in The Guardian). Critics attended when all three plays were performed on the same day, causing the Sunday

Times critic to conclude, "For those who remain wary of committing themselves to such a marathon, I should add that there are two hours between each play, and the West Yorkshire Playhouse, which must be one of the most attractive and user-friendly theatres in Britain, serves great, reasonably priced food – still rare in the poncey south".[210]

After Leeds, *Wars of the Roses* went on tour to ten other venues, but only one of them, The Yvonne Arnaud Theatre in Guildford, in the 'poncey south'.

Co-productions with other touring companies which were regular visitors to the Playhouse also allowed new work to be seen. The earliest example is *The Hanging Man*, a co-production with, and devised by, the Improbable Theatre Company.

The starting point for *The Hanging Man* is the story of a cathedral architect who decides to hang himself in the building he feels unable to complete. Unfortunately, death – a character in the play – decides not to let him die, leaving the man suspended there throughout the play – except when the actor comes out of character (and the noose) to tell the audience how painful it is to hang there. Improbable indeed! Improbable Theatre have a particular way of working: their productions are directed, designed and scripted through improvisations during the rehearsal process. Two of the team for this production, Julian Crouch and Phelim McDermott, were partly responsible for the very successful *Shockheaded Peter* which started its life at the Playhouse in 1998 before touring worldwide.

As part of the process of creating *The Hanging Man* for the Playhouse, the Improbable team conducted interviews about death with members of the Heydays community programme. The production continued to evolve once previews had started, which perhaps explains why the press night was ten days after the opening one (and why the production was an hour shorter when it opened at the Lyric Theatre Hammersmith, the other co-production partner, six weeks later). Stephen Snell, the Playhouse's Head of Wardrobe, was part of the play's design team, which won the 2003 TMA Best Designer Award. Like

Shockheaded Peter, the play went on to tour internationally; its US premiere was at the Ohio State University just six months after its West Yorkshire Playhouse opening. That theatre's promotional material reproduced glowing reviews such as "Mesmerizing, fascinating, hilarious, and terrifying" (Yorkshire Evening Post) and "A triumph of theatre, at turns genuinely funny and inescapably moving... see it now" (Bradford Telegraph & Argus).[211]

Cornwall-based Kneehigh Theatre was a regular visitor to the Playhouse, and 2004 saw the first co-production, also with the Lyric Theatre Hammersmith and the Bristol Old Vic. This was *The Bacchae*, an adaptation of the Euripides classic, directed by Emma Rice. Like Improbable Theatre, Kneehigh had a distinctive style, in particular the use of visual imagery and humour. *The Bacchae* was described as "cheerful anarchy" and "rollicking tragedy". By the time this production opened, Kneehigh had, since their first visit in 2002, acquired a loyal fan-base because of their distinctive, accessible style. Audiences who were a little uncertain about a Greek tragedy were reassured, reported the Independent on Sunday:

"The Playhouse audience clearly weren't sure, at first, what to make of Emma Rice's Bacchic chorus: a bunch of shorn-haired, bare-chested blokes slipping into gauzy white skirts and giving us a few balletic twirls. By the end, though, the punters were whooping and whistling".[212]

2007 saw another West Yorkshire Playhouse-Kneehigh co-production, *Brief Encounter*, based on the 1945 film and the Noel Coward play. Once again Emma adapted and directed the production. Its success led to a long tour, and in 2018 a revival which was performed in a cinema on London's Haymarket. Also in 2007 was *Rough Crossings*, a stage adaptation of Simon Sharma's book, directed by Rupert Goold. This was principally the work of Headlong Theatre, but the Liverpool Everyman and Playhouse, the Lyric Theatre Hammersmith, and the Birmingham Rep were also co-producers. The play tells the story of Black American slaves who fought with the British during the American Civil War in return for their freedom and a passage to England – but were betrayed and abandoned in Nova Scotia. The stage adaptation was by Caryl Phillips, at that time a Professor of English at Yale University. Caryl was born in St. Kitts, but his family came to Leeds when he was just four months old. A lifelong Leeds United supporter, returning to Leeds for *Rough Crossings* was quite special:

"There are so many feelings. I used to walk past the Quarry Hill flats twice a day on my way to school from where I lived on the Whinmoor housing estate and when the flats were razed the Playhouse was built. There is so much that is symbolic to me about the new and the old Leeds contained in that and for me to have a play on there – I want to be visibly and vocally a part of the city. Maybe some ten-year-old kid will see the story and see how I was able to grow up here and navigate my way through life and be proud to come from this place."[213]

The co-productions that became a significant dimension of the Playhouse's programming in the 1990s and 2000s, though motivated by financial pragmatism, also brought a beneficial cross-fertilisation of talent from other regions. The Playhouse continued to be a hub that nurtured and advanced its actors, writers and crew. When the Guardian newspaper published a series of interviews in 2020 on the theme of 'Theatres That Made Us', Emma Rice identified the Playhouse as the theatre that changed her life:

"It inspired me as a creative leader. In the early 2000s, it was West Yorkshire Playhouse that committed to Kneehigh and, over several years, built us a loyal and passionate audience. We became part of the family, and Leeds our second home. The workshops were world-class with prop, set and costume makers weaving, sticking and nailing magic into the bones of the theatre. The building was democratic and porous with community groups such as Heydays and The Beautiful Octopus Club showing us how to create, enjoy and treasure life.

"The cafe was delicious and cheap, the foyer buzzed with school groups, and the bar opened late with staff and audiences mixing with the company. Theatre was just something else that happened in that building, an easy extra step to take – and it thrived and we prospered. WYP (now Leeds Playhouse) epitomised the word 'welcome' and the people came. Astonishing."[214]

ACT TWO, SCENE EIGHT

On occasions, regional producing theatres get involved in co-productions with commercial organisations. Such productions are mostly mounted prior to a national tour or a London transfer. If these transfers are successful, the regional theatre should benefit financially. Sometimes, however, success at the regional theatre does not mean success elsewhere.

FIVE GUYS NAMED MOE by Clarke Peters
2nd September 1994

On occasions, often in respect of musicals, the West Yorkshire Playhouse has co-produced with commercial organisations. The first of these was *Five Guys Named Moe* which opened the 1994-95 season in the Quarry Theatre. This was a co-production with leading theatrical producer Cameron Mackintosh. *Five Guys Named Moe* was devised by Clark Peters as a celebration of the songs of Louis Jordan.

By September 1994 *Five Guys Named Moe* had been running at the Lyric Theatre in London's West End for well over four years and had won Olivier Awards for Best Entertainment and Best Theatre Choreographer. A Broadway production had opened in 1992. Both the West End and Broadway productions had been choreographed and directed by Charles Angiers, who then came to Leeds for the same purpose. This was effectively the musical's regional premiere, with touring dates arranged until Spring 1995.

The cast at the West Yorkshire Playhouse included twenty-one -year-old Jason Pennycooke who was born and grew up in the Chapeltown area of Leeds, where he first got involved in youth dance theatre. He trained at the Northern School of Contemporary Dance. Like the whole cast, he was praised by Alfred Hickling in the Yorkshire Post:

"The performances are sheer professionalism honed to a dazzling degree but special mention should be reserved for Leeds's own Jason Pennycooke, dapper and dynamic as Little Moe."[215]

Other reviews gave insights into how well *Five Guys Named Moe* was received by Playhouse audiences. Kevin Berry wrote in The Stage, "An outstanding, monumental, foot tapping, rousing triumph. The Playhouse is used to success but I have never known such uninhibited involvement from an adult audience and never seen so many folk on their feet for a thunderous standing ovation".[216]

After the tour, the West Yorkshire Playhouse production transferred to another London theatre, three months after the original West End production had closed. Keeping the same cast, it ran for over seven months; it was also filmed live and released as a VHS tape. Jason Pennycooke has continued to perform in, but also to choreograph, West End musicals, and his film credits include the Elton John biopic *Rocketman*. In 2017 he was chosen for the original cast of the much-anticipated London production of *Hamilton*, for which he received an Olivier Award nomination. This Leeds boy did good!

The Playhouse worked with Cameron Mackintosh again in 1998 on what was that year's Christmas production, *Martin Guerre,* a musical by Alain Boubil and Claude-Michel Schonberg who are best known for their two big successes: *Les Misérables* and *Miss Saigon*. *Martin Guerre* is set in sixteenth century France and is based on the true events of a man returning from war and taking on a false identity, which leads to an unexpected love story.

Martin Guerre had opened in London in July 1996 to poor reviews, leading to a number of rewrites. Then, unusually, the production was closed down whilst more substantial changes were made. When it re-opened, critics were invited to take another look. The reviews improved, but *Martin Guerre* nevertheless closed in February 1998, with Cameron Mackintosh reportedly losing £5 million.

It was generally felt that the relative failure of *Martin Guerre* was in part due to the production becoming too grand for a musical that was much smaller in scale than the other Boubil-Schonberg successes. Relevant here is the size and shape of its London theatre: the Prince Edward, which seats over seventeen hundred people, has a proscenium arch stage, a dress circle, and a grand circle.

The Playhouse production was effectively the third rewrite and included four new songs. In the Quarry Theatre it did become smaller in scale, including with a reduced-size cast and orchestra. It was given new blood with a change of director and choreographer. Cameron Mackintosh was happy that this production was happening away from the London spotlight and appreciated the Playhouse's support. In a programme note he wrote that because the writers were "dissatisfied with some aspects of their work and wanted to try to achieve their original dream, [Jude Kelly] immediately said 'well that is what the West Yorkshire Playhouse is for' and *Martin Guerre* had found the platform to fight its final battle. Only time will prove whether it is third time lucky but I know already that the brilliant new production team that we have assembled to create this new version couldn't be luckier to work in such a vibrant theatre which, thanks to Jude, is as inspiring in its staff as its atmosphere."[217]

In turn, critics appreciated the more intimate theatre. Sheridan Morley thought that this *Martin Guerre* was "now seen to much better advantage in the wraparound warmth of the West Yorkshire Playhouse rather than the old and narrow cinema-stage of the Prince Edward in London".[218] Most critics felt that it was much improved. James Christopher, in The Times, said, "Mackintosh has shed pounds (millions of them), half the company and most of the original songs to change the dream tabloid spectacle that opened at London's Prince Edward into a fierce musical animal... Maybe this West Yorkshire Playhouse experiment really does bode the future of the musical."[219]

After its eleven-week run at the Playhouse the production toured UK cities for six months, ironically visiting theatres with an auditorium much more like the Prince Edward in London. But unlike *Five Guys Named Moe*, it did not finish with a London run. Cameron Mackintosh did mount a North American production (with yet more re-writing) directed and choreographed by Conal Morrison and David Bolger, who had been responsible for the Playhouse production. It visited a number of American cities, but a transfer to Broadway never materialised.

The Playhouse has also been involved in work with other commercial production companies. Such co-productions are usually mounted with a UK tour or a London transfer in mind. *The Postman Always Rings Twice* (2004) is a good example. Co-produced with, amongst others, the Ambassador Theatre Group (ATG), the director Lucy Bailey and others in the production team including designer Bunny Christie had worked together before at the Birmingham Rep. There, a similar play, *Baby Doll* (another stage adaptation of a film) had transferred to the National Theatre.

The Postman Always Rings Twice was actually a stage adaptation of the novel on which the films were based. It was staged in the Quarry Theatre which allowed for a spectacular two-level set, a massive neon sign, and a coup de théâtre when a car crashes through the roof of the diner and hangs there for the rest of the play. Reviews were mostly favourable, particularly about the set design and the acting. The Financial Times praised the male lead actor:

"As Frank, the always formidable Patrick O'Kane stands comparison with John Garfield in the classic film version, which is praise indeed."[220]

As planned, the production transferred to London seven months later, but to a much smaller theatre (the Playhouse Theatre) and with one significant cast change. Frank was now played by Val Kilmer. The theatre was the first problem with the transfer:

"*The Postman Always Rings Twice* has been packed off to London from the West Yorkshire Playhouse. Alas, much has been lost in transit. It isn't helped by having the two-storey set – fly blown diner downstairs, murder most foul upstairs – squashed into a stage a third of the size of the one in Leeds."[221]

This was a serious mistake, given the importance of the set to the production. What had been a coup de théâtre in Leeds looked silly in London:

"It is even more mystifying why [the car] had to remain there throughout the whole of the second act, causing all sorts of health-and-safety implications for the cast, who had to try to act around it. The resulting tableau, with the car's headlights alternatively dimming and brightening, would have been considered odd even by Salvador Dali."[222]

A more serious problem, however, was the cast change. Presumably it was expected that the addition of a Hollywood star would attract bigger audiences. However, almost every London critic panned Val Kilmer's performance. Those who had also seen the production in Leeds and remembered how the relationship between the two lead actors had 'sizzled', felt that this was now lost. The Guardian's critic was typical:

"At West Yorkshire Playhouse late last year, you felt as if you could see the steam rising from the stage as Charlotte Emmerson's Cora ... and Patrick O'Kane's young drifter Frank coupled violently on the floor of the roadside diner. Now with O'Kane replaced for the London run with Hollywood star Val Kilmer, it is the theatrical equivalent of Horlicks. Quite simply he fails to give satisfaction. Not only is the chunky movie actor too old for the role but, despite the fact that he throws the furniture about and snarls at all the appropriate moments, he has all the stage presence of a damp tea-towel."[223]

Unsurprisingly, the production lasted for just three months in the West End. Lucy Bailey had more success in later directing the West Yorkshire Playhouse production of *Dial M for Murder*, another film adaptation. This was a co-production with Fiery Angel. After Leeds, the production toured to seven other English regional theatres. Four years later, the production toured again, to nineteen other theatres in England and Scotland.

As well as *Five Guys Named Moe* and *Martin Guerre*, the Playhouse also co-produced several other musicals, often pre-London runs. *Bat Boy – The Musical* was based on an American tabloid newspaper story about the discovery of a half-boy-half-bat in a cave in West Virginia. The musical focused on how the local community reacted to him, and about his insatiable appetite for blood. The musical started its life in an off-Broadway theatre in 2001, so the West Yorkshire Playhouse production was the UK premiere. If the subject matter wasn't surreal enough, even more so was the intention of the American producers to organise a donation campaign with the National Blood Service in Leeds!

Reviews in Leeds, mostly by local newspapers, were mainly good, seeing it as a fun summer production, albeit a weird one. The Yorkshire Post critic, Nick Ahad, lavished the most praise, calling it "a musical that is as hilariously brilliant as anything seen in the region in recent years" and concluding, "if there is any justice, Yorkshire will be able to take great pride in the fact that a show which premiered here will be in the West End".[224]

Unfortunately, the London critics didn't agree. The headlines said it all: "The brat boy from hell leaves us all in the dark"[225]; "Sharp teeth but no point" [226]; "Half bat, half boy and half-baked";[227] "Flight of fancy to drive you bats".[228]

Interestingly, in Leeds the regional Guardian critic saw it as a cult hit in the making, giving a four-star review: "slick, sick and compelling production... the ensemble playing is a joy"[229] whereas the Guardian's critic in London, Michael Billington, gave *Bat Boy – The Musical* one star, with the comment, "quite what it is doing on a West End stage, after a run at the West Yorkshire Playhouse, is a mystery".[230]

Once again the difference between theatres might be significant. At the Playhouse it played in the Courtyard Theatre with a three hundred and fifty-seat capacity, and in New York at the Union Square Theatre with a five hundred-seat capacity. It transferred to London's Shaftesbury Theatre, with more than fourteen hundred seats on three levels. Despite the reviews, the production did at least last in London for five months.

2007 saw another commercial co-production musical, *Bad Girls*, transfer to London. Based on the prison-set television drama, the reviews both locally and nationally were quite good (this time The Guardian critics gave it four and three stars respectively). Nick Ahad in the Yorkshire Post once again predicted London success:

"If I were a gambler, I would bet that this show will end up in the West End before long."[231]

He was right – but it only lasted for three months (at the Garrick).

The Playhouse's most successful commercial co-production was not a big musical, but a 'small' comedy with just four actors. This was another Fiery Angel co-production. The play was *The Thirty-nine Steps*, an adaptation of the Hitchcock film version, written by Patrick Barlow, already well known for similar productions with the National Theatre of Brent: epic plays performed by just Patrick and one other actor. However, *The Thirty-nine Steps* came about after the original idea of Nobby Dimon, who founded, together with Simon Corbele, North Country Theatre to tour plays to rural venues in North Yorkshire. With a Yorkshire Arts grant, in 1996 they toured their version of *The Thirty-nine Steps*, which was based on John Buchan's book rather than the Hitchcock film. There were further tours elsewhere in England over the following years. It was in 2002 that Edward Snape, the director of Fiery Angel, suggested that Patrick Barlow might rewrite the script, keeping the idea of four actors playing all the one hundred and more characters in the story – as well as moving the props and scenery!

It took another three years of negotiations before the production finally opened at the West Yorkshire Playhouse in June 2005, directed by Fiona Buffini. Reviews were positive apart from the Yorkshire Evening Post critic who wrote, "It's big and clever... but it's just not that funny."[232], though the Post's Nick Ahad's view differed: "If you are willing to treat this show for what it is and not expect a faithful adaptation but a night of fantastic comedy, you will not be disappointed". [233]

This time Nick did not predict West End success – but he should have done. After Leeds there was a short three-week tour, but it took another year before *The Thirty-nine Steps* got to London. Redirected by Maria Aitkin, it ran first at The Tricycle (now the Kiln) Theatre in Kilburn, and then at the Criterion Theatre in Piccadilly Circus – where it played for nine years, making it at the time the fifth longest running play in West End history. It started to win awards, beginning with the 2007 Olivier Award for Best New Comedy. Success led to a US production, firstly in Boston and then on Broadway in early 2008, where it ran for two years and received six Tony Award nominations including for Best Play and Best Direction, also winning the Awards for Best Lighting Design and Best Sound Design. The latter was given to Mic Pool who of course had worked on the original West Yorkshire Playhouse production. Since then there have been further UK tours, and productions across the world. *The Thirty-nine Steps* is an example of the West Yorkshire Playhouse, with its unique attributes and special northern magic, functioning as a launchpad for what was ultimately to be a block-busting production.

ACT TWO, SCENE NINE

Some regional theatres, for example the Theatre Royal in York, have a tradition of producing Christmas pantomimes. Others concentrate on staging big musicals with family appeal. Success is crucial: these often effectively subsidise other productions in the season. If musicals are produced at other times of the year, the appeal might be broader than to just regular theatregoers.

SINGING IN THE RAIN based on the MGM film
7th December 1999

ALTHOUGH NEVER A VENUE FOR CHRISTMAS PANTOMIMES, the Playhouse has often staged musicals based on American films at this time of the year. *High Society* was the first of these, staged in 1991. This was followed by *Gypsy* in 1993, and *The Sound of Music* in 1994. For *Gypsy*, the role of Rose (the 'entertainer' Gypsy Rose Lee) was played by Sheila Hancock, and for this part she won the 1994 Regional Theatre Award for Best Actress.

In 1999 an adaptation of the 1952 film *Singin' in the Rain* gave the Playhouse its most successful musical so far. *Singin' in the Rain* is a spoof of the film industry, set in 1927. There had been another stage musical version of the film back in 1983, directed by and starring Tommy Steele. Jude Kelly chose *Singin' in the Rain* for Christmas 1999 because the turn of the millennium reflected the film's theme of the transition from the old silent movies to the new 'talkies':

"I was thinking about the Christmas musical for the Playhouse. We were hitting the millennium and suddenly whether it was the Web or the Internet, everybody was into new technology and I realised that *Singin' in the Rain* was entirely about new technology hitting the film industry."[234]

New technology was a central part of the West Yorkshire Playhouse production. Three large screens dominated the stage, and onto these were projected computer-generated graphic images, pop video style sequences of, for example, rows of tap-dancing legs, spoof black-and-white movies acted in rehearsals by the cast. Technology was also used both in the film's famous title scene and at the finale: a 'waterist' had been employed to ensure that the rain was as realistic as possible.

If some critics questioned why there was a need for a stage version of such an iconic and perfect film, they were nevertheless taken in by the joy of the production and the quality of the dancing. Kevin Berry, in The Stage, concluded:

"Turning a film musical into a stage production takes artistic nerve, especially a film teeming with favourite songs and stars. Jude Kelly triumphs with *Singin' in the Rain* … and it really is an astonishing achievement. Kelly's previous Christmas musicals have been memorable and exciting, but this show reaches an entirely new level."[235]

On the first night, the lead actor (playing the Gene Kelly part) slipped over during the title sequence but quickly recovered. As the Daily Express critic wrote, "Recovering with a comic 'ouch' he got an enormous round of applause. They should keep that gaff in every night – it works a treat."[236] If nothing else, it was a reminder that, unlike the movies, live theatre does not allow for retakes!

Rain also poured for the finale, with the whole cast splashing around in white wellies, sou'westers and plastic macs. Loving this finish, The Independent critic wrote, "short of bringing on Esther Williams for a spot of backstroke, or showering us with banknotes, it's hard to see how this could stop the show in a more determinedly show-stopping manner".[237]

Trevor Nunn, then Artistic Director at the National Theatre, came to see *Singin' in the Rain* immediately prior to the last performance at the Playhouse and expressed a desire for the production to transfer to the National Theatre – and this happened. It opened in the National's Olivier Theatre four months later. Initially programmed for just one month of performances, it returned as their Christmas production in December 2000.

Some London critics were less impressed than those in Leeds. Nicholas de Jongh described the three screens as "redundant distractions from the main event".[238] Kate Bassett, in the Daily Telegraph, commented, "The snag is that these jazzy doodles don't stop the bare, black stage below looking gloomily spartan". She also doubted the intention of the production: "Gene Kelly's choreography was pushing the boundaries of dance by using the trick of cinema (several takes necessary, dubbed singing, etc.). You can't hope to match that on stage".[239]

If the production was less well received in London, certain factors are relevant. Firstly, it opened in the summer so was not, as in Leeds, a Christmas alternative to pantomime. Secondly, it opened in a theatre which, whilst not unlike the Quarry Theatre in design, is a much bigger space. The Olivier Theatre seats 1,150 people, including a circle level seating over five hundred. Thirdly, it opened at a time when some were questioning whether Government-subsidised theatres like the National should be staging musicals – or Ayckbourn plays, which the National was about to do at this time. Nevertheless, *Singin' in the Rain* at the National Theatre fulfilled one of Trevor Nunn's intentions: to bring the best regional work to the South Bank.

Whatever the reservations, following the second run at the National Theatre, *Singin' in the Rain* won that year's Olivier Award for Outstanding Musical Production. There was then talk of a West End transfer, but this did not happen. However, the production returned to the West Yorkshire Playhouse, with a new company, at Christmas 2001 for an eleven-week run, prior to a UK tour lasting until the following Christmas. Publicity for the tour focused heavily on the 'rain'. The Wolverhampton Chronicle even published a Rain Fact-file, with figures such as the litres of water used at each performance and the time taken to fully dry the stage. Regional reviewers had a field-day with their headlines, which were also very positive: "Oh, Water Show", "Water Carry On", "Flooded With Talent", "What a Brolly-good Show", "Tapping a Rich Vein", "Applause Didn't Rain, It Poured" are just some of them.

Very occasionally the Playhouse has produced a musical other than at Christmas. The most successful of these, in 1998, was *Spend Spend Spend*. This is the story of Viv Nicholson, from Castleford in Leeds, who in 1961 won £152,319 on the football pools, equivalent to several million pounds today, and went on to spend her winnings in the manner of the musical's title.

Viv's story had already been told in a book and a television play. This musical version of her story, by Steve Brown and Justin Greene was always likely to be a success. It was very much a Yorkshire story, and there was a lot of local media coverage even before the production had opened. Viv's willingness to be interviewed, and her presence on the opening night, helped considerably, and the production itself was very much a crowd-pleaser. A variety of music styles were included, mostly catchy and memorable songs. Moments such as a deluge of five pounds notes bearing Viv's face from above the audience were guaranteed to please. Above all, through dialect, regional humour, its portrayal of a local mining village, and because the story was one that audiences already knew, there was always going to be a sense of Yorkshire ownership about the production.

Nevertheless, London critics came to see *Spend Spend Spend*, and reviews were positive. The word "exhilarating" was used by several critics, and the 'Yorkshire-ness' was appreciated, if a tad patronisingly: the Daily Express described *Spend Spend Spend* as "a cracking new flat cap musical",[240] while the Mail on Sunday liked the style of the production: "It's as bold and brassy (and proud of it) as only a Yorkshire lass like Viv … can be".[241] Other critics appreciated its contrast with other recent musicals both in terms of the subject matter and the simplicity of the production:

"After the procession of recent musicals set far away in time or place – in France, endlessly in Grubby parts of America – a musical focusing successfully on an English life is an exhilarating experience."[242]

"Well-acted and mercifully staged without the usual vast hydraulic set, this show has an effortless down-to-earth ebullience which wins you over."[243]

Perhaps inevitably, some London critics measured success against other English musicals, notably those of Andrew Lloyd Webber, and speculated on a London transfer. There was indeed a West End production, which played for ten months from October 1999 at the Piccadilly Theatre but with a new director and lead actors. Barbara Dickson played the part of Viv, which had been performed by Rosemary Ashe in Leeds.

Jude Kelly's last production at the Playhouse was also a musical – but the fact that *The Wizard of Oz* opened in March rather than at Christmas rightly suggests something rather different. There were already clues: in May 1999 Jude had directed *Deadmeat*, for which the Courtyard Theatre had been transformed into a 'nightclub' – a multi-media environment complete with huge video screens. Some actors, including Ian McKellen, appeared only in digital form. Then came the three screens central to the production of *Singin' in the Rain*.

The Wizard of Oz was another multi-media production incorporating a team of eight actors who also acted as puppeteers for these creations. They performed alongside all the video effects, animation, and the appearance, on one of the screens, of Patrick Stewart as the wizard. Particularly effective was the way in which actors stepped through their filmed images onto the stage. Images were also projected onto a transparent screen at the front of the stage, effectively a 'fourth wall'. Some critics disliked this feature, feeling that it distanced the actors from the audience: "I only got a good look at Dorothy's pert, pretty face when she came out for her curtain call, and no one would hear her warbling Over the Rainbow if she wasn't, like the rest of the cast, heavily miked".[244] Another critic felt the actors were too preoccupied with keeping in sync with the video images. More generally, most were very impressed with the technology, but some felt that this was all at the expense of the story itself. The Yorkshire Post critic concluded, "How (the witch) met her end, we hadn't the foggiest. Whatever had happened to polish her off disappeared in the general melee – although it appeared to be Dorothy's doing. We were left looking at each other and saying 'what?' Something vital to the storytelling got lost in the technical wizardry. Surely some lesson here – such as less is more?".[245]

Taking over from Jude Kelly as Artistic Director, Ian Brown's first Christmas show at the Playhouse was a substantial part of his second season at the theatre, opening at the beginning of December 2003, and running until the middle of February 2004. This was Alan Bennett's adaptation of *The Wind in the Willows*, by Kenneth Grahame, which he originally wrote for the National Theatre in 1990. For some critics, a production in Leeds was not before time:

"Ian Brown's delightful production feels less like a revival than a homecoming. Bennett's soul may be by the riverside, but his heart remains in Leeds."[246]

In the programme Ian announced that this production marked a new direction for the Playhouse: a big increase in the amount of theatre produced for family audiences. He saw this as happening not only with Playhouse productions, but by attracting touring companies known for high-quality children's work.

The Wind in the Willows was indeed highly successful in attracting family audiences, perhaps partly because critics praised the production for appealing to children and adults alike: a typical conclusion was, "This show is pure magic. And if you don't have any children to take, take yourself, because judging by the loud adult guffaws that rocked the theatre, it is something that appeals to all ages".[247] Critics were full of praise for the lead actors, and several also delighted in the Brummie-accented galumphing carthorse. They equally praised the set:

"Yet, almost stealing the show from under their furry noses is Dick Bird's great set, which transports the audience from river to wood to various boltholes with ease – oh, and a car, a train, a barge and a boat."[248]

In his programme notes Ian also explained that Playhouse staff had been working hard to make the building a fun, welcoming place for families. Chairman Bernard Atha praised this work at the next Annual General Meeting, suggesting that initiatives such as a front of house buggy park, themed children's menus in the restaurant, children-sized ice-creams and juice cartons had helped to make the West Yorkshire

Playhouse "the premier family Christmas Venue in the region".[249]

Christmas 2003 also marked the beginning of there being a second production for families at the Playhouse. Alongside *The Wind in the Willows* was *The Elves and the Shoemaker*, an adaptation by Mike Kenny of the Grimm's fairy tale. Mike Kenny's involvement with the Playhouse went back to his acting with the Theatre In Education company at the first theatre. *The Elves and the Shoemaker* was directed by Gail McIntyre, separate from her work with the Schools Company. Performances took place in the Barber Studio because the Courtyard Theatre was being used for another Christmas-friendly production, *Blues in the Night*, essentially a compilation of blues and jazz music. The success of *Blues in the Night* led to a revival in Christmas 2004, so Mike Kenny / Gail McIntyre's production of *Pinocchio* also played in the Barber Studio. By now, their work had gained a good reputation for originality and invention, and for encouraging imagination. Reviewing *Pinocchio*, Kevin Berry in The Stage wrote, "With the names Kenny and McIntyre on the credits one expects excellence but it is impossible to predict how the excellence will be achieved. That is the excitement of their work".[250]

From 2006 these now annual Christmas productions did play in the Courtyard Theatre. They continued until 2012, in that year with Mike Kenny's version of *Sleeping Beauty*. Becoming known as 'Big Stories for Little People', these productions were always produced with audiences as young as four in mind. Occasionally the storylines were criticised for being too 'dark', but Mike Kenny made no apology:

"Kenny sees one of the main purposes of children's theatre as dealing with the dark and the dangerous. It is after all only make believe."[251]

What he did do was strip back stories to their essence, and the productions concentrated on storytelling, music, characters and imagination, rather than elaborate sets and props. Typically, a small company of actors between them played many different characters. This occasionally led to the criticism that productions were too minimalist. As Rod McPhee, in the Yorkshire Evening Post, put it, "asking [children] to suspend reality to such a degree in a theatre is unreasonable. Why? Because if there is ever an arena in which you can provide a visual kaleidoscope of images and sounds then this is it".[252]

For many others, however, simplicity was everything:

"Imaginations are set free. Nothing is beyond anyone's grasp. When a bird flutters over Pinocchio, it is Kay [one of the actors] simply wriggling his fingers."[253]

The Big Stories for Little People were perfect for families with children perhaps too young for the Christmas productions in the Quarry Theatre, partly because they were a cheaper alternative to these, and to pantomimes at other theatres.

Ian's success with *The Wind in the Willows* in 2003 put pressure on him to live up to the standard the following year. He was also aware of the importance of the Christmas production financially:

"If the Christmas show failed, you were in big trouble: how were you going to recover the loss?"[254]

The Lion, the Witch and the Wardrobe had already been announced for 2004, even before the run of *The Wind in the Willows* had begun. The production of *The Lion, the Witch and the Wardrobe* used Adrian Mitchell's adaptation of the C.S. Lewis novel, written for The Royal Shakespeare Company some six years earlier. Whilst reviewers were not as gushing with praise as for *The Wind in the Willows,* at least one saw it as a triumph:

"Well, Ian Brown has done it again! Not content with putting on a superb family Christmas show in 2003, he has gone one better this year with *The Lion, the Witch and the Wardrobe*, which I can only describe as amazingly spectacular."[255]

One difference between the two productions was that whilst *The Wind in the Willows* is essentially pure fun, there is a darker side to C.S. Lewis's story, which perhaps appealed more to the adults in the audience. The other difference related to the set: *The Lion, the Witch and the Wardrobe* had a much simpler one, dependent more on overhead projection screens: "The designer has chosen a minimalist set, relying on excellent costumes and on the audience's imagination to create the world at the back of the wardrobe."[256] But for Nick Ahad of the Yorkshire Post, this was a disappointment. His criticism was similar to those made of the Mike Kenny-Gail McIntyre productions:

"The most disappointing aspect is the set. To meet the standard set by last year's would have been difficult. It feels as if the production staff knew this and tried not to bother, and instead created something that demanded a stretch of the audience's collective imagination. Nothing to criticise here, but one wants the magic of theatre to help our imagination along on the journey."[257]

Regardless, the production was a big box office success, helped by a feature piece on BBC Look North television. Consequently *The Lion, the Witch and the Wardrobe* was revived in 2007, amid claims that that the 2004 production was the most successful Christmas family show in the history of the West Yorkshire Playhouse. This time a different Yorkshire Post reviewer praised the set as a simple "masterpiece of ingenuity" and concluding – "Prepare to be enchanted, thrilled, amazed and even to shed a few tears when you experience the magic of Narnia … this must be the best Christmas production ever staged at the Playhouse".[258]

Alice in Wonderland the following year (2005) was a co-production with the Birmingham Repertory Theatre. It was much more of a musical, with Carl Davis being the composer. Perhaps partly with the Birmingham Rep's main stage in mind, the thrust area of the Quarry Theatre's stage was not used. Instead, a proscenium arch was created, in front of which was an orchestra pit. More than one critic was disappointed by this, saying, "The strength of the modern main stage is that it creates a rapport between player and watcher. So to artificially create a barrier – and for a Christmas show aimed at trying to engage children – seems curious".[259] This perhaps explains why some critics found the production somewhat flat and lacking in fun.

Overall the West Yorkshire Playhouse's reputation in musical theatre production and children's productions alongside adult drama had achieved excellence. Trevor Nunn recognised this when he brought Leeds's production of S*ingin' in the Rain* to the South Bank in fulfilment of his ideal to bring the best regional work to London, though one London critic's affirmation of this production is still nuanced by the capital's attitude to the regions: "There is great ingenuity and skill in the theatre outside London, and it deserves more than the little encouragement it now gets".[260]

ACT TWO, SCENE TEN

Arguably, regional producing theatres should occasionally take risks. International work is significant in this respect. Success can enhance the theatre's reputation both nationally and internationally.

THE BEATIFICATION OF AREA BOY
by Wole Soyinka
26th October 1995

WHEN JUDE KELLY APPEARED on the radio programme *Desert Island Discs* in May 2002, she was asked to name the West Yorkshire Playhouse production of which she was most proud. Her answer was *The Beatification of Area Boy*, by Wole Soyinka, which played in the Courtyard Theatre in the Autumn of 1995 – perhaps the best example of the Playhouse's international work.

The first connection Nigerian playwright, novelist and poet Wole Soyinka made with Leeds was through studying at Leeds University in the 1950s. In the years after Leeds he became equally well-known as a political activist, one consequence being a two-year prison sentence starting in 1967. In 1973 Leeds University awarded him an Honorary Doctorate and in 1986 he received the Nobel Prize for Literature. In 1995, when *The Beatification of Area Boy* was produced in Leeds, Wole was in one of his periods of exile from Nigeria.

It was Jude Kelly herself who invited him to write the play, when she encountered him at a university event in 1989. Nothing happened until, in 1995, Jude received a copy of *The Beatification of Area Boy*. Wole was keen for the play to be produced at the Playhouse, given that a staging in Nigeria had become impossible:

"My plans were to produce the play in Nigeria towards the end of last year (1994) but by then the police were stamping on anything which had the slightest connection with Wole Soyinka's writings."[261]

Producing the play in Leeds became possible when funding was attracted from a Swiss producer, after which Jude went to Lagos to audition, in secret, Nigerian actors. Seven were recruited there; the rest of the large cast was mainly made up of Nigerians living in England and Switzerland.

The play is subtitled 'a Lagosian kaleidoscope', appropriate because the action takes place over one day in the city, and introduces a diverse number of characters. The 'area boy' of the title is the security guard of an opulent shopping mall; he is separately organising other area boys – street gangs extorting money from the rich people visiting the mall. The audience learns more about his life and those of the poor street traders outside the mall. There is plenty of humour and music, but the play has a darker side, being a microcosm of post oil-boom Nigeria. For example, the woman selling street food gives her memories of the horrors of the civil war. The clearing of the space outside the mall for a grand wedding involving two wealthy Nigerian families mirrors the recent clearing of a nearby squatter camp by the army which displaced a million people.

Reviews of *The Beatification of Area Boy* were good, but given the content, Charles Spencer arguably summed things up best:

"There are times when criticism seems almost impertinent, and this world premiere of Wole Soyinka's latest play is one of them."[262]

Wole attended some of the rehearsals. However, not wanting his whereabouts to be too obvious, he was not present for the opening night. Sadly, on that day his fellow Nigerian playwright, Ken Saro-Wiwa was sentenced to death. He and eight others were hanged during the play's run in Leeds, and on that day, a minute's silence was held prior to the performance. Understandably the Nigerian actors had been reluctant to be interviewed about their country. However, they honoured Ken Saro-Wiwa in a wreath-laying ceremony alongside local politicians and other city dignitaries.

The success of *The Beatification of Area Boy* led to an international tour in 1996 with performances in Denmark, Sweden, Switzerland and Germany, followed by a short run in New York.

With productions like *The Beatification of Area Boy* the Playhouse furthered its reputation as a theatre of national standing. Jude

Kelly and other Playhouse staff would begin to receive invitations to contribute to international theatre festivals and conferences, and in turn to host such events. The first international invitation came as early as 1993 when the Playhouse was invited to represent Britain at Italy's International Festival to be held in Venice and Rome, celebrating the work of the eighteenth century playwright Carlo Goldini. The Playhouse was the first major British company to perform a play from the Italian classical repertoire in English in Italy. *The Servant of Two Masters* was performed in the Quarry Theatre prior to the performances in Italy, with a cast including Toby Jones.

Then in 1995 Jude Kelly visited the University of Thessaloniki in Greece to lecture students on drama. This was beneficial in forging links with the British Council which organised the visit. Jude subsequently attended a conference in Amsterdam where directors, producers and administrators discussed British and international theatre collaborations, and later that year she was invited by the University of Toronto to participate in an international conference alongside big-name directors such as Robert Lepage, Robert Wilson and JoAnne Akalaitis.

Early the following year the Playhouse developed and launched the first European Directors' School, attended by twenty-six participants from seventeen countries. One of the invited tutors was Robert Sturua, Artistic Director at the Rustavel Theatre in Tbilisi, the capital of Georgia. Another Georgian director, David 'Doi' Dioashvili, participated. As proof of the success of this school in developing international links, Doi would return to the Playhouse later in 1996 with his regular designer and composer, to direct Arthur Miller's *The Crucible*. As Jude Kelly said:

"Bringing Doi and his team to interact with a group of nineteen British actors is part of the Playhouse's drive towards a truly integrated international programme, which invigorates all who come to the Playhouse and all who work here through exposure to vital and unfamiliar new ideas."[263]

Unfortunately the critics were mostly unimpressed with this production. Labelling it as 'director's theatre', many found it gimmicky in ways that worked against the text; they made similar comments about the music. The worst criticism came from Charles Spencer in the Daily Telegraph:

"It is also pretty clear that (Doi) has failed to understand the piece. The whole point about the Salem witch trials is that there *weren't* any witches. Here, however, he has the hysterical Betty Parris flying around the stage like a possessed Peter Pan, entirely robbing the play of its main thesis."[264]

In 1998 Jude was invited to take a play to Japan's International Solo Performance Festival in Tokyo. She approached Kay Mellor: the result was *Queen*, which Kay both wrote and performed. The 'queen' is a famous soap opera actress at the very end of her career, which coincides with the death of Diana, the Princess of Wales. The play explores the theme of celebrity fame and its consequences. Following Japan, Kay agreed to rework the play and perform it at the Playhouse. Of this acting experience, she was to say, "You have to remember I hadn't been on stage for six years, so I was completely terrified … In hindsight, I was barking mad to use a one-woman show as my return to stage acting".[265]

2004 saw a stage version of George Orwell's *Homage to Catalonia* which partly came about as an idea of the Artistic Director of Newcastle's Northern Stage Ensemble, Alan Lyddiard. His company had already produced very successful stage versions of two other Orwell novels: *Animal Farm* and *1984*. When he discovered that Calixto Bieito, his equivalent at the Catalan-based Teatre Romea, had a similar idea, he asked the British Council initially to negotiate a meeting. It took almost two years from this first meeting to the first performance at the West Yorkshire Playhouse in May 2004. Along the way, as well as the Playhouse, Paris's Bobigny Arts Centre came on board as co-producers, as did the Forum Barcelona 2004 cultural programme, making the projected £160,000 budget a reality. A bilingual script was written by the Catalan writer

Pablo Ley and the English playwright Allan Baker. Josep Galindo from Barcelona was chosen as director. Ten actors were chosen: five Catalan; five English, only one of whom understood Catalan. Fortunately the funding allowed for extended rehearsal time.

Language was not the only international challenge. At the Playhouse, Ian Brown was aware of the logistical challenge:

"It's easy to want to be international, but doing it is much harder. [It takes] a lot of behind the scenes work to set it up. There are different tax regimes, different conditions of work, different languages – there's less freedom across borders than you might expect. This is why it doesn't happen more often: people don't have the time or resources to do it."[266]

What emerged was a highly impressionistic production, not too dependent on the languages, although surtitles were provided. Critics were divided, but Michael Coveney's five-star review in the Daily Mail found it "one of the best evenings of political theatre in living memory".[267]

The production included film and stills footage, and the stage was filled with bottles, boots, books, clothes, and oranges; Coveney felt that because of all this, "an overwhelming picture of Orwell's war emerges in all its absurdity, filth, danger and betrayal".[268]

But reviewer Lynne Walker gave it only one star, as "a muddle-headed approach to a serious subject".[269] She disliked the way the actors were 'kept busy' lining up the props in rows, even if this was to give an impression of the tedious nature of the war. She also felt that the "constant murmur of percussive noise and a painfully loud eruption of a punk-rock number in which everything that can be thrashed most emphatically is [thrashed], suggests that the creators just don't trust the original material to hold our attention. When Orwell despairs that the situation – no rifles, tin hats, maps or boots – is more like a comic opera than a war, he might be describing Josep Galindo's production itself".[270]

Kinder reviewers acknowledged the ambitious nature of the production and recognised the significance of the ensemble approach of the company. Looking back, Ian said:

"I was proud to do it. It was a risk, it was exciting, it could have worked, but it didn't. It was a style of [international] theatre that Britain doesn't understand. You get hammered when it doesn't work, but I still don't regret going ahead with it".[271]

Jude Kelly had arguably displayed an intuitive instinct when she connected with Wole Soyinka at a chance meeting that resulted in the production of *The Beatification of Area Boy*. During her time at the West Yorkshire Playhouse and especially from this production onwards, the theatre's national and international standing proceeded to build.

ACT TWO, SCENE ELEVEN

How do you measure the success of a regional producing theatre? Is it just about attendance statistics and consequent income? Is it about the number of London transfers? Is it about attracting 'star' actors? Is it about success in staging productions particularly relevant to the community which the theatre serves? Or is it about productions which are of interest nationally, ones that people will travel longer distances to see?

.

TENTH BIRTHDAY PARTY
8th March 2000

ON 8TH MARCH 2000 THE WEST YORKSHIRE PLAYHOUSE celebrated its tenth birthday. A large party was held, with a speech given by the Rt. Hon. Chris Smith MP – at that time the Secretary of State for the Department of Culture, Media and Sport. A video giving a potted history of the first ten years of the Playhouse, was produced and screened at the event.

In those ten years the Playhouse had gained a national reputation, in part because productions were regularly reviewed by the national newspapers. The theatre was also winning UK awards including, after just four years, the 1994 Prudential Award for Theatre, given for excellence, creativity, innovation and accessibility. In addition, over the first ten years the Playhouse had won twelve Theatre Management Association Awards (now the UK Theatre Awards), a nationwide celebration of the outstanding achievements of theatre across the UK. These awards included Best Actor, Best Actress, Best Musical, Best Director, Best Designer, and Best Show for Children and Young People. Particularly special was the 1996 Award for Most Welcoming Theatre, the first time this had been awarded to a theatre in the north of England.

As the theatre celebrated its tenth birthday, it was soon to achieve, with *Singing in the Rain*, its first transfer to the National Theatre in London. At the start of those ten years, the West Yorkshire Playhouse had been heralded as the 'National Theatre of the North'. Early on, the theatre lighting expert and author, Francis Reid, commented, "perhaps the greatest compliment I can offer to all concerned is to suggest that the West Yorkshire Playhouse is the national theatre that we failed to build on the South Bank".[272]

So had the Playhouse become the national theatre of the north? Francis Reid's comment relates more to the building design. In this respect, the National Theatre on the South Bank had three, larger auditoria. More likely, however, the claim to be the National Theatre of the North was a reference to the programme and productions.

Richard Eyre was Artistic Director at the National Theatre when the West Yorkshire Playhouse opened in 1990, and Nicholas (Nick) Hytner was an associate director. When Nick was appointed as Artistic Director in 2001, he was surprised to learn that when it was founded in 1963, "the National had no charter. There is no founding document that announces what kind of work it should do, and who it should do it for".[273]

Interestingly a 1908 handbook by Harley Granville Barker, who back then was proposing a Shakespeare Memorial National Theatre, had suggested the following aims:

"to keep the plays of Shakespeare in its repertory; to revive whatever else is vital in English classical drama; to prevent recent plays of great merit from falling into oblivion; to produce new plays…; to produce translations of representative works of foreign drama, ancient and modern; and to stimulate the art of acting through varied opportunities which it will offer to the members of the company."[274]

Nearly a century later, Nick considered that this was essentially the work that the National Theatre should be doing.

With this in mind, it is useful to compare the National Theatre's programme with that of the West Yorkshire Playhouse in its first year. In that year (April 1990 to March 1991) the National Theatre presented sixteen new productions. Two were Shakespeare plays (*King Lear* with Brian Cox and *Richard III* with Ian McKellen), and four were considered 'classical', by Racine, Sheridan and Miller, as well as two others, by Moliere and Dario Fo, which were presented in the Cottesloe Theatre by the Education Department as part of a national tour. New productions of two recent plays, by Berkoff and Ayckbourn were included, plus six new plays, four of which were by established playwrights: Trevor Griffiths, Christopher Hampton, David Edgar and Alan Bennett. Apart from the latter's *The Wind in the Willows*, which was the Christmas production in the Olivier Theatre, new work was presented in the National Theatre's smallest space, the Cottesloe (now the Dorfman) Theatre. In 1990-91 the National Theatre also received seven touring productions, mainly by international companies (Johannesburg, Bucharest, Dublin, Taiwan, Quebec).

In the same period the West Yorkshire Playhouse presented an equal number of productions (one more if you include the Theatre in Education production of *The Poor School*). There were no Shakespeare plays (not until March 1993 did the Playhouse produce one: *The Taming of the Shrew)* however there were three 'classical' plays – by Shaw, Ibsen and Synge, and new productions of recent plays by Neil Simon and Ayckbourn. Unlike at the National Theatre, there was one musical revival: *Carousel*.

However, in comparing the National Theatre with the West Yorkshire Playhouse for 1990-91, the biggest difference was in respect of new plays. There were ten of these at the Playhouse, half of which were world premieres (or in the case of *The Maple Tree Game*, a British premiere). Three of these world premieres were performed in the larger space of the Quarry Theatre. A closer examination of these plays reveals that, with perhaps the exception of *Sunsets and Glories* by Peter Barnes, they were not written by established playwrights. Also they were plays with smaller casts by comparison with the National Theatre, where the plays by Griffiths, Edgar and Hampton had casts of between fourteen and sixteen actors and Alan Bennett's *The Wind in the Willows* had a cast of thirty-five. In 1990-91 the Playhouse received ten touring productions, all regional or national theatre companies – including the Royal Shakespeare Company's production of *Les Liaisons Dangereuses* by Christopher Hampton.

This comparison shows that, even in its first year, the work at the Playhouse, just in terms of plays produced and received, was as substantial as the National Theatre, even though the latter used three auditoria. However, the biggest difference relates to the amount of Arts Council funding. For the period

1990-91, the National Theatre received a grant of £9,140,000. The West Yorkshire Playhouse received just £600,000. No wonder that the National could afford a cast of thirty-five!

The vast difference in grants merely reflected the reality of Arts Council drama funding. The Consultative Green Paper on Drama in England, published in May 1995, admitted that the two national companies, the National Theatre and the Royal Shakespeare Company, in 1974-75 accounted for 34% of the total Arts Council drama funding – and that this had risen to just over 50% in 1985-86,and had remained at 46-50% ever since. The report also admitted that "in the recent period of falling funding levels, the nationals' success has created growing tension with regional theatres that are increasingly unable to sustain the range and quality of work expected of them".[275]

Nevertheless, when the Arts Council completed its appraisal of the West Yorkshire Playhouse in 1992 it did so on the basis of the theatre's commitment to provide a national institution based in a region. The committee therefore appraised 'national artistic leadership'. Ironically, given the comparison of funding with the National Theatre, it concluded:

"National leadership for any artistic organisation is not simply the result of greater resources – there are, for instance, leading theatre companies funded at less than one tenth of the level of this company. It is earned; either through innovation or achievement of the highest standards. The West Yorkshire Playhouse aspires to both of these, but it is not yet there."[276]

It criticised the standards of productions as generally disappointing and stated that the quality of work needed to improve in order to "increase attendances and earn the national tag".[277] The report acknowledged the achievement of a British premiere of *The Maple Tree Game* by the banned Czech playwright Pavel Kahout, but commented that "unfortunately the company has not spent sufficient time building on successful international links such as this. Improved artistic contacts with artists abroad can only help to improve the company's national profile…"[278]

In response, the artistic and executive directors and the Board of Governors pointed to the report's own statistics regarding performances (558 in 1990-91 by comparison with 268 at the Birmingham Rep, 497 at the Haymarket Leicester and 357 at the Crucible Sheffield) and argued back, that "the number of productions statistically increases the possibility of an occasional show not fully reaching the national standard to which we aspire".[279] Not surprisingly, they also pointed out the financial requirements of 'artistic excellence', and argued for additional Arts Council funding.

However fair or unfair the Arts Council's criticisms of the Playhouse (considering that the theatre had been open for less than two years when the appraisal was completed!), they did raise questions about what could or should be expected of a national theatre based in a region. Put simply, is it about scale, or about quality? If it is the latter, how could a regional theatre be expected to achieve the world-leading work expected of the National Theatre or the Royal Shakespeare Company?

Nevertheless, just as the Arts Council appraisal was completed, a new play of national significance, *The Gulf Between Us* by Trevor Griffiths, opened in the Quarry Theatre. The play was written in response to the first Gulf War. Trevor was by 1992 a well-established playwright with plays produced by both the Royal Shakespeare Company and the National Theatre. Trevor's previous play, *The Piano*, had opened in the Cottesloe Theatre in 1990; interestingly, therefore, he chose to open *The Gulf Between Us* in Leeds, expressing deep cynicism about London audiences and critics:

"I know how to write a well-made play to satisfy these aged white males who live in the fucking metropolis. But I've never been interested in doing only this. In fact, I'd sooner tap dance".[280]

The Gulf Between Us had a cast of just seven, and five of these were Palestinian actors – chosen because "it's not a play about Palestine or Israel, but Palestinians are much more political than almost anybody else in the region by virtue of their own history; and that hunch, about the essential contribution they would make to the production, has proved right".[281]

Despite his feelings about London premieres, Trevor was disappointed that the play did not transfer there or elsewhere. As an article in Tribune reported:

"Opening in Leeds in January 1992, at a time when snow was paralysing the city, *The Gulf Between Us* still managed to attract good audiences. 'I was there every night and it was responded to in a very passionate way. It was a dazing experience: people came out bumping into tables, staring at the walls, not wanting to speak'. Despite this, none of the London theatres would touch it. 'I feel as if I've been ring-fenced, says Griffiths. 'The play was not allowed to break out of Leeds'."[282]

The National Theatre's loss was arguably Leeds's gain: just the kind of play that a 'National Theatre of the North' should have been producing. Over the next years there were many more productions which would enhance the Playhouse's national reputation.

Two years later came the swansong of the theatre's first Resident Director, Matthew Warchus, whose final play was a revival of Sam Shepherd's *True West*, about two brothers, set in a kitchen in suburban southern California. Perhaps because it had been agreed that the play would transfer to London's Donmar Warehouse after Leeds, the production attracted Mark Rylance to the lead role. Mark had previously worked at the National Theatre and with the Royal Shakespeare Company, notably as Romeo and Hamlet.

True West was performed in 1994 in the Quarry Theatre with a cast of just four actors. Mark unusually shared the lead role with another actor, Michael Rudko: they exchanged roles on alternate nights. Whilst most national critics waited until the production opened at the Donmar, The Financial Times' Alastair Macauley reviewed *True West* as it opened in Leeds. He was full of praise:

"Congratulations to Leeds' West Yorkshire Playhouse and to director Matthew Warchus for staging this play, and to casting two superlative actors. This production clinches what I have felt for some time: that the West Yorkshire Playhouse is the most vital and refreshing English theatre outside London today."[283]

Reviewing the production in London, The Guardian's Michael Billington acknowledged its origin at the "increasingly powerful West Yorkshire Playhouse", concluding, "There is no more exciting acting than this to be found in the London theatre".[284]

After *True West*, Mark Rylance went on to play Macbeth at the National Theatre.

Just three months after *True West*, another Playhouse production was a national success: *The Winter Guest*, a new play by Sharman MacDonald. Her previous plays had been produced by London's Bush and Royal Court Theatres, in the West End, and at the National Theatre. This new play was commissioned by Ruby Wax and Alan Rickman, and like *True West* a London transfer was also planned in advance, this time to the Almeida Theatre. Alan Rickman directed the production, a play which, without a plot as such, observes the lives of four couples, including two elderly women and a pair of schoolboys. This time the national critics came to Leeds to review the play, and gave particular praise to the female actors (Sheila Reid, Sandra Voe, Phyllida Law and Sian Thomas). They also praised Robin Don's spacious set design for ingeniously combining "the interior of a house with a detailed depiction of the promenade, the snow-covered beach and the ice-locked sea. It is both bleak and beautiful, and you can almost feel the sharp chill in the air".[285] Michael Billington felt that the set "grabs you before anything else",[286] but the Yorkshire Post's Lynda Murdin thought that "the subtlety of much of MacDonald's text is almost overwhelmed by the visual strength of Robin Don's design".[287]

The setting for the play became real life one night when Playhouse audiences found themselves trapped at the theatre after snow fell in Leeds for twelve hours. They were stranded all night, as were staff and actors who served soup and entertained with songs and sketches!

Back in 1990, after *Sunsets and Glories* opened to excellent reviews, Jude Kelly observed that the play had received "the greatest national acclaim to date; the theatre needs this acclaim as it helps to entice better actors".[288] The theatre's attraction of 'big name' actors due to this 'national acclaim' was certainly demonstrated in the last season of Jude Kelly's time as Artistic Director – a season which was also something of a Yorkshire celebration: three plays by Bradford's J.B. Priestley, one of which starred another Yorkshireman, Patrick Stewart. In this 'Priestley: Making Time and Space for Theatre' season, two of the plays were relatively safe choices: *Eden End* and *Dangerous Corner*. The latter was a co-production, with the commercial

company Really Useful Theatre, which guaranteed a West End transfer. However, it was a much less well-known Priestley play, *Johnson Over Jordan*, which gained national attention – and was the most daring and riskiest part of the season. The risk was obviously lessened by the casting of Patrick Stewart. As Jude Kelly admitted:

"I'm not sure it would have been possible to have such an obscure piece unless the actor playing Johnson was someone the audience wanted to see."[289]

Patrick Stewart had worked as an associate artist with the Royal Shakespeare Company for seventeen years, followed by work at the National Theatre. However, it was of course his role as Captain Picard in *Star Trek* that had brought him international fame. Patrick and Jude had worked together before. During her sabbatical year from the Playhouse in 1997, Jude had directed Patrick in a production of *Othello* in Washington DC. The production was significant because of the casting: Othello was white, whilst Iago and all other parts were played by Black actors. Jude and Patrick's working relationship was a success: Patrick was clear that, "long before it opened, I knew not only that I'd found a great friend but also a director I wanted to work with again, who was good for me. Some directors take what you can already do, and use it. Others, like Jude, see what you can do and push you to do more than that".[290]

Johnson Over Jordan was perhaps Priestley's most experimental play, influenced by the German Expressionist playwrights. It opens at the moment of Johnson's death, he being an ordinary but good man, who only by looking back on events in his life can appreciate his achievements. What follows is a series of dreamlike memories of his life, the action taking place in three different settings: his insurance office, a nightclub and an inn. In the original 1939 production, the action was augmented with ballet and masks, as well as elaborate lighting effects. There was a cast of twenty-three actors, and the music, composed by Benjamin Brittan, was performed by a twenty-piece orchestra.

The West Yorkshire Playhouse production, over fifty years later, was the first professional theatre revival, although there had been a BBC television version in 1965 with Ralph Richardson recreating his original role as Johnson. As the audience entered the Quarry Theatre, Johnson was already on stage in a hospital bed, and as the auditorium lights dimmed, he died. By comparison with the original production, Jude Kelly's was simpler with a cast of just ten actors and a musical score performed live by two pianists. Nevertheless, once again she used video projection: Patrick Stewart's face was enlarged onto a white brick wall – which disintegrated during the action. The text was also updated with present-day references.

The original production of *Johnson Over Jordan* had by all accounts been a spectacular flop, but Jude Kelly justified her decision to revive the play:

"In terms of whether *Johnson* was a success or a failure, I wasn't entering into it in order to do a great revival, but I do feel that I want to pay homage to Priestley's risk-taking. It is a great responsibility. Because although I don't think that Priestley considered it to be a masterpiece, he was incredibly proud to have done it and very sad that people didn't recognise him for having taken those risks. There is a responsibility in terms of saying that this play was worth writing and is still very much worth doing."[291]

Unfortunately, whilst critics admired her risk-taking decision to revive the play, most felt that it was a mistake to do so. John Peter concluded that "The problem is the play itself: an hour and forty minutes of brain-racking tedium. This is Priestley's worst and most excruciatingly self-admiring play…"[292] while Kate Bassett found that "Priestley's dialogue is scarcely more sophisticated than Enid Blyton".[293] Several critics thought it was a mistake to modernise the setting and alter the text: "they misguidedly pander to a modern sensibility with mention of 'going clubbing', homosexual marriages and animal rights campaigns".[294]

These critics all saw the play as a period piece, opening significantly just before the start of the Second World War. The loss of this context was well explained by Rhoda Koenig:

"In the original play, Johnson had a speech (now a brief remark) about his fear of death, stemming from his years, like Priestley's, in the trenches of the First World War. Priestley may have meant to suggest that, after such horrors, a man has a need, and a right, to grab life at every chance he gets. In the muddle that is *Johnson Over Jordan*, however, such ideas never come to light, much less strike sparks." [295]

Sadly, despite the casting of Patrick Stewart, the production achieved an average attendance of fifty per-cent, much less than the other two Priestley plays, performed in the Courtyard Theatre.

The new Artistic Director, Ian Brown, also managed to attract a 'star name' in his first season. *Pretending to Be Me* was devised and performed by Tom Courtney ('Sir' Tom Courtney since the previous year, in recognition of his forty years on stage and screen). Tom was born in Hull eighteen years before Philip Larkin's arrival in the city. The play was a compilation of Larkin's letters, poetry, and prose, and set in 1974 on a single day as he moves home and reflects upon his earlier life.

Tom chose to perform the play at the West Yorkshire Playhouse because he wanted to work with Ian Brown again. Ian had directed Tom's other solo performance in *Moscow Stations*, an adaptation of the novel by Venedikt Yerofeyev, at the Traverse Theatre in Edinburgh in 1994. The reviews of *Pretending to Be Me* were good, firstly in respect of Ian's production: "Ian Brown's deft direction gives the play an understated, fluid rhythm".[296] They also praised Tom's performance – often more than the play itself. One reviewer compared this with that in *Moscow Stations*, "one of the finest things I've ever seen", concluding that "[*Moscow Stations*] allowed Courtenay to display his special strengths: emotional candour, profound vulnerability, an unsentimental ability to

admit to human weakness and acknowledge pain. And those qualities, less intensely and more wryly expressed, now give unity to a somewhat structureless piece". [297] Another reviewer wrote, "A performance to treasure; indeed a tour de force which should be forced to tour".[298]

It didn't tour, but the success of *Pretending to Be Me* led to an immediate West End transfer: an eight-week season at the Comedy (now Harold Pinter) Theatre. As the new Artistic Director, Ian Brown had immediately made his mark. Was this to be the forerunner of many future successful productions with Ian at the helm?

ACT TWO, SCENE TWELVE

A company of actors performing a number of plays in repertory can be a special experience for both actors and audiences. For the actors, they will likely develop as an ensemble, as they grow and trust each other. Audiences get to see the actors' ability to take on a range of parts. This, in turn, can only be good for the relationship between actors and audiences.

THE SEAGULL by Anton Chekhov
29ᵗʰ October 1998

ANOTHER EVENT OF NATIONAL SIGNIFICANCE occurred in 1998 when Ian McKellen and Claire Higgins arrived to work at the Playhouse as part of a company of eleven actors, the Courtyard Company. For six months they were to present a season of three plays: Chekov's *The Seagull*; *Present Laughter,* by Noel Coward; and Shakespeare's *The Tempest*. The idea of the company had come about through conversations between Ian and his friend Michael Cashman when Ian had visited the Playhouse to see Michael in the productions of *The Merchant of Venice* and *Gypsy*.

Ian's first visit to Leeds had been thirty years earlier when he played Richard II and Edward II (by Christopher Marlowe) for the Prospect Theatre Company on tour at the Grand Theatre. Both he and Claire had worked extensively for the National Theatre, and were also both at the Grand in 1990, the year the West Yorkshire Playhouse opened, with the National's tour of *Richard III*. For Claire, coming to Leeds was coming home: she was born in Bradford and grew up in Leeds.

Ian was attracted by the idea of working in a smaller theatre space, and saw being in a company as an opportunity to relive his roots in repertory theatre: "I simply wanted to go back and have the experience of being at the service of one community that I am able to get to know and live amongst for a time …"[299]

Somewhat provocatively and maybe to court publicity, prior to the first play opening, Ian gave an interview to The Independent newspaper, and was reported as saying that he was disillusioned with London theatre audiences and might never work there again. The story was picked up by other newspapers and became a criticism of London audiences as being all-white, middle class – or semi-comprehending tourists! The Guardian, too, referred to Ian's distaste for white middle-class [London] audiences [300] and he was also reported as saying that he might stop working in impersonal, larger theatre spaces

such as in his last post (the Royal National Theatre in London). In this respect, the Courtyard Theatre was perfect for him.

Unsurprisingly, when the London critics arrived in Leeds to review the first of the plays, *The Seagull*, they were quick to point out that the audience "gave every sign of being solidly and predictably bourgeois"[301] and that "there were only a handful of non-white faces in the West Yorkshire Playhouse; at least a third of these were on the stage, playing servants".[302] Georgina Brown, in The Mail on Sunday, somewhat cynically asked if the 'real' audience in Leeds was "the chap who clattered out of *The Seagull* at the interval, muttering, rather as the Russian audience had done at the play's premiere, about its pointlessness and pretentiousness".[303]

Nevertheless, the reviews were very positive about the production, with several critics welcoming the traverse layout of the auditorium with the audience seated on two sides and close to the action; also the performance of Ian McKellen earned particular praise. Notable was how he had made so much of the relatively small part of Doctor Dorn:

"McKellen gives simply his best performance in several years. What a wily old fox this actor is: his eye in a split second can show the audience his understanding of a whole relationship, his timing can create a haunting change of mood with a mere pause or change of tempo."[304]

Other cast members were equally praised, especially by John Peter of the Sunday Times, for whom it was his theatre event of the year:

"Claire Higgins was a magnificently ghastly, preening Arkadina, and Timothy Walker's Trigorin matched her subtly with his overweening self-absorption. Three young actors – Claudie Blakley (Nina), Will Keen (Constantin) and Clare Swinburne (Masha) – gave performances of unforgettable intensity."[305]

London critics admitted being envious of what the Playhouse had already achieved - "Lucky Old Leeds" - and wished the production could be seen further afield. They also looked forward to the next two plays from the Courtyard Company, acknowledging the potential of a repertory season.

Next up was *Present Laughter* which played over the Christmas season, directed by Malcolm Sutherland who had worked at the Playhouse the previous year, adapting and directing the stage version of Ian Banks's novel, *The Wasp Factory* (with Martin Freeman in the cast). Now an associate director at the Playhouse, his production of *Present Laughter* gained many positive reviews. Perhaps inevitably, again these concentrated on Ian McKellen's performance. Critics who were used to seeing him in more serious roles acknowledged his ability in comedy as well: "McKellen demonstrates – sometimes breathtakingly – just how consummate his acting technique is. He knows more of the science of acting than almost any other; here he makes comedy out of that science".[306]

One critic thought that one or two other actors were miscast, but acknowledged that this can be a problem with a small company. Others valued seeing the same actors in very different parts to those they had played in *The Seagull*.

As with *The Seagull*, Jude Kelly herself directed *The Tempest*, her fourth Shakespeare production at the Playhouse. Critics came with high hopes, having enjoyed the other Courtyard Company productions, and appreciating what an ensemble company can achieve. But there was considerable disappointment. They disliked the way an enchanted island had become a bleak prison and were unimpressed by a Prospero dressed in grubby, worn-out clothes. They found his polythene cloak and all the other plastic sheeting filling the stage somewhat bizarre. Several critics cited the way Prospero calls up the storm by dropping a toy boat into a tin bath as inappropriate gimmickry. They accepted that there were plenty of good ideas in the production but felt that they often went nowhere. Whether intentional gender-blind casting, or once again the drawback of a small acting company, critics found the male parts played by women somewhat ridiculous.

Whatever the critics' reservations, the Courtyard Company experiment was obviously a great success, with John Peter concluding "it is the great glory of British theatre that a regional house can do work of such commanding excellence".[307]

Even after two productions, the Yorkshire Post's critic recognised that the actors were "showing energy and versatility that makes you wonder why we've waited this long for rep".[308] After reviewing all three productions, one critic commented on how seeing actors in a range of work allows you to notice connections and contrasts between both the characters and the plays. For another critic, the company demonstrated the value of a group of people working together as a cohesive creative team:

"Only when you see the same actors in different roles can you really understand what acting is all about, how the actor combines his personality with the demands of different roles. Such work is both self-effacing and heroic."[309]

A few critics did suggest that the 'curse of companies' meant some actors being miscast. On the other hand John Peter, in reviewing *Present Laughter*, commented on two particular actors, Clare Swinburne and Claudie Blakley, and their contrasting parts in the first two plays:

"Watching these two young actresses soon after seeing their wonderful performances as Masha and Nina in *The Seagull* is to realise the wealth of young talent in the British theatre ready to be challenged and stretched by imaginative and caring directors."[310]

Clare went on to win the 1998 Ian Charleson Award for her performance as Nina in *The Seagull*, an award for the best classical stage performances in Britain by actors under thirty years of age.

Whatever the critics' reservations about *The Tempest*, the Courtyard Company experiment was obviously a great success. The Guardian's Michael Billington hoped that it might cause a return to the concept of permanent acting companies. Actor Simon Callow, writing in Country Life, opined:

"This, surely, is the way theatre must go: the concentration of talent in the capital is scandalous and wasteful, and some sort of central organisation must be created to make it possible for regional theatres to be able to sustain this sort of artistic enterprise at this level of talent and glamour."[311]

Arguably this central organisation already existed – the Arts Council – with the financial power to sustain regional theatres.

So – are the people who go to the theatre in Leeds the same as in any other part of the country? By the end of his season of working in Leeds, Ian McKellen had decided that this was, after all, the reality. However, others might argue that the audiences who have elected to go to productions of *The Seagull*, *Present Laughter* and *The Tempest* are the same as in any other part of the country.

ACT TWO, SCENE THIRTEEN

Productions of Shakespeare plays regularly feature in the programming at regional theatres. Should such productions be traditional ones, concentrating on the text and the actors above everything else? Does transposing the play to a modern setting add meaning and relevance to it? Is there a place for productions where the director imposes his/her, often radical, interpretation of the play?

HAMLET by William Shakespeare
25th October 2002

IN HIS AUTOBIOGRAPHY, Bernard Atha remembers Jude Kelly's decision to depart from the West Yorkshire Playhouse in 2002. In replacing her, he was aware that she "would leave a great hole in the way the Playhouse operated. Her imagination, persuasive powers, complete self-confidence, extraordinary energy and ability to see opportunities and grab them were unlikely to be found in whoever we appointed".[312] As chair of the Board of Governors (since 1981) Bernard set up an appointments committee and was determined to find "someone who had the same artistic and cultural vision as the founders of the Playhouse".[313]

Some of those shortlisted for interview were already known to the Playhouse, one being Ian Brown, who was already Associate Artistic Director. Ian was selected as the new Artistic Director and Chief Executive because, in Bernard's recollection of the committee's decision, "I think we all felt that after the excitement and artistic success of Jude Kelly we needed to ensure that the theatre was in safe hands and the artistic standard maintained".[314]

Ian's first work at the Playhouse, back in 1998, had actually been something of a baptism of fire. Previously, at the Citizen's Theatre in Glasgow, he had directed the original stage version of Irvine Welsh's novel *Trainspotting*. This explains how he came to direct the world premiere of Irvine Welsh's *You'll Have Had Your Hole* at the Playhouse. The play is set in a recording studio; the action includes the torture and homosexual rape of a man who is gagged and suspended from the ceiling for much of the play. Press night attracted not only the London critics but several from Scottish newspapers. Their reviews focused much more on the play than Ian's production, and were probably the Playhouse's worst-ever criticisms: "I believe, the most obnoxious and contemptible play I have ever sat through"[315];

"the saddest, sickest, most vile play I have ever sat through"[316]; "an hour and forty minutes of undiluted banality"[317]. But The Observer, at least, found Ian's production "gruesomely effective". [318]

Ian Brown took over from Jude Kelly in the summer of 2002, but prior to that, as Associate Artistic Director, he had directed *The Comedy of Errors,* for which he updated the play to a 1950s Mediterranean setting and used a cast of thirteen young actors – intended as a way of creating a boisterous, fast-moving production with youth appeal: "*The Comedy of Errors* is a good starter play for a young audience, it's a fun Shakespeare. If you are going to take a young person to their first Shakespeare, that wouldn't be a bad one to start".[319]

Although *The Comedy of Errors* had only attracted lukewarm reviews and attendances, Ian nevertheless chose another Shakespeare play, *Hamlet,* for his first production as Artistic Director. One difference was that the cast included two familiar faces from television: Christopher Eccleston and Maxine Peake, both making their Shakespeare stage debuts.

A different kind of decision-maker was now at the helm. To revisit Jude Kelly's approach: she had waited for three years before programming and directing a Shakespeare play, and she was to establish her own 'ways' with Shakespeare. Critics had felt that her production of *The Taming of the Shrew* was well worth the wait, with Kevin Berry, in The Stage, commenting, "Seldom can an audience have laughed so much and for so long when watching a Shakespeare play. This interpretation of *The Taming of the Shrew* is supremely, gloriously funny … without doubt a theatrical gem".[320]

Most other critics praised the production's humour and energy. For a time, at least, they welcomed what was to become typical of Jude's Shakespeare productions – invention and gimmickry:

"When the programme notes remark that Shakespeare "needn't" be played in ruffs, doublets and hose, you can bet that what you are about to receive is not the bog standard Bard.

And so it is with the interpretation that Jude Kelly has dreamed up. Dreamed is an apt word, for the surreal scenes witnessed here would enhance any of the audiences' pillow borne imaginings. Why not, when the stage is strutted by a 20s aviator, a Boar cavalryman, a capped and gown scholar, and – since this play opens on a passenger ship and not in a hunter's forest glade – by mariners in sou'westers and oilskins. But nonetheless engaging for that? There ensues a circus of scampering activity and a carnival of boisterous banter which last night was followed closely by a rapt audience noticeably on the edge of their seats".[321]

Jude undoubtedly welcomed the conclusion of the Daily Telegraph critic who "cannot recommend this *Shrew* highly enough: the production proves the West Yorkshire Playhouse to be the National Theatre of the North".[322]

A year later Jude would direct *The Merchant of Venice* with Nichola McAuliffe once again in a lead role. As with *The Taming of the Shrew*, the production was welcomed for being a fresh interpretation, this time of a difficult play. John Peter in the Sunday Times concluded that "with this performance Kelly has placed herself in the front rank of Shakespearean directors".[323]

However, Jude's subsequent productions would often be criticised as 'gimmicky'. This was the case both with the Courtyard Company's *The Tempest* and her 1995 production of *King Lear*. The 'scoop' for the latter was Warren Mitchell; the cast also included Playhouse regular Michael Cashman, and Toby Jones as the Fool. Jude had wanted Tom Courtenay to play Lear, but Warren himself – who had played the part in Australia seventeen years earlier – approached Jude – and she apparently cast him on the spot.

Warren Mitchell was, of course, best known for his part as Alf Garnett in *Till Death Us Do Part*, which he had been playing since 1965. Interviewed in Leeds by the Yorkshire Post, his interviewer tells of how, as Warren crossed St. Peter's Street to get to the theatre for rehearsals, some road-workers would shout "'ello Alf", but that he didn't mind: "He misses Alf after

playing him on and off for 24 years. And they're hardly likely to shout 'ello King Lear' now, are they?".[324]

Warren had already had success in major demanding theatre roles. In 1979 he won an Olivier Award for his performance as Willie Loman in *Death of a Salesman* which previewed at the Grand Theatre in Leeds before opening at the National. A year later he had played Davies in Pinter's *The Caretaker*.

Reviews for *King Lear* were mixed, several critics feeling that the production was too 'busy' so that it lost direction, and was indeed at times "gimmicky". It was felt, for example, that the mix of medieval and modern costumes and the choice of music and props added little. Benedict Nightingale, in The Times, reported that "the Fool, a roly-poly alternative comic with a model weather vain for a coxcomb, is seen hanging himself. A bread knife substitutes for Edmund's sword, cans of lager for period tipple. I was just about willing to buy a King of France who fired a water pistol at his rival, Burgundy, but not one who ended the play by appearing, flagged by frogmen and motorbike couriers, to annexe England".[325]

Critics were also divided on Warren Mitchell's performance. Michael Coveney concluded that "this performance is one of outstanding character, warmth, pathos and sensitivity from an actor scaling Everest after memorably negotiating the twin peaks of Pinter and Arthur Miller",[326] while Charles Spencer, using the same metaphors, thought differently: "Actors often talk, rather pretentiously, about great roles being like mountains that they have to climb. On this occasion, Mitchell... seems content to potter about in the foothills".[327]

Most reviews mentioned that Warren stripped naked in the storm scene, and also the heaviness of the rain during this scene, and some questioned the necessity of all this: "At the height of his dementia he does a full-frontal strip that director Jude Kelly presumably thought essential, though others may beg to differ",[328] and, "might it not be a tad insensitive to put a practical rainstorm on stage while Yorkshire Water has a drought order in force?".[329]

Yorkshire Water might have been equally unhappy with Jude's last Shakespearian production, in 1999. This was *Macbeth* in the Courtyard, which attracted a lot of preview publicity for Mario Borza, employed as a 'waterist'; having previously worked on *Singin' in the Rain*. Consequently, as Jeremy Kingston commented, there was "water, water everywhere. Dead bodies are wrapped and sunk in pools. Water cascades from gantries. From the underside of the table, Lady Macbeth crawls under to wash her hands".[330]

The production was set in 1970s eastern Europe. The weird sisters were portrayed as mothers wearing pictures of their missing children. Overall, Jeremy Kingston concluded, "So what with the water, some unexciting performances elsewhere and the interludes of news commentary in Slavonic tongue, this is a *Macbeth* where the hurly-burly's never done and the play is lost not won."[331] Other reviews made similar points, reflected in headlines such as "Bogged down in the rain" and "Superb actors triumph over director's foibles". One review lamented that, having approached his favourite Shakespeare tragedy with trepidation, "After suffering for years from the megalomaniac whims of directors who seem to lose sight of the power of the words and use the staging of Shakespeare's plays to experiment with increasingly bizarre settings, my worst nightmare seems to be coming true again".[332] In what must surely have been a first, Jude Kelly's *Macbeth* was reviewed in 'Plant and Control Engineering' and three other heating, ventilating, and plumbing magazines!

Ian Brown was thus to represent a sea-change in the style of the Playhouse's Shakespeare direction:

"For me, bringing the text of a play to life is more important than putting my stamp or concept onto a play".[333]

Given Jude's productions, it was hardly surprising that the critics in 2002 welcomed Ian's *Hamlet* in which he pared things right down. The Metro liked that "in sharp contrast to his predecessor Jude Kelly's rainbow-hued, multimedia extravaganzas, new artistic director Ian Brown's first major production is a stripped down affair".[334] He and most reviewers appreciated the vast bare stage, a fortress of dark wood, the absence of furniture, and minimal props – and not a drop of water in sight! The Guardian critic liked that in this production, "The play is indeed the thing"[335], while the Mail on Sunday critic liked that "Brown's account is admirably clear and staged with impressive economy".[336]

The critics seemed happy with something of a 1920s East Europe setting. The only unusual aspect of the production, the play-within-a-play scene being a silent movie, was also well liked. And one critic commented on another significant directorial decision:

"A few months ago, I complained .... that the West Yorkshire Playhouse, like other theatres in the North, tends to use local accents only for comic parts in Shakespeare. So it was good to find both Hamlet and Ophelia played with Northern accents."[337]

Ian wanted his *Hamlet* to attract a younger audience, hence his invitation of Christopher Eccleston (to whom he had given his first break with the TAG Theatre Company) to play the lead: "Chris will attract an audience that wouldn't usually come to see *Hamlet* and he is an actor of now. And it's good to see an actor that is 'now'".[338] Asked whether 'film stars' were the future of the West Yorkshire Playhouse, Ian replied, "well, yes and no, there's no point in putting on plays that no-one wants to see. There's no question that audiences love to see people that they recognise and admire".[339]

Almost all the reviews confirmed that this was good casting: "His performance is bewitching", "most accomplished", "a compellingly successful portrayal", "a truly bravura performance", "a thrilling, nervy stage presence". Ian must have been particularly happy with The Daily Telegraph's Charles Spencer's comment:

"During the second half of Ian Brown's fine new production of *Hamlet*, I briefly stopped watching the stage and took a look at the audience instead. The place was packed, and everyone, from teenagers to oldies, seemed entirely caught up in the events onstage. There was that atmosphere of rapt concentration that is the hallmark of all the best productions of Shakespearean tragedy."[340]

Ian Brown was to direct four further Shakespeare plays during his decade as Artistic Director. The next was *Twelfth Night* in 2005. He reset the play in the 1930s French Riviera, again intending it to be 'family friendly'. As with *Hamlet* he wanted a production which, without gimmicks, concentrated on and promoted clarity of the text itself. His approach was similar when directing *As You Like It* (2010): the set was simple with few props. Commenting on the designer and the composer, The Guardian critic admired that "though Ruari Murchison's design has trees everywhere, the view is unobstructed by anachronistic gimmicks, save for a beguiling suite of songs by Simon Slater … Delightful as it is, the music is for the most part where it should be: in the verse".[341] Another critic commented on how the lighting designer had contributed to creating a magical space.

The pre-publicity for *As You Like It* concentrated, nevertheless, on the set, which consisted of seventeen twenty-five-feet-high real trees supposedly 'sustainably sourced' from a forest in Wales. Once again the potential of the Quarry Theatre was demonstrated: "a huge production featuring an epic set – quite the most awesome ever seen in the Quarry Theatre… spectacular".[342] This time Ian kept the play in an Elizabethan setting, again allowing the audience to focus on the narrative's strength. Rosalind was very successfully played by Vanessa Kirby who had just achieved whirlwind success, aged twenty-one and just out of University, playing three leading roles at the Octagon Theatre in Bolton.

After *Hamlet*, the next Shakespearean tragedy directed by Ian Brown was *Macbeth* (2007), another deliberately stripped-back production focused on doing justice to the text. The set consisted of a stone wall at the back of the stage, and a metal spiral staircase. Lighting was used to show the location changes. Such a bare stage serves to heavily focus on the actors, and unfortunately, as a consequence, some critics felt that the casting was disappointing.

By comparison Ian's production of *King Lear* in his last season at the Playhouse was welcomed most of all for the casting: a strong ensemble, not just a vehicle for the 'star' actor. Nevertheless, Tim Pigott-Smith was unreservedly praised for his performance as Lear, the Daily Telegraph headline being typical: "Pigott-Smith scales the heights in a momentous performance".[343] More used to being in Stratford and London, Tim clearly enjoyed the experience of working at the Playhouse: "What you find up here is that the people who work for the theatre are absolutely dedicated to their jobs, and I think that they probably feel they are lucky to have their jobs. But conversely, the theatre is lucky to have them. There is a fantastic sense of teamwork here".[344]

Tim had waited for many years to play Lear, and having 'scaled the heights' some wondered where his career could go from here. Ironically, he went on to play another king, the future one, in Mike Bartlett's *King Charles III*, both in London and on Broadway. Sadly, Tim died suddenly in 2017.

Especially during Jude Kelly's time as Artistic Director, there were co-productions of other Shakespeare plays. There had in fact been another *Hamlet* just five years before Ian Brown's production, originating from London's Greenwich Theatre. Plus there had been one exceptional production when the direction was by Steven Berkoff, who also starred in it. This was the 1995 *Coriolanus*, which arguably could have opened at the National Theatre where Steven had previously performed and directed.

Steven had directed (though not acted in) a similar production in New York in 1988, but the Playhouse was its British premiere. He was initially reluctant to allow the critics in until two weeks into the run; understandably, given that some of the comments about his performance were to be unkind:

"Berkoff deploys his characteristic vocal arsenal as Coriolanus – the booms, the one-syllable bellows, the bass nasal

sawing, and the. Very. Slow. Delivery. The acoustics of the Quarry Theatre are not well suited to these vocal extremities (which he also encourages in his cast), and many lines rebound loudly but indecipherably off the back wall. His verbal violence may be over-compensation for its physical counterpart. Whisper it softly, but the lad's beginning to knock on a bit for this lark."[345]

"Nothing in Berkoff's version, alas, is more predictable than his own performance as a ranting little bully in gangster suit and boots. Never, even in the most elaborately mimed combat, does he look like a warlord. Vocally he repeatedly starts at the top, leaving himself no chance to build."[346]

The reviews led one cast member to write a complaint to The Guardian about their perceived unkind, unthinking and hurtful comments. Worse still, Berkoff wrote to The Sunday Times critic, stating that "since you are truly a theatrical thug, a right wing uneducated slob, you will be prohibited entrance to any of my shows again".[347]

Ian Brown's subsequent *King Lear* – the swan-song of his direction of Shakespeare at the West Yorkshire Playhouse – was by comparison a run-away success. Knowing that this was Ian's last season, some critics evidently took the opportunity to praise the production as his "crowning glory":

"This production must also represent a ... high directorial point for Ian Brown. It is, without question, one of his finest hours, and as he prepares to step down ... this represents a spectacular exit."[348]

ACT TWO, SCENE FOURTEEN

"BBC Northern Exposure is a 'BBC writersroom' focus on northern talent through a unique partnership programme, working with five theatres and fourteen other cultural partners across the North, from Merseyside to Tyneside. Our aims are to find and develop new writers for the BBC and to increase BBC production activity in the North."[349]

SUNBEAM TERRACE by Mark Catley 27th March 2003

AS WELL AS TOM COURTNEY'S *PRETENDING TO BE ME*, there were three more new plays in Ian Brown's first season at the Playhouse. One was a co-production of *The Hanging Man*, which was very much an Improbable Theatre production. The other two were *Sunbeam Terrace* and *Off Camera*, which were both in keeping with the season's Northern theme.

Sunbeam Terrace is the name of a street in the Beeston area of Leeds, just a mile or so from the theatre, where the playwright Mark Catley was born. His play was performed in the Courtyard, for which the space was reconfigured as theatre-in-the-round. The play is set in the bedsit of Drug Dealer (no proper names used) who is agoraphobic and on the edge of a nervous breakdown. He is visited by Hard Man who wants to clean up the neighbourhood, then by Lap Dancer and Teenage Boy looking for drugs. Their lives are revealed, watched over by Old Man, something of a ghostly guardian angel to certain characters.

Mark Catley's first theatre experience was acting with South Leeds Youth Theatre. He went on to study Performing Arts at Park Lane College. It was whilst studying for a degree in Drama and Theatre Arts at London's Goldsmith's College that he decided to concentrate on writing plays. He achieved all this despite seeing Beeston as a place where nobody went to the theatre, recalling that "I used to be scared of going to the Playhouse. I thought it was full of posh people".[350]

All of the cast of *Sunbeam Terrace* were from Leeds or Bradford. Hard Man was played by Mick Martin, and Young Boy by Dorian Smith who was chosen from thirty young men who attended auditions by way of two workshop sessions.

Sunbeam Terrace was partly a consequence of BBC Northern Exposure, a new writing initiative – part of the 'BBC writersroom' – set up to discover, develop and champion new and experienced writing talent UK-wide.

The play was directed by Alex Chisholm, who with this BBC funding had been appointed as the Playhouse's Literary and Events Manager, a post that had until then been left vacant for six years.

Thus Northern Exposure was born. As a consequence of Alex's appointment, the Playhouse was able to establish this annual festival of new writing, beginning in the summer of 2004. Continuing beyond the two years of BBC funding, thirteen new plays were produced in the Courtyard, the last season being in 2009.

As well as performances of another Mark Catley play, *Crap Dad* (which had previously toured with the Schools Company), the first season included two plays, playing in repertory with the same actors. One was *Coming Around Again*, set in a row of back-to-back houses in the Armley area of Leeds, also the home of the playwright Andrew G. Marshall. It simultaneously tells the story of three generations of the same family. The other play was *Huddersfield*, a surprising title given that the play is set in Serbia, written after its writer, Ugljesa Sajtinac, returned home to Serbia following a rehearsed reading of another of his plays at a drama festival in Huddersfield. Mirroring this, the play is about a group of young people, former schoolmates, who get together to celebrate one of their group returning from Huddersfield after ten years away. The play shows how their lives reflect the politics of their country at that time.

Reviewing the plays in this first Northern Exposure season, the Yorkshire Post praised the Playhouse for how this work demonstrated "what the new writing festival is all about – it provides the opportunity to see two very different plays and give an audience the chance to prospect for gold".[351]

Besides the plays in the Courtyard, other related new writing events formed part of the Northern Exposure festivals. These included work-in-progress performances, *Bus* being a good example. Produced in the Courtyard in 2006, it started as a twenty-minute piece performed at the previous year's festival. The writer Mark Kirby was from Leeds, and the play considers the contrasting residents of his city, asking who the city belongs to: those in trendy city centre apartments, or those living in the red-brick back-to-back houses? Having his play produced in the Courtyard was clearly a special moment for Mark:

"The thought of having a play on at the West Yorkshire Playhouse is pretty terrifying. I remember going to see the odd play there with school, always thinking about how massive and untouchable it was".[352]

His success was also partly because of his involvement in two other aspects of Alex Chisholm's work and Northern Exposure. One was the appointment of new writers-on-attachment to the Playhouse, which Mark had been offered in 2004. The other was his attendance at the annual six-week 'So You Want to be a Writer?' course, run by *Sunbeam Terrace* and *Crap Dad* playwright Mark Catley. Most of the other playwrights in the Northern Exposure festival seasons had also attended one of Mark's courses. Some had also been appointed as writers-on-attachment. One was Jodie Marshall whose first play, *Non-Contact Time*, was produced in 2005. This play also came about because of another of Alex's projects: the 'Lock-In'. Those invited to take part spent thirty-six hours over a weekend at the Playhouse with the expectation that by the end they would have written at least forty minutes of a new script. Afterwards Playhouse staff would help with re-writing prior to a semi-staged reading.

It worked for Jodie: "I sat there with a blank piece of paper on the Saturday morning, but by the end of Sunday the first draft of *Non-Contact Time* was written".[353] Her second play, *Tender Dearly*, was included in the 2007 festival season. Set in a shabby pub in Leeds, it observes five customers and staff, all borderline alcoholics. Ironically, although given a full-scale production and a stand-alone two week run, *Tender Dearly* was not so well-received as *Non-Contact Time*: "Marshall has abandoned the style that made her first play such a success. It is not a surprise that she wants to flex her muscles as a writer. She has much talent, but it is a shame she couldn't bring more of the modesty, realism and humour that made her first play such a hit".[354]

But allowing writers to flex their muscles is exactly what Northern Exposure was all about. *Safe*, included in the 2007 festival, was not the first play by David Hermanstein – that was *A Caribbean Abroad*, produced at the Library Theatre in Manchester in 2002. David had been given support from Eclipse Theatre, a consortium of regional theatres which included the West Yorkshire Playhouse, set up to promote high quality work from a Black British perspective. *Safe*, his second play, concerned the death of a young man involved in gang warfare and gun crime. The play focuses on the consequences for those left behind: his family and his girlfriend, now a single mum. *Safe*, like the other Northern Exposure plays, attracted national as well as local reviews. The Guardian's Alfred Hickling felt that the play betrayed David's inexperience as a stage writer (he had previously studied screenwriting) but recognised that "it will undoubtedly prove to be an invaluable learning experience".[355] Again, exactly what Northern Exposure was all about.

Both of the plays included in the final Northern Exposure season (2009) were by new writers who had attended the 2007 'So You Want to be a Writer?' course. *It's a Lovely Day Tomorrow* was written by Dom Grace and Boff Whalley who first met on the course. At that time Boff was better known as the guitarist with Chumbawamba. *Me, As a Penguin* was written by Tom Wells from Kilnsea in East Yorkshire. It was his first play, and as with *It's a Lovely Day Tomorrow* was developed through a series of masterclasses with the Playhouse's associate artist Colin Teevan. A new production of *Me, As a Penguin* toured in 2010, including to the Arcola Theatre in London. His subsequent plays have been produced at the Bush and Hampstead Theatres and by Hull Truck Theatre, and have toured nationally; *Jumpers for Goalposts* came to the Playhouse in 2013.

As well as Mark Catley, two more of the writers included in the Northern Exposure festivals went on to further work at the Playhouse. First was Tajinder Singh Hayer from Bradford. His first contact with the Playhouse was through the Black and Asian Writers Group. Prior to this he had studied Creative Writing at Bretton Hall College. His first play, *Before the Fight*, had been performed as a Summer Short in the 2003 Northern Exposure festival. Both this and his 2005 festival play, *Players*, were directed by Mark Catley. *Players* uses Asian culture as a starting point but is much more about male friendships. The production attracted actors which Tajinder described as an "A-list" cast, including Chris Bisson and Saraj Chaudhry, familiar faces from *Coronation Street*, *East is East*, and *Bend It Like Beckham*.

Of his experience of *Players* being included in the Courtyard's programme, Tajinder observed,"It was a fantastic opportunity to be given a chance by the Playhouse to write … It is really reassuring to have an organisation like that behind you, but it is also quite intimidating to have your stuff performed on such a high profile stage and with such respected actors".[356] The success of *Players* led to another of his plays, *Mela*, being given a full production at the Playhouse in 2008.

The following year's Northern Exposure festival included *Foxes*, by Alice Nutter. She was already well known in Leeds as a long-standing member of the music group Chumbawamba, but this was her first play to be professionally produced. *Foxes* is set in a Leeds tower block, where nineteen-year-old Loretta lives and looks after her younger brother. She begins a relationship with a Zimbabwean refugee in the flat next door. Their story raises the issues of immigration and racism.

As a measure of the importance given to the Northern Exposure work, *Foxes* was directed by Ian Brown. Interviewed about the production, he commented that including plays as part of Northern Exposure, "we're not putting quite so much pressure on one particular play – that it's got to succeed in reaching such and such a target at the Box Office or whatever. What the writer learns from the experience is invaluable. Even though it's being done on a bit of a shoestring, you still go through the whole process of putting something on stage. Alice has come to the auditions, she'll be there in rehearsal, she'll see how actors work, feel the pressure of the opening night, and then witness the response of an audience, and how that changes it. For a new playwright, that's like being blooded".[357]

Praising the play, Rod McPhee in the Yorkshire Evening Post described it as "amazingly well observed and fantastically written, it's hard to believe that this is Alice Nutter's first professional foray into penning plays. Yet, at the same time, the style is so fresh it bears all the hallmarks of someone who has just entered the theatre".[358]

Seven years later, Alice was back at the Playhouse with her play *My Generation*, the only piece of new writing in the 2013-2014 season. Another of her plays, *Barnbow Canaries*, was produced in the Courtyard Theatre in 2016.

The Northern Exposure plays also gave experience of directing to others involved at the Playhouse. As well as Mark Catley's direction of Tajinder Singh Hayer's work, two other plays were directed by Sarah Punshon, who was a resident trainee director at the Playhouse in 2004/2005. Another was directed by Sam Brown, who was a resident assistant director on secondment from the Birkbeck, University of London.

An interesting new departure came in 2006: Northern Exposure playwrights were given the opportunity to work on translations of plays by other writers. Six were paired with writers from European countries and were given literal translations of the plays. They then worked with the writers to produce an English version which reflected the tone and intention of the play in its original language.

Tajinder Singh Hayer worked with Andreas Flourakis from Greece. When he received the literal translation, "the plot was present and understandable, but the style and mood of the piece was hard to gauge – these were like landmarks hidden beneath lexical snowdrifts ... My job would be to reconnect those translated words to their emotional referents".[359] Also seen as a way of discovering and promoting new European playwrights, the project culminated in a week, alongside the Northern Exposure festival plays, which brought together all those involved, for readings, discussions, and performances.

Alex's work as Literary Manager also involved providing a script-reading service. Additionally, she organised a regular monthly open platform, *Thursday Night Live*, where anyone could submit a script for performance by professional actors. All this work reflected Alex's passion for nurturing fledgling talent in the local community: "If we continue to invest in the best regional writers, they can go on to become national writers and that benefits us and them".[360]

Mark Catley is the obvious example in this respect. He had two further plays produced in the Courtyard, but went on to become a successful writer for television: *Casualty, East Enders, Call the Midwife*, and many more series. In 2018 and 2019 he won BAFTA Awards for his scriptwriting.

In 2009 Northern Exposure unfortunately came to an end, thus in the following years there was little new work at the Playhouse: just two new plays produced in the subsequent four years. Of course there was still new work performed through visits by national touring companies throughout this period, including Tara Arts, Shared Experience, Paines Plough, Hull Truck Theatre, Frantic Assembly, Out of Joint, and Rifco. Only occasionally, however, were there new plays by local writers.

The situation substantially improved in September 2013 with the introduction of a new initiative, 'A Play, a Pie and a Pint'. The plays were shorts, performed either in the front-of-house foyer or the Barber Studio. Sometimes they were just script-in-hand readings, and always just for a small number of performances. These usually began at six in the evening., meaning that they would attract people who were also booked to see productions in the Quarry or Courtyard Theatre later that night. For a tenner, audience members got the three things in the scheme's title!

In the 2013-2014 season there were five new plays. Two were particularly successful both in terms of attracting new audiences and having an after-life. One was *Nine Lives*, by Zodwa Nyoni. She was born in Zimbabwe, and grew up in Leeds, attending Roundhay School and completing her further education in the city. She performed her first short play, about loss and migration, *Home Has Died*, in May 2012 as part of the Lift-Off festival at Leeds Metropolitan (now Beckett) University for that year's graduates on the Art, Event and Performance degree. In 2013 Zodwa co-wrote a verbatim play about markets in Leeds, performed as part of the Playhouse Transform 13 season.

Nine Lives is a play about a gay young man, Ishmael, who has fled Nigeria and is in Leeds waiting for a decision on his asylum claim. Zodwa wrote the play after visits to Meeting Point in the Armley area of Leeds, a drop-in facility for refugees and asylum seekers. She wanted to write a human story about the experiences of such people, not just the way in which they are processed. This is reflected when Ishmael says, "This letter says I'm a reference number. I'm an applicant. I'm circumstances. I'm outcomes. But it doesn't say that I'm real. It doesn't say that I exist. That I laugh. That I cry. I dance. I dream. I wonder. I want. I think. I question".[361]

The actor playing Ismael also plays all the people he meets whilst he waits, from a café owner to a teenage mother who befriends him. Reviews praised Lladel Bryant's performance as Ismael. One reviewer also praised the decision to perform *Nine Lives* in the Barber Studio: "In the incredibly intimate performance space, director Alex Chisolm had Ishmael really connect with the audience. His warm, honest and funny character established a bond with them right from the start of the piece, and had the audience laughing and staring in awe at Ishmael's story".[362]

The success of *Nine Lives* led to a national tour in 2015 and further performances the following year. It was performed once more at the Playhouse before the second Covid 19 lockdown in

November 2020, and also at the Bridge Theatre in London as part of their season of socially-distanced monologues.

The other successful play in the first 'A Play, a Pie and a Pint' season was *Playing the Joker* by Anthony Clavane, a sports journalist and Leeds United supporter who in 2009 published *Promised Land: A Northern Love Story* which won the British Sports Book of the Year Award. *Playing the Joker*, set in 1977, is the story of a young sports fan called Eddie who goes to the Queen's Hotel in Leeds city centre to try to meet his hero, the sports commentator Eddie Waring. Anthony describes the play as being about "Eddie Waring, Rugby League, Yorkshireness, revenge, revolution, betrayal and why trilby hats went out of fashion".

Interestingly, Anthony's first involvement with the theatre was at the Leeds Playhouse in 1977 when he worked there as an usher while studying for his A-Levels. He, like Zodwa, was a pupil at Roundhay School. After the Playhouse *Playing the Joker* toured to rugby league clubs in the north of England, and was then revived by Red Ladder Theatre in 2018, touring again for almost six months.

The 2015 'A Play, a Pie and a Pint' season included *Avocado* by the American playwright Eve Ensler, already well-known for her play *The Vagina Monologues*, first produced twenty years earlier. *Avocado* is a one-woman play, the story of a woman who has been subjected to human trafficking. In the play she is stowed away in near-darkness in a container of rotting avocados – hence the title – on a cargo ship. She is seeking to escape from trafficking to a place simply called Asylum; she tells of a life of poverty and sexual abuse. Like *Nine Lives*, *Avocado* returned to the Playhouse the following year, but this time as part of *The Fruit Trilogy*, all plays which dealt with the worldwide commodification of women. The three plays were co-produced with the 'Women of the World' festival (organised by Jude Kelly) at London's South Bank Centre. All the plays were directed by Mark Rosenblatt, Associate Director at the

Playhouse. Two years later, he once again directed *The Fruit Trilogy*, this time in New York.

'A Play, a Pie and a Pint' did not continue after 2015, but as with *The Fruit Trilogy*, further new plays were produced in the Barber Studio. 2016 saw *Blackthorn* by Charley Miles which played for six performances, having been chosen as part of the annual commitment to stage two pieces of new work by local writers. Charley had developed the play with Playhouse support: the Summer Sublets scheme, the playwriting course, and the Furnace festival. Charley is from rural North Yorkshire, where the play is set, and is inspired by her childhood there. One Guardian reader, Evelyn O'Neill chose *Blackthorn* as her play of the year:

"The story was simple; a tale of a boy and girl growing up together, falling in love, becoming almost incompatible adults yet still feeling the pull towards home and each other. The dialogue was pointedly regional, genuine and very witty. It was a rare example of romantic, rural writing and, although the story was a simple tale of young love, it resonated beautifully with anyone who has ever known Yorkshire, a small village, or a childhood sweetheart. A cracking good story and dialogue to make your heart ache."[363]

Blackthorn was chosen as a Finalist for 2016-17 Susan Smith Blackburn Prize for women playwrights. Charley then became a Channel 4 Playwright-in-Residence at the Playhouse. The play was revived and performed at the pop-up theatre in October 2018, following its four-week run at the Edinburgh Festival. Another of her plays, *Daughterhood*, would be performed at the Festival the following year.

Two other productions in the Barber Studio deserve to be highlighted. In 2017, there was *A Girl in School Uniform (Walks Into a Bar)*, which was only possible because the director raised £1,237 in less than a week using the Kickstarter website. After Leeds, the play transferred to the New Diorama Theatre in London followed by other UK dates. Then 2018 saw *What If I Told You?*, a dance and theatre performance, written and performed by Pauline Mayers. Pauline had previously been involved at the Playhouse with the 2013 Transform season and had worked with Red Ladder Theatre. An early version of *What If I Told You?* was included in the 2016 Transform festival. After performances at the Playhouse it was, like *Blackthorn*, produced at the Edinburgh Festival and elsewhere in the UK.

Of all the playwrights whose work was produced in the Barber Studio, Zodwa Nyoni went on to achieve most success: her first full-length play, *Boi Boi is Dead*, was included in the 2014-15 season in the Courtyard. This followed her year as a writer-in-residence at the Playhouse.

Boi Boi is Dead is a family story set in Zimbabwe. Boi Boi is a famous jazz trumpeter; the family members come together for his funeral. Conflicts arise between his long-term partner, his ex-wife and his brother. Boi Boi is present throughout, a ghostly figure observing the conflicts – and adding trumpet music to the play. Reviews were very positive about both the play and the direction, The Observer's Clare Brennan concluding, "The device of revealing a life as refracted through the memories of mourners, whose characters are simultaneously revealed through their interactions, can be a cliché [but] Zodwa Nyoni exploits it with sprightly ease and emotional depth ... she grippingly connects a particular situation to the universals of shared experiences through a wonderfully rich, humorous and densely poetic use of language".[364]Audience reaction was also positive, one reviewer describing the moment when Boi Boi's daughter sings as a coup de théâtre:

"When she sings... she brings the house down. It is wonderful. And so strong is the actual and symbolic impact of her performance that the packed house was stunned into silence. An audience pregnant with an emotional reaction, just one seeding clap would have brought the house down. Such confidence from [the director] Msamati, he allows a prolonged silence. And we sat in a great big, sticky tension that can only be achieved in live performance."[365]

Boi Boi is Dead won Zodwa the Channel 4 Playwrights Scheme, and like Charley Miles's play *Blackthorn*, *Boi Boi is Dead* was a finalist for the Susan Smith Blackburn prize.

A very different play by Zodwa was produced in the Courtyard in 2017. As well as being a playwright she also writes and performs poetry, as in her *Ode to Leeds*, the story of five young poets from Leeds who are chosen to compete in an international poetry slam competition in New York. Their life-stories are interwoven with their poems. The production, which was directed by James Brining, benefited from having the rapper and playwright Testament as consultant for the music and words.

Ode to Leeds was the last piece of local new writing before the theatre's temporary closure. The Yorkshire Post's reviewer had one reservation about the play being staged in the Courtyard, and looked forward to the future of the Playhouse:

"In truth, *Ode to Leeds* is a piece which may have worked better in the more intimate surroundings of a studio theatre, and struggles occasionally to fill the space of the Courtyard. Sadly, the Playhouse doesn't have a studio, but next year's redevelopment will right the wrong and audiences can hopefully look forward to a glut of new writing from new voices".[366]

The building scheme was about to begin, and the redevelopment of the Playhouse to include a new studio space was clearly being anticipated with optimism, as a stimulus for new creative voices.

ACT TWO, SCENE FIFTEEN

Peter Cheeseman, who pioneered theatre-in-the-round, is often quoted as saying that all theatres should be designed to self-destruct after seven years. This might be impossible, but it is certainly the case that their permanency hinders theatres reinventing their spaces in order to succeed and survive. The size of the stage and the rest of the auditorium also limits, in different ways, the range of productions that will work in the space.

PLAYHOUSE CREATURES by April De Angelis
4th April 2003

IAN BROWN'S FINAL PRODUCTION in his first season as Artistic Director was Alan Ayckbourn's *A Small Family Business*. It was a Yorkshire homecoming: unusually, this Ayckbourn play had not premiered in Scarborough but at the National Theatre in London in 1987. Alan was working there at this time with his own company, and a production of *A Small Family Business* needed the larger stage of the Olivier Theatre, so was also much more suited to the Playhouse than Scarborough's theatre-in-the-round. The set required was a two-storey house. Designed by Jonathan Fensom, he took on the challenge of the Quarry Theatre's stage:

"Normally if you have a house on stage you have it set back, but because the Quarry Theatre's a thrust stage, you would have a huge empty space and the front rows wouldn't see anything."[367]

The play requires the set to have six prominently-shown rooms, as well as glimpses of others through doors and serving hatches. Jonathan's set captured a specific 1980s style. Critics praised his design as much as the play: "You'd say that designer Jonathan Fensom had done a beautiful job if the domestic interiors weren't so meticulously hideous. I don't often rave about Ayckbourn, but this is the business".[368]

However, Ian's first season at the West Yorkshire Playhouse also included a new version of *Playhouse Creatures* by April De Angelis, which played for four weeks in the Quarry Theatre. It was directed by John Tiffany who had previously worked with Ian at the Traverse Theatre in Edinburgh. John was happy that the play was to be staged in the Quarry: in advance of the opening night, he said, "It deserves the Quarry. It's a new play, it's unknown and there's a lot to connect with the audience. There's nothing nicer than when you've got a big audience laughing together in the Quarry and *Creatures* is robust and funny".[369]

With a cast of just six actors, *Playhouse Creatures* is about women, including Nell Gwyn, who were, in the seventeenth century, the first to be allowed to act in theatres. Critics were mostly positive about the play and the acting, but several questioned the decision to stage the production in the Quarry: "[it] makes stylish use of a revolving stage, pin-prick-sharp lighting and echoey surround-sound design. What it palpably lacks, however, is atmosphere".[370] Kevin Berry, in The Stage, concluded, "The overall impression, though, is that this play has been stretched to fit the Playhouse's vast Quarry Theatre. It is an intimate piece requiring a confined, almost claustrophobic acting space". [371]

At the following year's Annual General Meeting, Bernard Atha summed up that despite excellent ensemble performances, the production had "appeared lost in the vastness of the space, contributing to a diminished atmosphere which was reflected at the Box Office".[372] *Playhouse Creatures* had indeed drawn a mere 15 percent average attendance. This compares very unfavourably with other attendances earlier in the season: *Hamlet* saw a 90 percent figure, and the touring production *To Kill a Mockingbird* achieved a 97 percent average. In respect of the latter, however, it is important to note that the production played over just five days – and such a play has 'school party' appeal.

Ian soon recognised that the Quarry Theatre was a much harder space to programme, by comparison with the Courtyard Theatre. Years later he reflected that "the Quarry works brilliantly for some things, no question. It's a very good theatre for many shows, but they've got to be shows, they've got to have a theatrical size to them". [373]

Although *To Kill a Mockingbird* was an exception, it has always been difficult to use the Quarry Theatre for receiving productions, mainly because these mostly tour to theatres with proscenium arch stages, meaning that the thrust of the Quarry Theatre stage is left unused, and consequently the play is distanced from the audience. An obvious exception is productions by Northern Broadsides because these are designed for touring to venues with very different auditoriums, from Scarborough's theatre-in-the-round to Skipton's auction market arena.

In the following seasons, Ian mostly programmed the Quarry with co-productions and musicals which benefited, as did always the big Christmas productions, from the size of the stage. Most of the theatre's own productions were of classic plays, ranging from the work of John Webster in 1613, via Shakespeare, John Ford, Ibsen, Coward, and Miller to Rattigan. They were productions which recognised the potential of the Quarry Theatre stage – something of which the Yorkshire Post's regular critic, Nick Ahad, was particularly aware. Reviewing *The Duchess of Malfi* in 2006, he commented:

"An enormous canvas, it needs something equally large to fill the space. Ian Brown … has pulled a smart move in programming this theatre classic, finding something which shows off his main stage at its grandest".[374]

Ian Brown's first Quarry Theatre production in the 2008-09 season was *Privates on Parade*, a play with music about a military entertainment unit posted to Malaya in 1948. It was definitely a 'show'. The local newspapers gave excellent reviews: "A theatrical triumph ... must rank among one of the best shows staged at the West Yorkshire Playhouse"[375], and "What a joy, what an absolute joy – *Privates on Parade* is a complete hoot from start to finish".[376]

But despite these reviews and high audience enjoyment, it achieved just 21 percent attendances – particularly surprising given that the original production of *Privates on Parade* by the Royal Shakespeare Company had had two successful runs in London's West End (1997,1998). There had also been several regional productions, a national tour, and a further West End production. It was also a perfect choice for the Quarry Theatre stage.

As a consequence, Ian saw the need to programme the Quarry Theatre in a slightly "more populist way", rather than choosing plays that "would challenge the audience and push their artistic tastes".[377] This perhaps explains why his next production was J.B. Priestley's *When We Are Married*, with a cast including actor and comedian Les Dennis. In the 2009-10 season, apart from a very successful Christmas production of *The Secret Garden* (an adaptation of the Frances Hodgson Burnett novel), his only other Playhouse production that season was Noel Coward's *Hay Fever*. As with *Privates on Parade*, the reviews in local newspapers were excellent:

"As farce demands, it's terribly convoluted but Ian Brown's direction never fails, every cog turns perfectly and there's not a slammed door or clutched bosom out of time."[378]

"Now this is how a classic should be done… Brown makes the play startlingly relevant, making it feel fresh and light, despite the play now being over eight decades old."[379]

However, like *Privates on Parade*, it was not a box-office success.

Looking back, Ian felt that in his time at the theatre, the Quarry Theatre was "an albatross round the Playhouse's neck. It's an incredibly inflexible space. You're stuck with seven hundred and fifty seats staring at you. I always wanted to be able to shutter down the Quarry so that you could change the auditorium's shape, you could have it as a five hundred-seater. On some nights it would have been nice for the audience to feel that they were not in a half-empty theatre".[380]

Despite his reservations about the Quarry, Ian is particularly proud of having been able to bring in several new associate directors, giving them a chance to work on a big stage with the benefit of a really good support structure around them. One of these was Nikolai Foster who grew up in Sutton-in-Craven, North Yorkshire. He had done work experience at the Playhouse whilst a pupil at South Craven School where he had acted and directed school productions. His first production on the Quarry Theatre stage, in 2007, was *Bollywood Jane* written by

Amanda Whittington. As the title suggests, it included music and dance, with a chorus of community dancers performing on a revolving stage.

Nikolai was responsible for four further productions during Ian's time at the helm, including two big Christmas productions: *A Christmas Carol* (2010) and *Annie* (2011). Both of these, like *Bollywood Jane*, had a community chorus of young people. Reviews of *A Christmas Carol* praised the production for avoiding the usual sentimentality. Similarly, *Annie* was praised as a fresh interpretation that avoided its cheesy, saccharin reputation. Annie received many four- and five-star reviews, the Daily Telegraph describing Nikolai's revival as "a slick, stylish, tightly drilled production".[381] The Independent saw it as "fast moving and spectacular"[382] while Kevin Berry (The Stage) reported that "Foster and his team use the full width, height and depth of the cavernous Quarry Theatre space to inspired effect".[383] The Yorkshire Evening Post reviewer concluded – "that this is a masterpiece of staging, there is no doubt".[384]

Earlier, in 2008, Nikolai had directed Peter Hall's stage version of George Orwell's *Animal Farm*. It was this production that made special, if very different, use of the Quarry's stage. As he explained at the time, "I wanted an empty space and that's what we've got – the entire Quarry stage. We've gone back as far as we can go and it is huge. But we've also brought the design right into the auditorium so the audience will feel very much a part of it".[385] He also described the production as a complete sensory experience. This vast stage was filled with muddy earth, in which the 'animals' moved. These actors carried and played musical instruments. One reviewer described this *Animal Farm* as an "intense, brutal and disturbing production... the last supper scene is a haunting finale as grotesque as an Hieronymus Bosch painting".[386]

With one exception (*Salonika* by Louise Page), all Nikolai's work as associate director was staged in the Quarry. He returned to the Playhouse in 2013 to direct *Sherlock Holmes, the Best Kept Secret*, by Mark Catley; back again in 2014, he directed the Christmas production of Irving Berlin's *White Christmas*.

ACT II

Since 2015 Nikolai has been Artistic Director at The Curve theatre in Leicester.

Sarah Esdaile followed Nikolai as an associate director, and, like him, all her work (with one exception) was on the Quarry stage. She enjoyed the challenge of working in this space and was not intimidated by it, feeling that "the stage is magnificent, as long as you have an epic design that is able to utilise it in a poetic, creative way".[387] She nevertheless acknowledges that there are plays which just 'sink' in the Quarry Theatre because "there has to be something epic, classical and weighty at the core of the play".[388]

Sarah is grateful to Ian Brown for allowing her to direct plays in keeping with her passion for big American drama, the first of which, in 2010, was *Death of a Salesman*. Working in the Quarry, a particular challenge for Sarah was directing the moments of intimacy in a way that would engage audience members throughout the auditorium. She fondly remembers one incident:

"I was sat at the back, frantically making notes during a preview. There was an older man a few seats down in the same row. He was crying. Knowing that Arthur Miller was concerned about how the play would affect men, both fathers and sons, I knew that his words had been successfully delivered".[389]

Sarah acknowledges the importance of her designer, Francis O'Connor, for this production, who chose to create a multi-level space that was both intimate and disconnected, reflecting the complexities and conflict in the lives of the characters:

"I wanted to convey something about the fractured lives of the Loman family, the fact that this was a space where four people were living together, but not really communicating."[390]

Death of a Salesman received four- and five-star reviews, one reviewer concluding that it was "quite possibly as quality a production … as you're ever likely to see",[391] while the Yorkshire Post's Nick Ahad opined that "contemporary productions of this play tend to try too hard to surpass the original. Esdaile doesn't fall into this trap. She simply tells

Miller's story as faithfully and as powerfully as she can. And it is magnificent… this is everything a leading regional theatre should be doing".[392] He concluded with:

"It is good to see the Quarry Theatre at the West Yorkshire Playhouse being used to its full potential again. Recent shows seem to have forgotten how extraordinary a stage this is. This production, if nothing else, will make you fall in love with that space all over again."[393]

The Yorkshire Evening Post reviewer similarly observed, "The stage, for example, is superb, clearly modelled on the split-level design of the original version that premiered in New York sixty years ago. And this is the Playhouse doing what they do best: making big, classic American plays even bigger. The set is spectacularly cavernous (one of the biggest you're ever likely to see in the Quarry Theatre)."[394]

The next play that Sarah directed in the Quarry was not a big American one, but Terrence Rattigan's *The Deep Blue Sea*. Again, her intention was to make sure that the "emotional heartbeat of the play translates right up to the trickier seats".[395] She remembers the first preview:

"There's this huge coruscating scene at the end of the first act where Hester screams after Freddie. Being the tour de force of an actor, [Maxine Peake] went for it, and I remember the audience stunned for about eight seconds before they clapped."[396]

This time, not all reviewers agreed about the Quarry setting. One enthused, "Never have I found myself so enchanted by a set. Ruari Murchison's angular London apartment is a platter of jutting panels, its triangular floor dislodged from a huge, horizontal picture frame. The Playhouse's version … is almost worth seeing for architectural reasons alone"[397]; however, another felt that the design was "handsome, with gauze walls that let us see the neighbours outside Hester's door. But the huge frame that runs round the set exacerbates the problems of playing an intense piece in this huge auditorium".[398]

Nevertheless, reviewers agreed about Maxine Peake's performance; typically:

"Most of *The Deep Blue Sea* is dominated by Peake, not just because of her near omnipresence, but her enchanting stage presence. This is very much her play, her moment – and it could very well be the making of her as a stage actor."[399]

Sarah's last production on the Quarry Theatre stage was another big American one: *Cat on a Hot Tin Roof*. She again acknowledges her brilliant designer, and the reviews praised the atmosphere he created:

"Francis O'Connor's design makes a splash of its own – evoking the opulence of the Deep South in its palatial scale, ingeniously dispensing with solid walls to emphasise how no secret is watertight safe, and tipping at one end into the lapping Mississippi."[400]

"It's not easy bringing the Mississippi delta to Leeds city centre – yet here its hanging moss and tea-coloured waters fill out every inch of the expansive Quarry stage. The production's exotic setting is so convincing, in fact, that it should probably carry a warning – as it's a rather rude surprise to suddenly find yourself navigating the busy city traffic upon exit."[401]

Sarah feels that this production taught her a lot about how sound can affect an audience's response to a play, and is grateful to Mic Pool who recorded a live jazz band and a gospel choir improvising alongside the rehearsals. However, looking back at her time at the Playhouse, she is most grateful to Ian Brown:

"As a young artist, what you want is someone you respect and admire, who believes in you, a parental figure who gives you a chance. So I worked my socks off not to let him down."[402]

After Leeds, Sarah continued as a freelance theatre director, but in recent years has worked in television, including episodes of *Eastenders* and *Call the Midwife*.

James Brining's first production at the Playhouse was *Sweeney Todd*, which opened the 2013-14 season. James had previously directed this Sondheim musical at the Dundee Repertory Theatre in 2010, a production which won the UK Theatre Award (formerly known as the TMA Awards) for Best Musical. David Birrell had also been nominated for Best Performance in a musical, and he recreated the lead part in the Playhouse production.

In a programme note, James explained that he had always wanted to revisit *Sweeney Todd* on a large scale. He also chose to revive it because he felt that "it has something important to say to us now, in Britain in 2013. It deserves its status as a classic, but its richness affords us the opportunity to explore it and interpret it afresh for today".[403] This explains why he moved the time setting from the Victorian period to 1979, when the musical was first performed on Broadway – which was, of course, the year when Margaret Thatcher won the General Election.

The production, set in a mental asylum, was something of a play within a play. The set was, as in Dundee, designed by Colin Richmond, using massive shipping containers on stilts amongst boarded-up buildings and corrugated iron. Reviews were good, and inevitably focused on this being James's statement of intent: "a brilliant beginning for Brining",[404] and "it's undoubted excellence makes a very healthy start".[405] The same Daily Telegraph reviewer, Dominic Cavendish, also made a general comment that the Quarry Theatre is "easy to empty, hard to fill". On the same issue Nick Ahad, in the Yorkshire Post, was also full of praise: "[Brining] has spent the last year learning how the Quarry Theatre works. He has got to grips with it like few others have over the past decade… accepting the vast, unwieldy Quarry stage and instead of battling against it, working with it". He concluded that "our patience has been rewarded with an epic, almost operatic, intelligent and visceral production of *Sweeney Todd*".[406]

The two productions which followed *Sweeney Todd* in the Quarry also 'got to grips' with the stage. First came the Christmas production, *The Jungle Book*. It was directed by Liam Steel, who was also an established choreographer and movement director. The production included live original music, dance, stilt-walking, masks and puppets. Some reviewers had doubts about the adaptation, by Rosanna Rowe, of the Kipling novel, although one critic concluded that it was "a stunningly dramatic interpretation, spellbinding for all ages".[407] However, critics were full of praise for the staging:

"Liam Steel's production is a visual delight, the Indian jungle bursting out beyond the bounds of the expansive Quarry stage to the walls of the auditorium in Laura Hopkins's verdant design. Couple this with the surround-sound of sound designer Fergus O'Hare, and the young audience feels enveloped magically by the animal kingdom… ".[408] As another reviewer put it, "The real star of the show is the magnificent set, which outdoes even the Playhouse's usually high standard and incites more than one impressed gasp from audience members as they settle into their seats. Designer Laura Hopkins has used the cavernous Quarry Theatre space to great effect; creating a wonderful jungle playground that calls out to the younger members of the audience to clamber on and start exploring".[409]

'Working with it' in respect of the Quarry stage was also the approach of Mark Rosenblatt when directing *Of Mice and Men*. This was another of the Playhouse-produced plays to be staged in the Quarry during the 2013-14 season. It was also Mark's first work as the theatre's Associate Director. He wanted to make full use of the expanse of the space; an epic staging to match the play's vast themes:

"We're responding to the Quarry, and the Quarry is massive … it immediately made me think of an open American landscape, and two men walking through it. So I wanted to use the space and acknowledge its expanse.".[410]

In the seasons that followed, James' programming for the Quarry Theatre followed a similar pattern to that of his predecessor. The theatre's own productions included classic plays by Arthur Miller and Anton Chekhov, as well as adaptations of Dickens's *Great Expectations* and Steinbeck's *The Grapes of Wrath*; there were two further productions of Shakespeare plays. As well as musicals at Christmas, James revived his original Dundee Rep production of *Sunshine on Leith*. He also directed Stephen Sondheim and James Lapine's *Into the Woods*, significantly a co-production with Opera North. Two of the Christmas productions, as planned, had a life beyond the Playhouse. *Chitty, Chitty, Bang, Bang* toured for eighteen months after the 2015 production. *Strictly Ballroom*, co-produced in 2016 with the commercial Global Creatures company, transferred to Toronto for a two-month run, and was restaged at London's Piccadilly Theatre in 2018, where it ran for eight months.

In addition to these Playhouse productions, James' first five years as Artistic Director saw a substantial increase in touring productions on the Quarry Theatre stage. As had become a tradition, every Northern Broadsides tour visited the Playhouse. Other companies, for example Kneehigh Theatre, regularly visited, having developed a loyal following at the Playhouse. There were also productions of plays based on well-known novels: George Orwell's *1984*, Sebastian Faulks's *Birdsong*, Jacqueline Wilson's *Hetty Feather*, and Khaled Hosseini's *The Kite Runner*.

The last Playhouse Christmas production before the theatre closed for redevelopment was to be highly significant. For the production of *The Lion, the Witch and the Wardrobe*, the Quarry Theatre was, for the first time in twenty-seven years, converted into the round, and audience members, as well as being placed in the main block of seating, were also seated on what is normally the stage. The audience thus surrounded the vast, circular stage. The intention was explained by the director, Sally Cookson:

"We're working really hard to make the audience feel fully included in the story, in our version, the beginning of the show takes place at the railway station from which the children embark on their journey to the countryside. So we're setting the whole auditorium as the railway station. Everyone who comes in is treated as an evacuee, which puts them in the same situation as the Pevensie children. Then throughout the story we are finding moments when we connect directly with the audience. That will be exciting I think – the audience will be aware of each other and at the same time will feel close to the action."[411] One reviewer saw another dimension to this staging: "Having the audience surround the stage highlights the Cirque du Soleil feel of the spectacular action".[412]

Another significant aspect of this production was that it was devised by the actors under Sally's direction – with support from others directing movement, fight scenes, puppetry, aerial displays, and music. Together they created the magic, without resorting to the latest technological special effects. This simple magic was highlighted in several reviews, with comments such as:

"With DIY scenery suggestive of children's own make-believe games, bedsheets become carpets of snow and suitcases turn into train carriages. But rather than breaking the enchantment, this simplicity makes us conspirators in it, as we collectively conjure CS Lewis's frosty parallel world."

The production attracted several five-star reviews in local and national newspapers, such as, "this new production leads us through the doorway and into the magical realm of Narnia, a land of snow, wood and deep magic. It is a hugely inventive, wonderfully escapist and ultimately heart-warming flight of fantasy from the director Sally Cookson and her ensemble cast of talented performers".[413]

The Lion, the Witch and the Wardrobe was, to coin a phrase, a rip-roaring success. Its run was extended for a week before the Playhouse's closure, and ultimately it turned out to have broken all box office records in the Playhouse's forty-eight-year history, having been seen by sixty-four thousand people.

ACT II

ACT TWO, SCENE SIXTEEN

"An effective regional repertory theatre is an essential part of the community it serves. It works with local children, young people and community groups. It contributes in many ways to the local economy, creating jobs directly and indirectly. A lively theatre is a community focus and a welcoming centre for visitors. It is as much a source for local pride and identity as a top class football team or a great cathedral."[414]

FIRST FLOOR
Grand Opening, 31ˢᵗ March 2009

BY THE TIME OF THE LAUNCH OF FIRST FLOOR (literally on the first floor of the St Peter's building owned by the Playhouse and adjacent to it), the West Yorkshire Playhouse had a nineteen-year history of programmes that reached out – as a matter of ideological principle – to schools and communities. In the introduction to the 2003 report on the Playhouse's programme of activities, Ian Brown wrote that an immense pleasure of his first year as Artistic Director had been "to discover and understand the work of Arts Development at the Playhouse. Over the years, Arts Development has reinvented the concept of creative education and has developed an international reputation for its unique and inspiring work with communities and individuals".[415]

Some of that Arts Development work with children and young people by which Ian was so inspired had been running continuously since the opening of the West Yorkshire Playhouse in 1990. Indeed, provision had begun even before the theatre had officially opened. The first was an event called 'Upfront', which consisted of ten sessions for young people, mainly from local youth centres, giving them the chance to explore backstage. Three hundred young people attended these sessions. Once the Playhouse opened, 'Playdays' were organised, each relating to a specific production. Sessions might include extracts from the play, parallel improvisations, talks by directors and designers; they might also focus on specific aspects of theatre such as lighting, costumes, stage management. These were offered to young people from colleges, training schemes, and secondary schools.

Next came the first regular provision, 'Playbox'. Under the banner of the Network Community Programme, this was a playgroup for children under five years. Activities included dance, music, and craft activities. Playbox was immediately over-subscribed. Also, in the first months that the Playhouse was open some one-off Network activities were provided for local primary and secondary schools. Children and young people had opportunities to perform on the stage; there were also activities relating to environmental issues. During the 1990 summer holiday, playschemes were organised, which included the opportunity to learn circus skills and culminated in the chance to perform in the Quarry Theatre.

The Network community programme continued to grow during the 1990-91 season: at the Annual General Meeting in September 1991, organisers reported two hundred and eleven events over the year. Many of these were one-offs, but there were occasional week-long events, such as a project called 'Crazy Cats' during the schools' summer holiday period which offered a chance for children aged nine to twelve to learn theatre skills, with a performance on stage for family and friends at the end of the week.

As part of their appraisal of the West Yorkshire Playhouse in early 1992, the Arts Council examined the Network Community Programme – and expressed concern that this was more about encouraging access to the building than about marketing value. Stressing the need for a development plan for this work, it was recommended that any developments in community work, including establishing relationships with other professional arts groups, should "accord with the primary need to produce plays".

Perhaps as a consequence of this appraisal, the provision for children and young people developed as a programme of regular activities which continued for many years. A weekly one was a play session for children under five and their parents, which evolved as arts sessions, also open to groups from nurseries and other playgroups. During school holiday periods, programmes of arts-related activities were organised, usually for under-sevens and for eight to twelve year-olds. These were often targeted at children and families who would not otherwise come to the Playhouse. Provision for older young people was made through 'Playhouse Partners' which offered tailored programmes for students and teachers, either on particular aspects of theatre studies, or related to a specific West Yorkshire Playhouse production.

Particularly because of the West Yorkshire Playhouse's financial situation in the early years, a lot of the work of the Community and Education Department (renamed the Arts Development Unit from the autumn of 1996) depended on external funding. The biggest example in this respect was the nationwide SPARK (Sports and Arts Towards Knowledge) initiative. It was also an example of how the Playhouse developed links with other organisations: in this instance, Leeds United Football Club; Leeds Rhinos Premier Rugby League Club; Education 2000 (a network of after-school clubs), and Leeds City Council services. Provident Financial was a major funder of SPARK in Leeds.

The pilot of SPARK took place in ten inner-city primary schools during the summer of 1998. The aim was to facilitate after-school arts and sports activities which would enhance such provision in the National Curriculum. The Playhouse ran a number of workshops with activities such as puppet-making, costume and characterisation sessions, scriptwriting, sculpture and lino-printing. SPARK also offered training for volunteers, a programme the Playhouse devised in partnership with Leeds Training and Enterprise Council and Leeds University. Sessions for teachers, parents, and play-workers, as well as volunteers, took place at the theatre on Saturday mornings. The pilot project culminated in a national conference in May 1999, held at the Playhouse, for which the theatre organised a display of children's work. SPARK continued from September 1998 with funding from the National Lottery's New Opportunities Fund. This funding was due to end in 2004 but new money through the Neighbourhood Renewal Fund and the Local Regeneration Fund allowed the work to continue for another year. After this, the Playhouse went on to support a pilot SPARK project in Bradford, with finance from Bradford-based Provident Financial. Playhouse staff then offered support for other theatres in England, Scotland, and Ireland which had become SPARK venues.

As well as SPARK, when Ian became Artistic Director in 2002 there were two other new areas of work which were to continue for many years. One was 'Creative Education' weeks. For one week each month, groups of primary school children came for a half-day programme of activities, often linked to the National Curriculum. There was usually a theme: for example, 'Pirate Adventures', using stories, movement and dance. In 2004-05, twenty-two schools were involved, and by 2009-10, fifteen hundred primary school pupils were taking part.

The second area of new work, 'Storymakers', was a very different way of promoting creative education. Groups of children in early years settings were sent a parcel, a box which contained items (for example, a star, a key, a piece of beautiful fabric) carefully chosen for their creative potential. The parcels would also contain a letter from the storyteller asking questions such as where the item might have come from, and to whom it might belong. In 2006-2007, the eighth year of this work, one hundred and twenty boxes were sent to forty-two different settings. More so than in the earlier years of community provision at the Playhouse, projects aimed to introduce participants to the theatre building, its productions and provision. So, with the Storymakers project, parcel items might link with specific productions for children.

As with SPARK back in 1998, other work with children was often dependent on external funding and so was time-limited. One such project was 'Whole New Worlds', which in 2003 received a grant of £25,000 from the Ragdoll Foundation. This project provided the opportunity for parents to take part in creative play with their babies. Again using boxes, these contained objects introduced one at a time over several weeks. These might be a musical instrument or a soft-toy fruit, chosen as ones that might build up familiarity and confidence. Final sessions were video-recorded so that parents could view how they interacted with their babies, and see how they learn.

Sessions mostly took place away from the Playhouse, at settings such as a prison mother and baby unit and a women's refuge. A dad's group also took part. The success of this project led to a conference at the Playhouse in 2004, which was an opportunity to share research findings and good practice. This was attended by one hundred and fifty delegates from the UK and abroad, including Early Years and theatre workers.

Another school-based project in need of mention is 'Sound Play', which began in 2004 with two years of funding provided by the National Foundation for Youth Music. This specifically targeted six Leeds inner-city primary schools and two secondary schools, ultimately involving four hundred students. The main aim was to support students in their transition between schools. The first stage of the project involved children engaging in music activities with a freelance musician. The second stage introduced another artist, for example a dancer or a choreographer, so that the children could experience a combination of art forms. Crucial to the work was bringing together the students from each of the schools, an opportunity to perform their work to each other, and at a later stage to family and friends. This also encouraged children and young people into the Playhouse building to rehearse or perform.

In addition to WYP Touring productions and related workshops, schools were also offered opportunities connected to specific Quarry Theatre and Courtyard Theatre productions. This could be one of the following: a meet-and-greet session, where the students met the actors and talked with them about the production they were about to see; a pre- or post-show talk; a 'Theatre Day', where students participated in practical activities at the Playhouse and then saw a matinee performance. The theatre also offered workshops on specific Shakespeare plays which schools and university students were studying, not necessarily ones with Playhouse productions. Usually facilitated by a theatre director, the aim was to bring the texts to life through practising verse-speaking alongside actors. Initially these were offered free to students, through 'Aimhigher' funding, a national organisation which aimed to widen participation in higher education.

Although at this stage the Playhouse had chosen not to offer a Youth Theatre programme, nevertheless, starting in 2007, the theatre hosted *The Shakespeare Schools Festival*. Over three or four days, all across the UK, every secondary school was given the opportunity to perform an abridged production of a Shakespeare play. In Leeds, local schools staged half-hour plays in the Courtyard Theatre to a paying audience.

One other way that schools could visit the Playhouse was by using the Cyber Café, which opened in February 2002. This was part of the UK Online network, a government initiative promoting public access to computers. Situated in the Playhouse restaurant area, it was equipped with fifteen desktop workstations, with other digital equipment available to use. A popular provision, in July 2003 the Cyber Café celebrated its ten thousandth user.

As early as 2004 the board of governors recognised that a dedicated space for work with young people was needed. Around this time, there was a change in the direction of national Youth and Careers services, coupled with the formation of the Connexions service, prioritising work with young people categorised as NEET (not in education, employment or training). The Playhouse's Arts Development Unit staff wanted to develop daytime work with fourteen to sixteen year-olds not attending mainstream schools, but recognised that this was not possible in the theatre building due to lack of space.

Meanwhile the St. Peter's building, purchased prior to the opening of the West Yorkshire Playhouse, was still just being used by the theatre for the Costume Hire Department, storage and a rehearsal space. The ground floor of the building was being rented out as The Wardrobe bar and night club. By 2006, the idea evolved of First Floor, a permanent arts facility for young people. On weekdays, the St. Peter's space would be used for alternative schooling provision, and at weekends and school holidays would offer accredited arts courses to disadvantaged young people more generally. It was estimated that the conversion of the building would cost £578,000, so a capital fund-raising campaign was launched. Christopher Eccleston, Jack P. Shepherd (*Coronation Street* actor) and Hilary Benn, MP for Leeds Central, agreed to be First Floor patrons. The project had the support of agencies such as Education Leeds, the Out of School Activities Team, and the Youth Offending Service. In preparation, the Arts Development Unit ran First Floor pilot projects, the first, in 2006, funded by Connexions West Yorkshire. Another pilot programme was a foundation course, leading to a Bronze Arts Award, an Arts Council qualification.

By June 2008 £444,000 had been raised, with funding secured from several charitable trusts. Arts Council England awarded £100,000. Smaller amounts were raised through local events, including a sponsored abseil event on the theatre's fly tower, in which even Councillor Liz Minkin participated. Additionally, the theatre box office introduced an optional one pound donation from ticket buyers. The remaining money was found through the City Council's Prudential borrowing scheme, a loan to be paid back over five years. Work on the building began in July 2008. At a later stage, grants were received from the Esmée Fairbairn Foundation and the Liz and Terry Bramall Foundation, which covered the first three years of running costs, including staffing.

First Floor thus opened in January 2009, with an official launch by Christopher Eccleston two months later. Initially the focus was on promoting awareness of the building and the opportunities for young people. This was done through open days and drop-in taster sessions that included a whole range of arts activities from creative writing to rap and DJ-ing. Following the successful pilots, a regular twelve-week programme for fifteen to nineteen year-olds, categorised as NEET, was offered, once again leading to Arts Award accreditation. These focused on a specific theatre style: for example, one programme linked with the production of *Othello*, meaning that participants were able to meet with Lenny Henry and work with this production's assistant director.

A year after opening, the appointment of a Musician-in-Residence to the staff team, funded by Youth Music, enabled First Floor to offer many further musical opportunities. Was this the heyday of the West Yorkshire Playhouse's outreach to the young people of Leeds?

ACT TWO, SCENE SEVENTEEN

Theatres in other European countries receive much more in public subsidy than do theatres in Britain – in Germany as much as eighty percent. Without comparable subsidy, British regional theatres are much more dependent on ticket sales and other income. When this income declines, decisions have to be made which can adversely affect not only staffing but artistic decision-making.

OTHELLO by William Shakespeare
14th February 2009

IN THE FINANCIAL YEAR BEFORE Ian Brown's arrival as Artistic Director in 2002, expenditure had once again exceeded income, resulting in an operating deficit of £263,850. Consequently one of Ian's first tasks was to break even. As recorded at his first Annual General Meeting, "When he took on Jude's mantle, Ian said he had committed himself to scrutinising the operation and, whilst still being ambitious, being leaner and keener with the ultimate aim of balancing the books, would be his objective".[416]

Hence cuts were proposed in respect of show budgets; namely, reducing actors' and musicians' wages; reducing crew numbers to two for every show; reducing marketing expenditure – and in particular reducing the production costs for the Christmas show by sixty percent.

Thus, after thirteen years of deficits, the year 2003-04 saw the achievement of an income surplus. This continued for another three years, but then 2007-08 saw a sixteen percent fall in ticket sales. This was in part attributed to the general downturn in the economy, but also to the continuing uncertainty about future developments on Quarry Hill. Effectively, there was an abandoned building site in front of the theatre, and access was difficult, whether by car or on foot. Decreased ticket sales also adversely affected income from sales in the bar, the restaurant, and from other miscellaneous sales. Again, the state of Quarry Hill also discouraged custom at other times of the day. Fortunately another financial lifeline was received, this time not from the Arts Council but from HM Revenue and Customs, in the form of a £504,000 repayment of VAT on production costs, following a change in case law. Another exceptional source of income occurred at this time: the sale of part of the staff car park. Half of the £2.14 million sale was received from Leeds City Council, who owned the land, which was sold to a company building the Skyline apartments. The Governors decided to set aside this money to safeguard the theatre's future.

At the start of the 2007-08 season, during the disappointing run of *Privates on Parade*, a press conference was organised to announce what would become another financial lifeline: Lenny Henry was to come to the Playhouse in February 2009 to play Othello. This was to be a co-production with Northern Broadsides, directed by Barry Rutter. At the time, Lenny was better known as a comedian, and as one newspaper commented, "To make your theatrical debut at fifty could be called brave, but to make your debut at fifty as Othello could be called madness".[417] The extent of the challenge was reflected in Lenny's reported response when Barry Rutter asked him play the part: "Are you sure you want to start with this? Isn't there some panto you want me to do first?".

Nevertheless, Lenny coming to the Playhouse must have been very good news for Ian Brown, who later reflected that people wanted 'stars' to be in the productions, but that it was mostly too hard to get such actors to come to Leeds. As he said at the press conference, "I think Lenny Henry doing *Othello* could be inspirational for a lot of kids, it could open it to a lot of people who would never dream of coming to a Shakespeare play".[418]

With perfect timing the press conference coincided with the start of another scheme – government-funded – offering free theatre tickets to young people aged under twenty-six. Nick Ahad asked whether the casting was just a gimmick, but conceded, "If the only way to fill the house is to stick a name on the bill that's more exciting to modern audiences than Shakespeare's, then sad though it is, that is the price we pay for our age's Faustian pact with the devil of celebrity".[419]

With so much at stake with this production, the reviews published after the press night must have been a relief to everyone concerned. They inevitably focused on Lenny's performance. With one or two exceptions – such as "Mr Henry is simply not ready to tackle a stage role of this magnitude"[420] –

reviews were positive. Perhaps the most gushing praise came from Charles Spencer, who had been expecting to review a theatrical car crash:

"This is one of the most astonishing debuts in Shakespeare I have ever seen. It is impossible to praise too highly Henry's courage in taking on so demanding and exposed a role, and then performing it with such authority and feeling."[421]

There were two particularly perceptive comments relating to the popularity of Lenny Henry; first, Mickey Noonan from The Metro observed that the rest of the company "desperately wanted Henry to do well", and that the goodwill and encouragement every time he walked on stage was "palpable".[422] Secondly, Susannah Clapp, for The Observer, noted how the audience "laugh[ed] often in this *Othello*. Not because Henry is clowning around. Or because he's self-important or ponderous. It's rather that familiarity with him – the fans are in – makes for an ease and intimacy with the play. Othello being talked of as 'sooty' is more than a fluting racial insult: it becomes ridiculous, intimately wounding: is that our Lenny he's talking about? Well, that's daft. So daft that it's laughable".[423]

Unsurprisingly *Othello* played to full houses at the Playhouse. A short tour followed. On the day that tickets went on sale in Scarborough, staff were giving out hot drinks to the long queue of people outside the theatre, and so many people were ringing to book tickets that the telephone system crashed. This was followed, unusually for Northern Broadsides, by a West End run. It played for four months at the Trafalgar Studios on Whitehall (now the Trafalgar Theatre). *Othello* was a significant source of income, and not just because of the excellent tickets sales at the Playhouse. After Leeds, the theatre received royalty payments throughout the run of the production in London.

Although *Othello* attracted excellent audiences, the rest of the Playhouse season saw a further decline in attendances, with the result that the financial year ended with a consolidated deficit of £232k. This would have been worse but for the outstanding success of *Othello*. The same applied in the following financial year, 2009-10, when the Playhouse received royalties for two other productions as well: *The History Boys* and *The Thirty-nine Steps*, which amounted to a total of £82,000, half of which was from the latter play's West End and touring productions.

When Ian explained, at the end of 2008, his intention to programme the Quarry Theatre "in a slightly more populist way", he nevertheless recognised that this auditorium was the 'financial engine house' of the Playhouse. Successful productions such as *Othello* were crucial in this respect. Whilst the Courtyard Theatre was, as intended, perfect for mid-scale touring, and had the advantage of adaptability of configuration, he also recognised that it was harder for this space to be cost-effective, even with good attendances. By 2009 Ian had concluded that "the Courtyard Theatre is a loss-making theatre unless there is a co-production in it". Until that point, he had nonetheless used this space for new and more challenging work, but thereafter there were just two more new plays in Ian's last four years at the Playhouse.

Reflecting on the problems of programming the theatres, Ian has concluded that, certainly at that time, there were simply not enough theatregoing people in Leeds to support the two auditoria with a total of eleven hundred seats. He also feels that in this period the West End touring circuit had "upped their game" so that the Grand Theatre in Leeds and the Alhambra Theatre in Bradford had taken away audiences from the Playhouse. He would have preferred to programme the theatre so that just one auditorium was open at a time, but that would have meant loss of income, and "we had a big infrastructure; I had a big responsibility for people's jobs; it was hard keeping that going".[424] He also felt that, for whatever reasons, the Playhouse had lost its loyal audience and hadn't found a new one. Consequently, as at many other regional theatres, the subscription scheme had collapsed.

Perhaps because of the precarious financial situation by 2008, a new post of General Director and Joint Chief Executive was created, and Sheena Wrigley was appointed to this post. Until then Ian Brown had been both Artistic Director and Chief Executive.

Sheena's first priority was the challenge of achieving a realistic budget for 2009-10. The need for this was urgent. As the Chair of the Finance committee made clear, "even using our reserves, as it stands at the moment, we will run out of cash in the middle of next year so the changes need to be fundamental".[425] As in 2002, cuts were proposed, this time in respect of marketing, maintenance and staffing. In respect of the latter, a wage freeze was seen as necessary, and the possibility of replacing front-of-house paid attendants with volunteers was also considered. Other necessary cuts inevitably affected the quantity and quality of productions. The number of productions was reduced: one fewer per year in each theatre. Ticket prices were increased, with reduced concessionary ticket rates and restricted availability. If all this was necessary, it was nevertheless recognised that such reductions, affecting all aspects of the theatre's work, would only be possible for just one year.

Good fortune came once again. Firstly, the box-office income was the best since the West Yorkshire Playhouse had opened, up twenty-two percent on the previous year. Secondly, the theatre was awarded a grant of £424,000 from the Arts Council's Sustain Fund, to "defray recessionary losses and maintain the artistic programme". Thus the theatre's deficit was eradicated, indeed a modest surplus achieved, and the theatre's financial situation – for the immediate future – was secured.

The development in 2010 of a formal business plan was arguably a sign of the times, in the sense of a shift in national (or in particular, governmental) values. 'Business Plan 2010' referred to the theatre as a brand – one in need of a "brand health check", starting with a rethink of its vision and mission:

"For the last four years, in order to continue with our current model of operation and create workable budgets, we have reduced production activity and committed to an increased level of co-production, we have cut commissioning and education work, postponed management improvements, training and capital investment and removed posts from a range of departments. Even before funding cuts we recognised that this was not sustainable. It contradicts everything we value".[426]

The plan acknowledged the priority of becoming financially stable and operationally strong. In respect of Playhouse productions, the business plan proposed longer-term planning as a way of achieving what was referred to as "signifier" productions; in other words, "theatrically ambitious 'must see' events which increase visibility and create a 'buzz' within the city, make an impact nationally, advance the art form or strengthen the cannon. They may be a significant new musical or play by an important writer/composer, name/guest of national stature, a really unusual approach to staging/concept, a fantastical collaboration".[427]

The plan recognised that whilst the Quarry Theatre could generate substantial income, poor audience figures could mean losing a lot of money. Consequently, it proposed that the focus should continue to be on recognisable titles and big names. The business plan also recognised that, if only for financial reasons, the Playhouse needed to attract a broader demographic.

The business plan also proposed that much more should be happening in the building besides the performances, and that those attending these should be offered a full-evening experience – not just the restaurant, but exhibitions and extra events. At other times, it was hoped that people would be attracted to use the public areas. However, it was recognised that "the slowing of the two major building projects on Quarry Hill have left the area in an appalling state of repair, which neither the Council nor the developers are prepared to take responsibility for. The unkempt nature of the car park and public walkways do not encourage people to this area of the city, especially at night".[428]

Specifically concerning finances, the plan proposed focusing less on sales-based income, especially the reliance on ticket sales (then forty percent of turnover). Whilst the latter could be improved by converting occasional attenders to regular ones, ticket sales were seen as volatile. Instead, the plan proposed investment in fundraising.

Should this business approach only be acceptable if new income streams continued, idealistically speaking, to be "the business of theatre"? Controversial territory was now being entered. For example, although hiring out spaces might indeed be a source of income, the difficulty with theatre hires was (as the Finance Committee was informed in early 2010) that these "can only be booked in around the other events taking place within the theatre".[429] The fact was, these 'other events' were community use, rehearsals, and so on. As a concrete illustration of a pragmatic, if not ideological, shift in priorities, the same committee would propose, only two months later, the moving of the Heydays community programme, which had always been held on Wednesday daytimes since 1990, to a different day of the week, on the basis that the theatre was turning away potentially lucrative business conferences wanting to use the building on Wednesdays.

Perhaps most significantly, the Business Plan articulated for the first time the pressing need for a repairs and renewal programme. The building was now twenty-one years old, and the necessity for a refurbishment and redevelopment of the Playhouse, partly to make it more visible amidst the larger developments planned for Quarry Hill, was now firmly on the table.

ACT TWO, SCENE EIGHTEEN

The rise of 'fringe' theatre has resulted in much more small-scale, experimental work, not necessarily performed in traditional theatre spaces. Are regional producing theatres able to incorporate such work into their programme? Or is the task of the Artistic Director, if only for financial reasons, to programme work for the main theatre spaces?

TRANSFORM
Grand Opening, 6ᵗʰ June 2011

JUST AS 'BUSINESS PLAN 2010' WAS PRODUCED, the Playhouse's management became aware of the likelihood of cuts to public funding. Both the Arts Council and Leeds City Council had announced the need to make savings. As Management prepared its budget for the last of Ian's ten years as Artistic Director, the 2011-12 situation was once again concerning. The Arts Council grant was reduced by 6.9%, and a further reduction from Leeds City Council was likely; furthermore this would be the last year of funding from West Yorkshire Grants, and to cap it all, Education Department funding for the Schools Company was to cease in April 2012.

However, once again the Playhouse benefited from another exceptional source of funding. In December of 2010 the theatre was chosen as one of five organisations across England to take part in the Arts Council's Action Research Programme, and was awarded £1.4 million for this work. The purpose of the programme was to investigate new ways of working in developing creative programmes and in strengthening the business operation longer-term. The money was partly used to fund new staff posts, including an Action Research Project Co-ordinator and an Action Research Communications Manager, a Change Mentor and Critical Friend. The money was also used for consultancy work, as well as research and development. The Action Research work was given the title of 'Transform', and yet another business plan was produced.

Some of the money was used to start-fund new commercial and artistic initiatives. The first of which, also using the name 'Transform', was a two-week-long series of events in 2011 running from 6th-18th June. For some of these, the Courtyard Theatre was converted into a smaller, more intimate space, but other areas of the theatre were also used. In line with purpose of the Action Research programme, Transform (quoting an interview with Associate Producer Amy Letman) was about "making people look at the theatre in a different way and experiencing it in a way they haven't before".[430] She explained that Transform was not necessarily about finding new audiences; however, the content of the programme was arguably targeted at a younger one. Elsewhere she commented that "if regional theatres keep doing the classic tried and tested bums on seats works then I really believe that in twenty years they won't be here any more... there won't be a need for them unless they are doing rewarding work that is urgent and relevant and of its time, which is what Transform is".[431]

Twenty-five events were programmed, many being one-off performances, some lasting no longer than fifteen minutes. The emphasis was on interactive events: for example, a karaoke booth where individuals could duet with video recordings of serving soldiers. Over five days, a theatre director and actors devised a play from scratch, but the rehearsal room was open to everyone to come along and influence the final production. There was a performance of *The Last Supper* by the Wau Wau sisters from New York, described as a 'cabaret-burlesque blasphemy'. Reviewing this for Leeds Confidential, Paul Clarke gives a flavour of the performance:

"The show closed with the Wau Waus recreating the Last Supper complete with satyrs, transvestites and random audience members who were all smiling fit to burst. Oh and the sisters are stark naked which might sound gratuitous but actually feels right as they had really bared themselves to us".[432]

Transform also included readings of three-minute short plays by new writers who had attended the theatre's 'So You Want to be a Writer?' course. Another local event was a performance by Leeds-based Imitating the Dog theatre company. A further dimension was that throughout the two weeks, the bar area of the Playhouse was transformed with a piece of installation art.

It should be mentioned that other ventures continued to take place in 2011 alongside the Transform activities. Projects were created by two local theatre companies: Slung Low and Unlimited Theatre. Slung Low developed an outdoor 'adventure' about the history of Leeds; Unlimited Theatre's project was about people of all ages playing old-fashioned games.

How successful was Transform? Well, in terms of attendances, this was overall recorded as fifteen percent, and more than half of the tickets issued were complementary. One online reviewer questioned whether or not the events achieved what was intended:

"What I witnessed was – although competent and often diverting – nothing transformative… the Transform event seemed like an excuse for industry types to get together and engage in a load of chin stroking and back slapping. What I was subjected to was the perpetuation of the exclusivity of the theatre: writers, actors, directors, making art either for themselves, each other or for the sake of it… the impression I garnered was that it wasn't really meant for me… So how the WYP is expecting to address the transformation of the theatre without actively engaging the potential punter in the discussion and execution is beyond me".[433]

Nonetheless, Transform took place again in 2012, this time described as a 'festival', spanning two weekends in April. Previewing the 2012 programme the Yorkshire Post's Nick Ahad commented, "Last year it was a little tricky to write about Transform, the festival of new work staged at one of the flagship theatres in the region. It wasn't that there was not enough to tell readers about – more that there was too much, and what there was could be considered either a little esoteric, or possible a bit difficult, or just downright virtually impossible to explain".[434]

Nick anticipated that 'Transform 12' would be a much more significant event, partly because it had had a longer planning time. A good example in this respect was a show called 9. Three months earlier, the Playhouse had invited local people to audition, with the plan that nine would be chosen to perform a five-minute solo piece as part of a full-length show. It was hoped to attract people who had never before considered acting and might not even have been to a theatre before. Once selected, the nine people were to be supported by directors and designers in producing their work.

9 was performed on two evenings in the Courtyard Theatre. Rod McPhee (The Yorkshire Evening Post) welcomed 9 as "an innovative and imaginative way to invert the normal dynamic which sees ordinary members of the public watching actors recreate fiction. Here ordinary members of the public appear on stage to tell their true-life stories". Whilst acknowledging that some of the stories were more successful than others, he concluded, "what's impressive is the use of communication beyond the usual recital of lines. Surprising moments of music, song, dance, and graphics are frequently employed alongside the expected lighting effects, occasional pieces of set and props.[435]

In the Yorkshire Post, Nick Ahad highlighted three impressive stories:

"The ones that rose high above the benchmark were Shazia Ashraf who is a brilliantly funny performer taking the fact that she can't play the piano to hilarious heights, Sheila Howarth who danced in the face of potentially terminal illness and Emi Neilson who acted out the fantasies of the desk bound wage slave".[436]

Other Transform 12 events included, as in the previous year, a play which started with writers, directors, and actors coming together in a rehearsal room without a script. Another event, You: The Player involved the 'audience' taking part in an interactive journey through the corridors, workshops and other spaces in the Playhouse building. There was also a performance by Curious Directive, a theatre company made up of scientists and theatre-makers. Your Last Breath told four stories spanning several decades, all linked by the idea of freezing humans and bringing them back to life at a later time. Originally performed at the Edinburgh Fringe Festival the previous year, it was performed on the Quarry Theatre stage, but with the audience entering the auditorium from the front and with much of the seating screened off to create a studio theatre space.

Other theatre companies, mostly local ones, took part in Transform 12. Perhaps as a consequence, the purpose of the festival seemed better thought-out. Comparing it to the rest of the Playhouse's work, Sheena Wrigley observed, "It doesn't mean by any means that you'll never see us do another Tom Stoppard or William Shakespeare production here... But it means that where those (new) ideas are very exciting, we can potentially put more resources in the hands of those artists, and they might produce some very striking pieces of larger-scale work."[437]

The decade saw the establishment not only of Transform, but a further outreach programme that served to realise the theatre's idealistic founding principles of reaching into the community and encouraging innovation. In 2011 a short season of new work called 'Furnace' took place, co-ordinated (as was Transform) by Amy Letman, who enthused that it was "an opportunity for the Playhouse to support different ways of creating theatre and ... bring new and exciting artists into the building to discover the work they want to create and give them a space to do it".[438]

Like Transform, Furnace was repeated in 2012, once again a showcase for works in progress, or ones not appropriate for productions on the Quarry or Courtyard stages.

Both Furnace and Transform continued and thrived. In 2013 Transform took up the theme 'My Leeds My City', focusing on local communities and artists. Once again, some performances took place in non-theatre spaces, but within walking distance of the Playhouse. 2014 similarly saw performances in non-theatre spaces, but within the Playhouse building; that year, however, the festival took place over just one weekend. From 2015, funding issues were resolved by the festival becoming independent of the theatre, though still coordinated by Amy Letman. It is now a citywide event attracting theatre work both nationally and internationally.

Apart from the Coronavirus closure period, Furnace, too, has continued every year, hosting many other theatre companies including RashDash which became an Associate Company of the Playhouse. 2022 saw the eighth annual Furnace programme, with a number of workshops as well as readings and performances of works in progress. Despite funding challenges and commercial pressures these two ongoing projects (though Transform is no longer under the Playhouse's umbrella) uphold the theatre's founding ideals.

ACT TWO, SCENE NINETEEN

According to the 2021 census, 18.7% of the population of Leeds identified as Asian, Black or a mixed or multiple ethnic groups. This compares with a figure of 13.8% in 2011. The breakdown of these figures is as follows: Asian, Asian British or Asian Welsh – 9.7%; Black, Black British, Black Welsh, Caribbean or African – 5.6%; Mixed or Multiple ethnic groups – 3.4%. To what extent do audiences at regional theatres like the Leeds Playhouse reflect the ethnic groups of the communities which the theatres serve? Equally, do the plays, the writers and the actors reflect these communities?

WAITING FOR GODOT by Samuel Beckett
3rd February 2012

AS WELL AS TRANSFORM AND FURNACE WORK, a central objective of the Action Research programme was:
"to re-ignite the relationship between the Playhouse and Minority Ethnic communities and artists. The impetus is a desire to enrich the programme and connect with the diversity of communities of West Yorkshire and Leeds".[439]

In order to achieve this, three areas for development were identified: to strengthen the diversity of Playhouse productions on the Quarry and Courtyard stages; to build more creative collaborations with Black and Asian professional companies; and to expand the Playhouse's community ambassador scheme. The latter would concentrate on the Chapeltown and Harehills communities – building links, developing participative programmes, and growing audiences for the main stage productions.

Two productions were considered important in respect of these developments. First was *The Wiz*, a revival of the 1974 Broadway musical, an African-American retelling of *The Wizard of Oz* story, which had also been adapted as a film in 1978 with Diana Ross and Michael Jackson. *The Wiz* uses soul and Motown-derived music to tell the story. Another co-production with the Birmingham Repertory Theatre, it was directed by Josette Bushell-Mingo. Better known as an actor, ten years earlier she had set up 'Push', a London arts festival showcasing new Black drama, opera and dance. With performances at the Almeida Theatre, the Royal Opera House, and Saddler's Wells, the aim was to encourage mainstream institutions to take on diversity in a much more visible way.

The production in Leeds saw an all-Black cast joined by a sixteen-member community ensemble. As an example of linking with local communities, this ensemble included teenage twins Tila and Tavelah Robinson from Chapeltown, who had previously been involved with *Carnival Messiah* when it was revived at Harewood House in 2007.

The second production, later in 2011, was *Waiting for Godot* – another co-production with Talawa Theatre. While *The Wiz* was primarily a Birmingham Repertory Theatre production (which Josette had suggested to their artistic director a year earlier), *Waiting for Godot* was much more a West Yorkshire Playhouse production, which then toured to four other theatres. It was directed by Ian Brown, his last production as Artistic Director. The significance of this *Waiting for Godot* was that it had, for the first time in Britain, an all-Black cast. This was not colour-blind casting: the production was a new interpretation of the play.

Talawa Theatre was founded in 1986 to nurture talent in emerging and established artists of African or Caribbean descent. This has not necessarily been about new writing: for example, one of their first productions was a Black-cast version of *The Importance of Being Earnest*. The aim of Talawa Theatre has been "to provide opportunities for Black actors, to use Black culture to enrich British theatre, and to enlarge theatre audiences among the Black community". [440]

Regarding the Playhouse's staging of this production, Ian Brown similarly argued that "it also brings in a potentially different audience and you want the audience to be as wide as it can be. If all plays look like plays for white audiences, then you have to do something to change that, to broaden it".[441] Ian clearly believed in the decision to use an all-Black African-Caribbean cast:

"Ultimately it's still the same play but it certainly lends itself to this interpretation. Hearing voices that are not Irish or English, giving it West Indian accents instead, suits it very well and it becomes a play about Black people rather than the Irish tramp story we're used to. Culturally, doing the play this way, we see it slightly differently and it makes us think about what the rope around Lucky's neck may suggest. It alerts you to the possibility about slavery without saying it, and we've also thought about the Windrush generation who came with such high hopes but have lost all that power, status and hope".[442]

For Patricia Cumper, Artistic Director of Talawa Theatre at the time, *Waiting for Godot* "talked about a great many experiences that would resonate with Black Britons. It talks about a world where you wait for someone else to tell you whether or not your life can improve, of constantly having to negotiate with someone who holds themselves just out of reach. It speaks about having to sleep in a ditch and endure regular beatings, of living in uncertainty and fear. It also explores the power of friendship forged against adversity yet it also looks at how power makes those who have it insensitive to those they hold power over".[443]

Jeffrey Kissoon, who played Vladimir, believed an all-Black cast would "force audiences to contemplate some very specific images. There are many references in *Waiting for Godot* to war, conflict and suffering, and in particular to bones... There are many images in the play that are reminiscent of the master-slave relationship, and of course that automatically resonates... There are also many references to skulls and the dead, and for me that conjures up an image of the ocean filled with bones from the transatlantic slave trade".[444]

In respect of the relationship between the Playhouse and minority ethnic communities and artists, it was appropriate that the objective of the Action Research programme used the word 're-ignite'. Early in 1986 the Playhouse had produced an Ethnic Minorities Action Plan. Two specific and measurable proposals were that there should be two representatives of the ethnic community in Leeds on the Theatre Board, and that a forum be established drawn from community groups of African/Caribbean origin. The Action Plan was very much about attracting Black and Asian people to the theatre's existing productions – through targeted advertising, press releases to ethnic press and radio, and so on. Nevertheless it was proposed that a minimum of five percent of other activities – films, talks, concerts, exhibitions – should be specifically for the Asian and African/Caribbean communities.

Clearly the Playhouse's relationship with local Black and Asian communities had become more substantial since the theatre's first opening. The inclusion of Temba Theatre Company's *Glory!* in the first season at the West Yorkshire Playhouse had been a statement of intent – though this itself had received some criticism and disappointment that "only one black group, the 'safe' Temba Theatre Company, is included in the first programme".[445] At the time, the theatre responded that there were only one or two other Black companies nationally that could produce work for an auditorium the size of the Quarry Theatre.

Once the Courtyard Theatre opened, smaller-scale Black and Asian companies were able to tour to this space. Kali Theatre Company visited the Playhouse in 1991 with their inaugural production of *Song for a Sanctuary*, a play about domestic violence and abuse within the Sikh community. Also in 1991, two of the Playhouse's own productions, plays in the *Lifelines* series of new writing, were by Black writers. Then April 1994 saw the first Black Arts Week funded by the Arts Council following a joint application by the Playhouse and Black Expressive Theatre Enterprises. The week started with a gospel choir concert directed by Geraldine Connor who had already worked at the theatre as a regular composer and music director. Many of the singers had performed in the gospel choir in the previous year's production of *All God's Chillun Got Wings*. On another evening, a variety night showcased Black Arts in the region including poetry, dance, music and comedy. Alongside these and other events were Caribbean food days, a carnival costume exhibition, a book fair, and free foyer events.

Two plays were also included in the programme. *The Black Hole* by local writer Ansell Broderick was a space adventure for families, promoted as 'a close encounter of the Black kind'. The other play was *Moor Masterpieces* by Leeds-born Sol B River, performed by two actors from the cast of *The Merchant of Venice* which was on at the time in the Quarry Theatre. *Moor Masterpieces* is an emotional journey through Black history, where the actors represent Othello, James Baldwin, Solomon, Duke Ellington and Martin Luther King. They talk about the past, the present, slavery and liberation. Following the production of *Moor Masterpieces* Sol was appointed as Writer-in-Residence for the next two years. During this time, *Moor Masterpieces* was revived for a Schools Company tour, finishing with two more public performances at the Playhouse.

The 1994 Black Arts Week also included a day conference on the future of Black Theatre in Britain. Perhaps as a consequence of this and of the week more generally, the Playhouse decided to create the post of Black Arts Coordinator. Garfield Allen was appointed, starting in June 1995. Before then the Playhouse held its second Black Arts Week, and other Black arts events were featured in the spring season, including an early version of *Carnival Messiah* based on Handel's oratorio, which would receive a full-scale production at the Playhouse four years later.

Once in post, Garfield produced a three-year plan for Black Arts Development, emphasising the development of African/Caribbean work within the mainstream programme, and challenging the "misleading stereotypes of African and Caribbean art forms, frequently viewed as exotic (low status) arts". A stated objective was "to dispel the myth that African and Caribbean theatre and arts are of minority interest, by encouraging a wider audience to attend, utilising a creative and pro-active marketing strategy".[446]

A further Black Arts Week was held in May 1996, but from 1997 the programme became a month-long one to coincide with October's annual Black History Month. Throughout this month, the Playhouse presented a photographic exhibition, 'Being There', which focused on the experience of three generations of Caribbean people since the 1950s. Tours and workshops were organised for Leeds schools as well as for Heydays members. The month saw visits by two major theatre companies, which broadened the focus. Examining the politics of South Africa, The Market Theatre of Johannesburg presented *The Good Woman of Sharpeville* (an adaptation of Brecht's *The Good Woman of Szechwan*) directed by Janet Suzman. Tamasha Theatre presented *A Tainted Dawn*, about the partition of India fifty years earlier. For Garfield this production was a springboard in developing, specifically, South Asian arts activities.

That Black Arts Development influenced the Playhouse programme throughout the year is illustrated by three productions in the months before and after Black History Month. In May 1997, following the success of *Beatification of Area Boy* two years earlier, the Playhouse produced another play from Nigeria: *Things Fall Apart*. This was an adaptation of the novel by Chinua Achebe. Set in the nineteenth century, it is about one man's stand against colonialism, and the consequences for his village when different cultures and religions collide. The play was adapted by Biyi Bandele who came to England in 1990 when his first play won a British Council sponsored playwriting competition, judged by Alan Ayckbourn, and was performed in Scarborough at the National Student Drama Festival. In September 1997 the Playhouse produced the British premiere of *The Other War* by the Eritrean writer Alemseged Testai, about the plight of women living inside occupied enemy territory in a revolutionary situation. November 1997 saw another British premiere: *Jar the Floor* by Cheryl L. West, about four generations of African American women. Also in 1997, plays by Black and Asian writers had featured in the *Sevenx7* season of new writing.

Did all of this make Black audiences roll in? Despite all efforts, in 1999 Jude Kelly expressed her frustration that "a lot of work had been done with Black actors but... members of the Black community were actually very indifferent attenders at the Playhouse. There seems to be a difficulty in striking up partnerships with the Black community."[447] This perhaps explains why Garfield had been keen that Black History Month events should not solely be held at the Playhouse; he proposed satellite activities in Chapeltown, and in schools and colleges.

1999 saw the community production of *Carnival Messiah* in the Quarry Theatre, but also *Who's Boss?*, written and directed by Ansell Broderick, in the Courtyard Theatre. Ansell was born and grew up in the Chapeltown area of Leeds. He had been involved at the Playhouse for some years, including working with the Theatre In Education team. Another of his plays, *Roots and Boots* had had a short run at the Playhouse in 1997, ten years after its first production at the Mandela Centre in Chapeltown. *Who's Boss?* was a Playhouse commission, first performed as part of *Sevenx7*, but then given a full production. He called it a 'Hipopera', as the play is written in verse and was accompanied throughout by a synthesiser and a live DJ. The play is the story of a Black man in jail awaiting trial for drug-dealing. Through flashbacks, the play looks at how this man coped in a white society.

The reviews for *Who's Boss?* were disappointing, but also quite revealing. Sheena Hastings, in the Yorkshire Post, opined that "a confusing story is further scrambled by several scenes rendered in a patois so most of the (mostly white) audience would have been left clueless about what was being said. Cultural accuracy has an important place, but if some universal theme about good, bad and redemption is to be understood then we've really got to be able to follow the story. This was a good opportunity for the white majority to carry the message home. But what was it?".[448] Meanwhile Nigel Cliff, in The Times, objected to "astonishingly crude white stereotypes", concluding that "the West Yorkshire Playhouse is to be commended for giving space to a new local voice, but *Who's Boss?* left me feeling angry for all the wrong reasons".[449] Karen Joyner, in the Yorkshire Evening Post, concurred, "It is hard to see what Broderick is driving at with his story … On the surface it is a clichéd tale which would never have seen the stagelights if it had been written by a white author. All blacks are victims, all whites are villains, and every stereotype about each skin colour is emblazoned across every line".[450]

Between the production of Carnival Messiah in 1999 and its revival in 2002, there was only one play produced by the Playhouse which could be considered part of Black Arts Development. This was *Hijra* by Ash Kotak, which Ian Brown directed the year before his appointment as Artistic Director.

Somewhat controversial at the time, *Hijra* tackles the subject of homosexuality and transvestism in the Asian community. Ian had directed the original production at the Theatre Royal Plymouth, which transferred to the Bush Theatre in London a year earlier.

A change of Artistic Director might have effected a new methodology for achieving Black inclusivity. From his appointment to the role in 2002, Ian Brown continued where Jude Kelly left off, programming plays, as Jude had done, which gave opportunities to local Black writers and directors. His first season included *Off Camera* by Sheffield-based Marcia Layne. Her first full-length play, it is about two young women, both second generation Jamaicans. Jamaica is where the play is set and where they are on holiday in search of love. The cast also includes two local young men; they are looking for a way to escape the poverty they live in. Marcia won the 2003 Alfred Fagon Award for plays written in English by a writer from the Caribbean or of Caribbean heritage. *Off Camera* was directed by Femi Elufowoju Jr., who had been appointed as an associate director at the Playhouse. His previous involvement at the theatre had been as an actor in *Beatification of Area Boy* back in 1995.

In the same year, Femi also directed Euripides's Greek tragedy *Medea* – and took on the part of Jason at short notice. With an all-Black cast, the production merged the traditions of Greek theatre with that of Nigerian Yoruba drama. A review in Leeds Student opened with:

"This play was in all honesty the most electrifying I have ever seen on screen or stage. At certain moments, notably the opening and final scenes, the tension in the auditorium became almost palpable".[451]

As well as *Off Camera* and *Medea*, 2003 saw *Two Tracks and Text Me*, another play by Sol B River, directed by Joe Williams who was born in Leeds and attended Intake High School which specialised in the performing arts. In *Two Tracks and Text Me* twelve-year-old Louise is being abused by her father. Her text message cry for help brings her into contact with three young men, initially too preoccupied with their own lives to help her. The production was a multi-media one, using poetry, music, dance and video. The Yorkshire Post's Sheena Hastings raised the question of how to make such a play and production appeal to a wide range of theatregoers. When she interviewed Sol about this his response was simply to express the hope that the Playhouse's older audience would have the will to embrace a play "which is supposedly more experimental, and on the face of it, aimed at younger people who don't necessarily go to the theatre that much".[452]

After 2003, apart from the Playhouse's Northern Exposure and Theatre In Education plays, Black and Asian work was more prominent with visits from touring productions. Four companies that focused on South Asian work were regular visitors (Kali Theatre, Rifco Theatre Company, Tara Theatre, and Rasa Theatre) and the productions of the local Asian Theatre School, developed with the support of Red Ladder, all came to the Playhouse. Pilot Theatre, the York-based mid-scale touring company producing theatre for younger audiences, brought *East is East* in 2007, and *Sing Your Heart Out For the Lads* the following year. These plays, by Ayub Khan Din and Roy Williams respectively, in different ways both tackled the subject of racism in Britain.

There were also touring productions from Eclipse Theatre, founded in 2003 with the aim of addressing the absence of Black Theatre on the regional mid-scale touring circuit. Eclipse was originally a consortium of three regional theatres: the Birmingham Repertory Theatre, the New Wolsey Theatre Ipswich, and the West Yorkshire Playhouse. They brought two further plays by Roy Williams to the Playhouse (*Little Sweet Thing* and *Angel House*). Then at the beginning of 2009 the Playhouse worked on a co-production with Eclipse Theatre, a play with a very local story. This was *The Hounding of David Oluwale*, adapted by Oladipo Agboluaje from Kester Aspden's book of the same name. David Oluwale came to England from

Nigeria as a stowaway in 1949 aged nineteen. Struggling with finding employment, he was arrested for disorderly conduct during a police raid on a nightclub. He spent periods in prison and in a psychiatric hospital, ending up homeless on the streets of Leeds, until in May 1969 his body was found in the River Aire, after which it transpired that two police officers had regularly inflicted violence on him. They were eventually convicted and imprisoned for assault, but not for manslaughter as many had hoped. The play is not a piece of verbatim theatre but a drama which effectively brings David back to life as he tells his story, mainly to the detective who investigated the case of police brutality.

After Leeds, this production toured to four other regional theatres. Significantly, at Leeds, it was estimated that two fifths of those who saw the play were new to the Playhouse.

In summary, in the years since the Action Research programme, the Playhouse has continued to develop the relationship between the theatre and minority ethnic communities and artists, but this happened largely through its community engagement programmes rather than the work on the Quarry and Courtyard stages. Hence in the theatre's 2021 'Plan for Change', there was acknowledgement that "through the fifty years of the Playhouse, whilst the organisation was established for and continues to be a place that aims to serve all our local communities, we know we haven't always delivered on this aim, losing the trust of some Black people and communities along the way".[453]   The Plan therefore suggested staffing changes, aiming to "build more meaningful and positive relationships with Black communities in Leeds".

ACT TWO, SCENE TWENTY

The National Association of Youth Theatres believes that all young people have a right to participate in high quality, engaging, challenging and meaningful theatre experiences. As drama provision in schools declines, regional theatres are uniquely placed to offer personal and educational development to young people. They can also support other theatre companies in their work with young people and communities.

GIRLS LIKE THAT by Evan Placey
18th July 2013

WOULD A NEW ARTISTIC DIRECTOR bring change and innovation? In August 2012 James Brining replaced Ian Brown. James arrived at the Playhouse at a time of change, a consequence of the Arts Council-funded Action Research programme that had just been completed. Developments mostly related to the work which James was initially to focus on, as well as work which allowed the theatres and other spaces to be used in different ways.

Unusually, James chose not to direct any productions during his first year in post:

"I've decided not to direct any shows myself in the spring season, I want to address lots of things about the theatre itself first. I want to look at where it is placed, where it is heading, which areas I want to contribute to most. If I was directing in spring, then I would have to have my head in that already, but I want to take my time to get to know the place and set out the direction of travel."[454]

This in itself was a statement about the direction of the Playhouse's work: that the work other than in the two theatres was as important as the productions in these spaces.

There were some new developments resulting from the Action Research programme. In addition to the Transform festivals, new ways of supporting emerging and developing artists were introduced. Just one month after James Brining's appointment, the Playhouse Youth Theatre was established. Another innovation was the Summer Sublets scheme to support Yorkshire-based artists by making available free studio and rehearsal space, giving professional development and advice, and giving feedback on performances of work in progress. In 2013, fifteen individual companies were supported in this way.

Support on a more regular basis was given to Unlimited Theatre which was based at the Playhouse from 2012. A year later RashDash became the second associate company. Both were given use of office space, rehearsal space and meeting rooms, plus mentoring and organisational support. They were also given the opportunity to present work during the Transform festivals.

Opportunities for these regional companies to perform were also opened up with the introduction of 'Open Season' launched in 2013, which was to be held annually in the month of July. An example from the 2015 season was *Gipton: The Musical*, a show about the history of the Gipton estate in Leeds, the result of eighteen months of research by local residents with the support of the Space2 arts organisation in East Leeds. Space2 had previously used the Playhouse for performances by community groups alongside professional artists. Participating in Open Season was also an opportunity for existing groups at the Playhouse to perform: young people from First Floor; older people from Heydays.

The first Open Season was also a performance opportunity for members of the Playhouse Youth Theatre, which was established in September 2012 to, "open up and open out the expertise and resources of the theatre by engaging young people in creative opportunities".[455] Thus the first Open Season (2013) gave the first performance opportunity for the Youth Theatre's considerable membership: one hundred and twenty young people aged eleven to nineteen had immediately signed up, and different groups had been formed based on age. Whilst most were interested in acting there was also an opportunity to learn backstage work, tutored by Playhouse production staff. Some writing and performance workshops were tutored by the writer Evan Placey who had been co-commissioned, along with The Birmingham Repertory Theatre and the Theatre Royal Plymouth, to write a full-length play. This would be performed separately by the three companies. The result was *Girls Like That*, performed for one night in the Courtyard Theatre.

The play explores the pressures on young people caused by advances in digital technology; specifically, the impact of 'sexting' on a group of young women. The story begins when the boyfriend of a teenager takes a naked picture of her then texts it around the whole school. Reviewed, appropriately, on the A Younger Theatre website, Adam Bruce (a student at York University) called it "an energetic and dazzling piece of theatre that captivates a vast age range of audience right from the start".[456] He also recognised the large amount of talent and potential among the young performers. Nick Ahad, in the Yorkshire Post, similarly concluded that "the show bodes well for the [Playhouse] youth theatre's future and perhaps might make more people take youth theatre a little more seriously".[457]

Following the success of *Girls Like That*, a group of the Youth Theatre members were invited to perform an extract at the Houses of Parliament, at the launch of an initiative by the Young Minds mental health charity, a programme focusing on cyberbullying.

In 2014 the Youth Theatre's fourteen to sixteen year-olds performed another new play by Evan Placey. *Pronoun* was about a transgender teenager and the impact on friends and family when this young person decides to transition. This play was commissioned as part of the National Theatre's Connections Festival, so was performed by youth theatres across the UK. It was again reviewed by Adam Bruce:

"*Pronoun* in itself is an example of a tightly-knit, well-crafted piece of theatre, but the issues surrounding it make it all the more captivating and interesting. The West Yorkshire Playhouse Youth Theatre's response to them is honest and mature, and the amount of hard work they have put into presenting *Pronoun* is incredibly evident. Their sensitive and perceptive approach to creating theatre really shines in this production, and makes them stand out as a well-rounded and solid youth theatre group and, more importantly, an engaging and provocative theatre company."[458]

The following year, the same Youth Theatre group performed *Immune* as part of the 2015 Summer Open Season. This was a play by Oladipo Agboluaje, who had written *The Hounding of David Oluwale* back in 2009. Co-commissioned with the Theatre Royal Plymouth and Royal and Derngate Northampton, the setting is a secondary school where pupils of one class are the only survivors of an apocalypse. The Youth Theatre was lucky in getting Fly Davis to design the set: she had done this for the previous Christmas production of *James and The Giant Peach*.

2017 saw a Youth Theatre production programmed for four performances in the Courtyard Theatre. *Zoetrope*, specially commissioned for the Playhouse, was written by Rebecca Manley. It examined mental health issues and the services available to young people. Rebecca wrote the play after running a series of workshops with the cast, where together they decided on the questions and themes the play should investigate. She also liaised with mental health agencies in the city. The play focuses on seven very different young people taking part in group counselling. The Leeds production had a cast of twenty-five, with others playing a chorus of doctors and nurses. Rebecca explained their significance:

"Many of the young people talked about being moved around in the system, with their counsellors/doctors/nurses changing frequently. Many of them said this was one of the biggest challenges and left them feeling confused, unsettled and unimportant. Presenting the professionals in the piece as an almost faceless mass was a way to represent this."[459]

Gemma Woffinden, who directed, won the Yorkshire Evening Post's Mental Health Champion of the Year Award, and the play was included in the programme for the European Festival of Youth Theatre in Birmingham in August 2018.

Before James Brining's time as Artistic Director, children and young people were often involved in Playhouse productions, but mostly the Christmas ones where the cast required child actors. From September 2014 (by which time the Youth Theatre had been successfully extended to include eight to ten-year-olds), children and young people were included in other productions, where their presence added an extra dimension. The first of these was James's production of Arthur Miller's *The*

Crucible, the opening play of the 2014-15 season. Three children were added to the already large cast (fifteen actors). Thus the Proctor children, unusually, were present in the production. Other, older members of the Youth Theatre also performed as Puritan girls.

One review suggested that the young people's presence was a strength of the production, such as in the scene when a dozen blank-faced girls respond to Abigail's lead in witnessing the devils in the eaves of the makeshift courtroom, and as "the spectral silhouetted figures of the girls witchily dancing in the woods".[460]

This production of *The Crucible* was also significant in that the cast included three actors who had just been appointed through the Playhouse's newly established Graduate Actors Scheme. They then spent eight months at the theatre, mentored by the artistic team. One of them, Verity Kirk from Harrogate, had just completed her training at RADA. She expressed her gratitude for this opportunity:

"When I was fourteen I performed at West Yorkshire Playhouse for the Shakespeare School Festival – I remember being amazed at what a trek it was to walk across the Quarry stage! To be back here, on that same stage, and to know I have months here to learn all I can, alongside talented people making brilliant work, means such a lot to me."[461]

The following season, members of the Youth Theatre again appeared on the Quarry stage, this time in an adaptation of Dickens's *Great Expectations*. They played the younger Pip, Estella, and Herbert Pocket. Reviewers commented on just how demanding the three parts were, particularly the younger Pip, for child actors. Simultaneously with *Great Expectations*, the Courtyard Theatre was staging the first production of *The Damned United*. Eleven young people were involved, mainly as a 'chorus'. One reviewer commented on how the play benefited from their involvement:

"There's … an energetic ensemble of young performers who play masked footballer and press reporters. The movements of this ensemble are fluid and focused, and maintain the energy of the play throughout to convey the themes of the piece and keep the audience engaged."[462]

But it was, arguably, the 2017 production of Shakespeare's *Romeo and Juliet* which most successfully used First Floor and Youth Theatre members. The director was Amy Leach who had just returned to the Playhouse as an Associate Director, having previously directed community tour plays *Little Sure Shot* and *Kes*. Amusingly, her first visit to the Playhouse, aged fourteen, had been to see the 1995 production of *Romeo and Juliet*. Amy's production was set in a present-day environment that could easily be seen as inner-city Leeds. She wanted to include young actors as the generation following Romeo, Tybalt, Mercutio and Benvolio:

"The young company are the people who witness the wiping out of the generation just above them. Of that generation, only Benvolio is left alive at the end of the play. Will the young generation be influenced by what they've witnessed and continue the cycle of violence? Or will they join together to break the cycle, and bring hope for the future?"[463]

Amy was assisted by Fiona McCulloch and Gemma Woffinden who were working at the Playhouse with First Floor and the Youth Theatre. They held auditions for the young people's company for *Romeo and Juliet*, and worked with them throughout the five-week rehearsal period, observing their progress:

"Even within the first week we could see a change in our Young People's Company, from being quiet and hiding towards the edge in the rehearsal room on day one to standing up tall, speaking out and interacting with each other and with the professionals in the room with ease. The impact has been equally noticeable on our professional cast, as they support and work directly with our young people to realise more visibly with this tale of youth."[464]

This was reflected in the thoughts of Callum Mardy, one of the young company, who had previously been part of the First

Floor scheme and was by then studying drama at Leeds City College:

"I think we all feel that in this production we are part of something really special. Amy has really made us feel that we are as important as the rest of the cast and even though we are only in rehearsals at the moment the feeling of being on stage is incredible. I have always been really interested in drama, but at high school I couldn't take part in any of the classes … I use a wheelchair and it just so happened that the drama department was on a level I couldn't access. First Floor was really important for me. It gave me a real confidence boost just when I needed it and without it I probably wouldn't be doing what I am now. For me acting is freedom and being part of *Romeo and Juliet* is the next step on the journey and I hope will show other people just what a young cast can do."[465]

Unsurprisingly this *Romeo and Juliet* attracted many young audience members, and on the first night there was spontaneous cheering and whooping enthusiasm. As the Yorkshire Post reviewer wrote, "There are good financial reasons for staging *Romeo and Juliet*. A staple on the school syllabus it guarantees decent tickets. It also generally guarantees much fidgeting and audible yawning. Not here. Whatever the faults of this production, it kept its target audience entertained and perhaps even proved to a few that Shakespeare is still relevant. Right now maybe that's enough".[466]

From the start of his 2012 appointment, James Brining evidently oversaw a burgeoning of youth engagement. Yet another youth project to be established early in his time at the helm was 'Primary Players' in 2014. This was work with school pupils aged seven to eleven who created their own versions of Shakespeare plays. Thus, considerably before the involvement in 2017 of First Floor and Youth Theatre members in *Romeo and Juliet*, young people had already appeared in Shakespeare on the stage of the Quarry Theatre. In July 2015, two hundred pupils from three Leeds schools presented their version of

Macbeth. Performed as part of the Summer Open Season, it was billed as bringing 'the tragedy of Macbeth to life as you've never seen it before'.

The following year, in the same season as the Playhouse production, Primary Players would perform Richard III – to a packed Quarry Theatre audience. Financial success aside, such attendance reflects the Playhouse's success in meeting an obvious demand for youth involvement.

ACT TWO, SCENE TWENTY-ONE

"The uniqueness of regional theatre lies in its ability to provide drama of relevance to its setting, rooting the theatre in its community"[467]

MY GENERATION by Alice Nutter
5th October 2013

JAMES BRINING PROGRAMMED *My Generation* by Alice Nutter as the opening play of the 2013-14 season in the Courtyard Theatre because he wanted the season to focus on Leeds. Alice's first play, *Foxes*, had been part of the Northern Exposure season in 2006, and her second play, *Where's Vietnam?*, Red Ladder Theatre's Fortieth Anniversary production, had visited the Playhouse in 2008. In between plays she had written for television, notably for three series produced by Jimmy McGovern: *The Street*, *Accused*, and *Moving On*.

My Generation started life as a radio play. Set in Leeds, the story spans two generations and forty years of one family, but with the backdrop of specific years and events: the Chapeltown area of the city at the times of the Yorkshire Ripper and the 1984 miners' strike; the rave culture in 1992; and finally 2013 (when the play was produced). Live music was performed throughout the show, and the reviews praised the play's ambitious structure and content, but its politics divided opinion:

"One woman on Thursday noisily walked out, muttering oaths and maybe thinking that loo in the opening scene was the best place for it – an extreme reaction – but others stood to cheer an incredibly hard-working performance."[468]

The Guardian reviewer found the writing "uneven, but when it's good it's fabulous, the soundtrack to the characters' lives is performed by a terrific band, and the performances are tough and committed, although in the rave scenes, drugged-up Ben does seem to be channelling Frankie Howerd. It's a show with heart and if the story needs twice the time to do it justice, it offers a glimpse of the way we were – and the way we are now".[469]

Alice herself was delighted that the Playhouse was committed to mounting a new play of such scale and ambition, and was happy that James "wants to find new plays that tell stories the theatre doesn't normally tell, and which speak to various different communities here in Leeds".[470] Soon after his appointment as Artistic Director, James had explained his reasons for putting both the theatre and city on the map through productions with an authentically northern voice: "It always slightly irks me that [Leeds] never seems to quite get the spotlight that in my head it deserves. Whether it's Alan Bennett, or Jeanette Winterson, or Caryl Phillips, or Simon Armitage, or Ted Hughes, there are brilliant artists from our part of the world. And I'm interested in employing the sensibility of those artists – and not just because they are northern but because they have a point of view".[471]

James Brining's focus on Leeds and the North was of course nothing new: the West Yorkshire Playhouse's commitment to northern voices and talent was part of the theatre's DNA, having been a founding principle. A strong precedent had been set by Ian Brown's first season as Artistic Director back in 2002.

A brief recap on this earlier period will serve to illustrate the extent of the Playhouse's ideological commitment to promoting northern theatre. Ian's 2002 production of *Pretending to be Me* with Tom Courtenay had followed another play about the poet, *Larkin With Women*, which had won the TMA Best New Play Award following its premiere in Scarborough three years earlier. The plays told of the three women in the poet Philip Larkin's life during his thirty years as librarian at Hull University. Ian's Northern theme had continued in 2003 with three revivals of recent plays. As well as Ayckbourn's *A Small Family Business*, there was *Four Knights in Knaresborough*, a comedy by Paul Webb, which imagines what these knights did having fled to Knaresborough Castle in 1170 after murdering Thomas a Becket. The play had premiered in London in 1999, so the Courtyard Theatre production, with a new ending, was seen as its northern homecoming.

Opening in the Quarry Theatre just two weeks later was *The Accrington Pals* by Peter Whelan, telling the story of the town's World War I voluntary army battalion of eleven hundred men (or 'pals'). Accrington was the smallest British town to form one of these. The play records how in the first twenty minutes of the Battle of the Somme in July 1916, two hundred and thirty-five of these men died and three hundred and fifty were injured. Particularly in the second act, the play focuses on the women left at home. The Playhouse production had a particular present-day relevance: the looming Iraq War. In the lead role was Greg Haiste, who at the start of his acting career had worked with Ian at the Traverse Theatre. At the Playhouse he had almost become a repertory actor, playing in *The Lady in the Van*, *Rosencrantz and Guildenstern Are Dead*, and *Hamlet* before *The Accrington Pals*. Greg grew up in Leeds, and in a Yorkshire Evening Post interview, said that acting at the Playhouse was a dream come true:

"Obviously this place opened when I was a teenager and I always had my eye on working there ... It really is a premiere league theatre, and I hope the people of Leeds don't forget that – I'm sure they won't."[472]

Ian's Northern commitment was also reflected in some of the touring productions. Hull Truck Theatre visited with another John Godber play, *Reunion*. Northern Broadsides brought a double bill: Shakespeare's *Henry V*, and *A Woman Killed with Kindness*, by Thomas Heywood, an early seventeenth century play set in Yorkshire. There were also two plays by Asian Theatre School, a company set up in 2002 in a partnership between Leeds's Red Ladder Theatre and Bradford's Theatre in the Mill. *Streets of Rage* is a piece about the Bradford riots of 2001, based on interviews with young people who were witness to these events. *Silent Cry* is about deaths in police custody, focusing on one family's campaign for justice following the death of their son.

Thus James Brining's northern programming in the subsequent decade was a demonstration of solidarity and continuity. In 2014, after *My Generation*, James scheduled a season of works by Alan Bennett, opening with *Enjoy*, which had previously been produced at the Playhouse in the Courtyard in 1999. This early (and less successful) Bennett work is set in Leeds. James's production again made good use of the Quarry Stage, with a coup de théâtre in the last minutes of the play.

The Alan Bennett season also included *Untold Stories*, a double bill of autobiographical plays based on Alan's childhood memories of Leeds. This was a regional premiere of the plays, which had opened at the National Theatre two years earlier. Alan Bennett was played by Reece Dinsdale, another return to the Playhouse since his role in *Wild Oats* twenty-four years earlier. Years later, Reece said that "being Alan Bennett was possibly the hardest thing I've ever had to do. You have to get Alan's permission to impersonate him on stage, so nothing's a done deal. You accept the part and then it's like waiting for the white smoke to appear at the Vatican".[473]

Untold Stories played in the Courtyard Theatre, but the Barber Studio was also used for the Alan Bennett season. Three of his *Talking Heads* plays for television, performed together, were a sell-out success, necessitating an extra week of performances. The final Bennett production was *Betty Blue Eyes*, a musical version of the film *A Private Function*. This was a co-production with three other theatres including the Mercury Theatre Colchester – whose artistic director, Daniel Buckroyd, directed. It was the least successful play of the season; the original West End production three years earlier had also not been a success.

Leeds as a city offers a breadth of multi-cultural and historical material which the North's creative community continues to harvest. The final production programmed by James for the Courtyard that year once again had Leeds at its heart. *Beryl* was a play about Beryl Burton, the world-champion racing cyclist from the Morley area of the city. It was written by actor Maxine Peake, who, like Alice Nutter with *My Generation*, had adapted her radio play for the stage – her stage-writing debut. The production was timed to coincide with the start of the 2014 Tour de France in Leeds. *Beryl* played to full houses, so the run was extended. James was delighted:

"Every night we see our audiences on their feet applauding not only the actors but also the astonishing achievement of an ordinary Yorkshire woman. A wife, a mother and an extraordinary cyclist. Demand for tickets has been so high, we've taken the decision to extend for a further week. It's a great end to Yorkshire's celebration of world-class cycling and fantastic that a new play is having such an impact."[474]

To date, *Beryl* has been produced in five other northern towns and cities, as well as at the Arcola Theatre in London.

ACT II

ACT TWO, TWENTY-TWO

"To avoid the sense of being 'irrelevant to many', the [theatre] sector must understand the needs of local communities, acting as a social destination, offering space and activities for both theatre audiences and other community members, without the inevitable expectation of buying seats"[475]

REFUGEE BOY by Benjamin Zephaniah, adapted by Lemn Sissay
9th March 2013

THE PLAYHOUSE HAS BEEN PARTICULARLY CONCERNED to provide for specific groups of people within the Leeds community. From its opening in 1990, the West Yorkshire Playhouse, through its Heydays programme, has offered older people arts activities on a weekly basis. In more recent years there has been provision for people living with dementia; the same applies for people with learning disabilities. The Playhouse also pioneered work with refugees, becoming the country's first Theatre of Sanctuary.

Refugee Boy concerns a fourteen year-old boy, Alem, whose parents are from Ethiopia and Eritrea. He has been brought to the UK by his father, who returns home leaving Alem behind to protect him from the war back in their country. The play charts his life in a children's home and in foster care.

When the Playhouse approached Benjamin Zephaniah about a stage adaptation, he agreed with the proviso that there be a new and local writer for the script. However, he was persuaded by Lemn Sissay to let him do it. Lemn was born in the UK but his family came from Ethiopia and Eritrea, and like Alem he grew up in children's homes and foster care. The play was directed by Gail McIntyre who had previously been responsible for the work of the Schools Company at the Playhouse.

An important aspect of this production was the programme of related events offered alongside the performances. These were organised in partnership with the Refugee Council and asylum seeker community leaders. There were events, projects and workshops for, with and about refugees and asylum seekers. One of the most successful events was a singing opportunity which resulted in the formation of a choir called Asmarina Voices ('asmarina' means 'united' in Eritrean). Open to refugee and asylum-seeking women, the members met for an hour each week. They sang at one of the performances of *Refugee Boy*, and continued to meet after the run of the play ended. Rose McCarthy, who worked for the Refugee Council and helped with the project, said – "We're so pleased to be working with the West Yorkshire Playhouse … Most of the clients we work with have really tough lives and they need a bit of fun. Singing has helped many of the women in the choir come to terms with their experiences, through the support, friendship and fun they have had. They have fantastic voices, and we were delighted they could showcase this at a performance of *Refugee Boy*." Rose reported that one of the women told her, "When we sing, I leave all my troubles behind and forget I am an asylum seeker. I felt so proud singing in the West Yorkshire Playhouse and was shocked that so many people wanted to hear us". [476]

Refugee Boy returned to the Playhouse for five performances in February 2014 prior to a tour of venues in England and Scotland. The Playhouse encouraged venues to organise additional events similar to those held in Leeds. In Glasgow the Citizens Theatre, in partnership with the Scottish Refugee Council, organised a series of free workshops in the six weeks prior to the performances, and this work was particularly welcoming of people from refugee and asylum-seeking backgrounds. The project culminated in a performance open-day of music, song, and storytelling prior to the final performance of *Refugee Boy*. And at the Waterside Centre in Sale, a photography exhibition, 'Committed to Represent', was mounted, outlining the work of the Greater Manchester Immigration Aid Unit; its director also gave a talk prior to one of the performances.

Refugee Boy was a coup that brought the Playhouse a new and unique status. The national City of Sanctuary organisation gives out awards to organisations that promoted sanctuary in their practice. The Playhouse applied for the award and thus became the first ever Theatre of Sanctuary. A pledge was made "to all refugees who come through its doors: that the theatre will address their deep concerns, in outreach work and in repertoire – and will create a place of refuge, of genuine welcome".[477]

Following the Award, the Playhouse held workshops aimed at building refugees' confidence, facilitated by Barney Bardsley who wrote an article for The Guardian describing this work:

"All performers need to use voice and body well, to get their message across. But imagine trying to speak out, when you hardly know the language; standing tall, when you may be weakened by malnourishment or mistreatment; feeling strong, when you are cut off from your own culture, not sure what tomorrow may bring. All this fragility – a sense of transience and insecurity – enters the room during refugee workshops. But so too does hope.

"Sometimes, I see young men physically bent by intimidation – maybe torture too. I hear women hardly daring to whisper, because their voices have been so suppressed. But by the end of a session, there is always transformation. It may be subtle, but change happens. And this is what we in the theatre can do. Listen. Encourage. Empower."[478]

Younger refugees were also offered the opportunity to meet up regularly at First Floor; the weekly Wednesday evening group attracted thirty to forty young people. As another opportunity for involvement, all ages could obtain complementary tickets for Playhouse productions. Overall, the aim as a Theatre of Sanctuary has been to help those seeking asylum overcome isolation and be given a sense of belonging and inclusion. The theatre also successfully promoted this practice to other theatres, such that in November 2019, the Playhouse hosted the first Theatre of Sanctuary Network Gathering, bringing together thirty-five individuals employed in theatre from across the network to promote sanctuary in their practice.

The Playhouse has also prioritised working with people who have learning disabilities. The Beautiful Octopus Club project had come to fruition in September 2002 when a club-night was held at the Wardrobe night-club, next to the theatre, attended by two hundred people. A club of the same name had been operating in London since 1995, organised by Heart n Soul, an arts organisation focused on developing the power and talents of people with learning disabilities. Heart n Soul came to Leeds for the first time to support the organisation of this event.

Crucial to Beautiful Octopus Club nights is the club crew. The role of workers, whether Heart n Soul or West Yorkshire Playhouse staff, is to support the crew in organising the event for themselves. In the first instance this was achieved through running three full-day workshops focused on the necessary skills, ranging from DJ-ing to designing and making night-club banners. A second club night took place a year later, by which time the crew of fourteen adults were meeting on a weekly basis. Members were learning all the skills necessary to run a night-club, including the very practical skills in managing the box office, the cloakroom, and so on.

By 2004 club nights were happening twice a year, and the need for a bigger venue was resolved by moving to Evolution on Kirkstall Road. Nights were always themed, and the venue decorated accordingly. The second night at Evolution, in March 2005, had the theme of 'Space', reflected in the crew's artwork displays, the video projections above the dance floor, and the costumes worn by crew members. There were performances, including one by Yorkshire Dance, as well as an Open Mic slot. That evening attracted four hundred and twenty people. In September 2006 the club-night theme was 'Over the Rainbow', linking with the Playhouse's upcoming Christmas production, and performances included one by the crew's Beautiful Octopus Band performing their own original music.

The choice of venue for the Beautiful Octopus Club was crucial. As Playhouse staff member Ruth Hanant said, "We chose to hold the event at a city centre night club to make the experience as close to a mainstream night out as possible. Beautiful Octopus Club is about breaking down preconceived ideas of learning disability and providing opportunities for adults with learning disabilities to socialise with their friends and families in a friendly and inclusive environment".[479]

A further move was necessary in 2007, this time to Leeds University Students Union. The club night there in March 2009 attracted six hundred and thirty clubbers, by which time the crew had increased to thirty members. As well as organising club nights they were now helping to develop a similar project, the Dandy Lion Club, for younger people with learning disabilities.

The Beautiful Octopus Club and the Theatre of Sanctuary work are community programmes that demonstrate another essential link in the Playhouse's DNA from its conception. A third dimension of community engagement has been 'Heydays' – a programme inaugurated when the West Yorkshire Playhouse first opened its doors. One hundred people had joined instantly, such that a waiting list had to be introduced. The programme offered a day of activities for those aged over fifty-five, including drama workshops, creative writing, discussion groups and craft activities. By 1991 membership had increased to five hundred with people travelling from all over Leeds as well as Wakefield, Bradford and beyond.

In later years, although still supported by Playhouse staff, the scheme was to be co-ordinated by a members' advisory group. The programme continued to offer a whole range of activities from photography to philosophy, music to meditation, dancing to DJ-ing. Each term would see specialist courses within these activities: for example the dancing group learning traditional Japanese dance one term, Bollywood routines the next. At the end of each term, activity groups would often perform to all members, or organise craft displays, with items for sale as a way of raising funds for future activities. Heydays was about both companionship and creativity. As one founder-member said, "Heydays has given me the chance to meet lots of different people from all walks of life. It has given me a reason to get out of the house. Heydays has given me enthusiasm for life and time to appreciate what it has to offer. At Heydays, we are constantly challenged, with new and exciting projects and activities. We have fun, help each other, learn new skills and broaden our horizons. There is a real community spirit which binds us together".[480]

After a day spent with Heydays, a Times Educational Supplement journalist reported "a definite buzz. Heydays is not, I am constantly reminded, an old folks' centre. The theatre is filled with people asserting their right to be valued and showing their value. The phrase 'people think we don't count' is often mentioned, but politely. 'Our brains are still working' is another mantra delivered with a smile. It is quickly followed by 'we have to remind people that they don't have to speak slowly to us'".[481]

Certain activities included in the Heydays programme were specifically organised to attract a wider membership. In 2010 when Mustapha Matura's play *Rum and Coca Cola* was playing in the Courtyard (a co-production with the Black British Talawa Theatre Company), Heydays members invited older people from Leeds' Caribbean community to a series of workshops. These included question and answer sessions with the director of the play, and with Talawa's Artistic Director. Another endeavour to broaden their demographic was the Arts Exchange Project in 2006. Members of five other groups, all being members of Leeds Older People's Forum, took part alongside Heydays: Amrit Day Centre, Leeds Gypsy and Travellers Exchange, Roscoe Methodist Church luncheon club, Aasra Women's Group from the Ramgahria Sikh Centre, and the Association of Blind Asians. Meeting together on a weekly basis, in turn each group led a session to share knowledge of an art form. These ranged from ceramics, foil embossing and glass painting to traditional folk dance. More than just a way of promoting Heydays, the project was about breaking down barriers and encouraging understanding of other cultures. One outcome was a recognition of what the groups had in common. Community Development Officer Nicky Taylor described how, "during the ceramics session there was an overwhelming consensus that making clay or mud models had been part of this generation's childhood, whether they grew up in Yorkshire or the Punjab!".[482] All this culminated in a celebration event in the Courtyard Theatre, where participants spoke about their experience of the project and displayed their artwork, and members of the Aasra Women's Group performed their Giddha folk dance.

Members established links with other areas of the theatre's work by forming a Playhouse Support Group which met each week to produce all kinds of props and decorations for Playhouse projects. For example they were involved in building the set for the Schools Company's production of *Whose Shoes?*; also with the SPARK project, for which they produced the story-sacks for use with four to seven year-olds. They were also directly involved with activities such as reading with children using the props and puppets included in the sacks.

On occasions, Heydays members performed in events beyond the Playhouse: for example, a Bollywood dance routine and a 'DJ Divas' performance at the International Day of the Older Person event at the Central Library. Sometimes, artwork was displayed elsewhere: for example, the 'Nutty Knitters' group created an Under the Sea display which toured the country to raise funds for the Royal National Lifeboat Institution.

Then came the turning point of the International Year of the Older Person in 1999. Members involved with that project came back with the question – why have we not formed our own theatre group? Thus the foundations were laid for the eventual Feeling Good Theatre Company. After four weeks of improvisation sessions, a first play evolved, and Leeds's Unlimited Theatre Company helped the group to attract funding to produce it. As Feeling Good member Jean Eckersley recounted, "There was a production at the end of it at the Leeds Metropolitan University Theatre and it was sold out. We had got the bug. We told them that we didn't want to disband. We wanted to form our own company".[483]

Like Heydays itself, the company was concerned to challenge stereotypical ideas of older people, instead presenting real and positive images. They mainly performed to community groups, nationally as well as in Leeds, and occasionally in schools, at festivals, at conferences. *Distraction Burglaries* for example, a forty-five-minute play which aimed to raise awareness of doorstep crime, was performed to Social Services groups not only in Leeds but in Manchester, Liverpool, Wakefield and Kings Lynn. That too was an improvised show, of sketches and songs, based on real cases of distraction burglary. Following the tour of northern venues, the company was invited to perform their play at a Trading Standards conference in London. In turn, this led to the making of a training video, with the help of Yorkshire Television, which encouraged other companies to perform the play.

Five years after the company was formed they decided to employ a professional theatre director to help with a 'bigger and better' play, *Whatever Next?* It was bigger in the sense that the play needed to be performed on a stage rather than on the floor of a community building. Exploring the themes of age, life and love, it was structured around a group of people embarking on a course about 'Agedology' which turns out to be a voyage of self-discovery. Lasting ninety minutes, it again involved dance and music, including rap. *Whatever Next?* was given two performances on a Saturday in July 2004, playing to a full house at each performance, even at five pounds per ticket.

In 2010 it was recognised that some members of the Heydays community programme were starting to show signs of dementia and were less comfortable taking part in the regular weekly activities. Hence specific ones were introduced, designed for people with that diagnosis. Weekly activities included reminiscence work, song-writing and other creative programmes. Nicky Taylor, the theatre's Community Development Officer at the Playhouse, introduced this work. As she explained, "people can use their past experiences, opinions and imaginations even when they're experiencing some of the challenges associated with living with dementia. We create unique, joyful experiences using arts activities that are inspiring and stimulating. It's all about celebrating people's skills and experience. By concentrating on the incredibly creative, positive contribution people living with dementia can make, we write poetry and songs, create beautiful artwork or use props and costumes to fire people's imaginations".[484]

This work was carried out in collaboration with Leeds City Council's Peer Support Team and Leeds Libraries, Museums and Galleries. Nicky also recognised that people living with dementia might need support in order to attend performances at the theatre. So, staff training was introduced to help in making the Playhouse a dementia-friendly organisation. A bigger step was taken in December 2014, when the theatre held its first specifically adapted and dementia-friendly performance, which was also a UK first. The production was Irving Berlin's *White Christmas*. Advance preparation included organising singing sessions for community groups so that people were familiar with the songs in the show. At the theatre a more relaxed environment was created through, for example, not dimming the lighting in the auditorium as much as usual. The production was also adapted: lessening the sound cues; removing strobe lighting sequences; avoiding full blackouts on stage. A quiet room was organised for anyone feeling uncomfortable in the auditorium, but the fact that nobody used this facility suggests that the 'friendly' approach worked well.

In all, over four hundred people attended the performance: people living with dementia, their carers, their family and friends. This included more than sixty members of the Tea Cosy Memory Café in the Rothwell area of Leeds, one of the organisations with which the Playhouse liaised in preparation for the performance.

The logistics of getting many frail people and wheelchair users to their seats was a challenge. But, as James Brining commented, "Many people I spoke to haven't been to the theatre, or out at all, for years; it took the level of support we put in place to achieve this. We 'made' Christmas for a lot of vulnerable people and their families".[485] And one of the attendees said afterwards, "It were a great pleasure, and I've not been to anything as nice and as outstanding as the whole issue was. It's been a real pleasure for me to be here today. It'll remind me for a long time about how nice a day it was. And the people who I've met all day have been beautiful, really nice people".[486]

The West Yorkshire Playhouse continued to innovate in this sphere of community engagement. In early 2015 a new project was set up with funding from the Paul Hamlyn Foundation called 'Our Time', involving poetry and drama sessions for people living with dementia. Where appropriate, those taking part did so alongside their partners. Further dementia-friendly performances were organised: *Beryl* in 2015, and the Christmas productions of *Chitty Chitty Bang Bang* and *Strictly Ballroom* in 2016 and 2017 respectively.

Meanwhile, the Playhouse shared their practical experiences with two other theatres – in Leicester and in Derry/Londonderry. Both theatres organised their own dementia-friendly performances: *Oliver!* and *Aladdin* respectively. The choice of musicals was intentional because they prompted people's reminiscences about previous theatre productions or films, as well as the songs themselves. In Leeds, *Beryl*, about the world-champion race cyclist from the Morley area of Leeds, was an exception: this was chosen because of all the references to people and places in Leeds, and because the play might stir people's happy memories of cycling in the city and beyond.

In view of the Playhouse's pioneering work, the theatre was approached by The Baring Foundation to produce a Guide to Dementia Friendly Performances, which was published in May 2016. Written by Nicky Taylor, in her introduction she enthusiastically promotes the idea of dementia-friendly performances:

"Many people with dementia have spent a lifetime attending theatre, concerts and music halls. A diagnosis of dementia can reduce confidence and increase isolation, leaving people with dementia and their supporters less likely to attempt such trips. As life becomes more mundane, these stimulating, meaningful activities assume greater importance, and present significantly increased potential for enriching lives.

"Our aspiration is to increase opportunities for people with dementia to access life-enhancing shows, reconnecting them to their local cultural venues and their communities. We hope theatres across the UK and beyond will find this practical guide an inspiration in advocating for and staging dementia friendly performances."[487]

It is indeed a very practical booklet, full of good ideas about selecting and adapting a show, preparing audiences, preparing the theatre on the day, and publicising the event. For instance, the booklet suggests providing song sheets for the show itself and encouraging people to sing along with the performers. This in itself is an example of how a dementia-friendly performance differs: such singing would not be allowed at regular performances.

The Playhouse went on to crown this impressive innovatory work when it achieved, in early 2018, another first: 'Every Third Minute' – a Festival of Theatre and Dementia, so-called because this is how often someone in the UK will begin living with dementia. Again with the support of The Baring Foundation, the festival was organised alongside the Courtyard Theatre production of *Still Alice*, based on the novel by Lisa Genova about a female university professor who is diagnosed with early-onset Alzheimer's disease. The play shows the changing relationship with her husband and her grown-up children. The Festival of Theatre was programmed by people living with dementia and their supporters. As well as workshops, discussion and music sessions, it included several short new plays – three of these commissioned by the Playhouse and co-written by people living with dementia and professional writers. The programme was both for people living with dementia and for anyone wanting to find out more about the subject. There was also a symposium for practitioners across the country. Events were not only held at the theatre but out in care homes all around Leeds.

The Every Third Minute festival was another significant community outreach initiative that had developed on James Brining's watch. The West Yorkshire Playhouse's staff have demonstrably been consistently committed to achieving this kind of outreach. Such possibilities for theatre to reach into society can only arise if its employees hold dear to the principle of theatre for all. An expression of this idealism rings out in Nicky Taylor's description of how "the idea for the festival came from the frustration that there were certain stories being told about dementia, but not necessarily a well-rounded story. We were hearing a lot about decline and loss. But that wasn't necessarily representative of the stories I was seeing and hearing on a daily basis here at the Playhouse, where people were being creative, they were finding friendship and laughter and fun [and] taking new adventures in the face of a really challenging condition. It's been an incredible experience of learning and has proved again and again how capable people are, how resilient they are. For us to learn from that can teach us a lot about our theatre practices. And also make sure we are a welcoming and supportive as we possibly can be".[488]

As for James Brining himself, the festival represented "a kind of summary, if you like, or a distillation of the many different bits of practice that we have been exploring and developing here".

ACT TWO, SCENE TWENTY-THREE

Some regional theatres mount productions of plays primarily intended to tour local community venues, such as social clubs and community centres. This can be a great introduction to the theatre's work. Audiences will likely be of people who are more familiar with the venue than with the theatre – where they may never have been to a performance.

TALKING HEADS by Alan Bennett
23rd June 2014 and 14th June 2018

'COMMUNITY TOURS' BECAME AN ARM REACHING OUT from the Playhouse once James Brining was at the helm. The catalyst, in the summer of 2014, was the production of three of Alan Bennett's *Talking Heads* monologues. It was decided to tour this production to venues within Leeds, visiting seven wards which were identified as 'hard to reach': Armley, Hawksworth Wood, Burmantofts, Gipton, Rothwell, Seacroft and Middleton. In each ward, the Playhouse recruited Community Ambassadors. These were motivated local people, who agreed to publicise the production, and afterwards continue to work in partnership with the Playhouse to promote the work both at the theatre and in their community.

Prior to *Talking Heads*, tours of West Yorkshire Playhouse productions had only been those of the Theatre In Education and Schools Company. There was one exception: in 2010 a production of Simon Stephen's *Country Music* played for just four performances in the Courtyard Theatre. After these performances the production toured to prisons around Yorkshire. The idea for this project came from Lisa Blair and Eleanor While, who directed the play. They were two further students on secondment to the Playhouse as part of their Masters degree course in Theatre Directing at Birkbeck, University of London. The play was originally produced at the Royal Court Theatre in London in 2004, following Simon's work running playwriting workshops in Grendon and Wandsworth prisons. The play tells the story of Jamie, a violent offender in prison for murder, but looks more at his younger life and his life after prison.

The success of the *Talking Heads* community tour resulted in another play, more specifically a touring production, the following year. This was *Little Sure Shot*, a new play with music, promoted as a family show. It told the story of Annie Oakley, the American sharpshooter who starred in Buffalo Bill's Wild

West Show. The production played for just four days in the Courtyard Theatre, and before and afterwards at the seven venues where *Talking Heads* had been performed. A further priority area was also identified, Chapeltown, and *Little Sure Shot* also played at the West Indian Centre in that ward. The cast of five featured three of the Playhouse Graduate Actors; Verity Kirk played Annie.

By 2016 the community tour had become an annual event, and a production of *Kes* toured that year. This time the production played for two weeks in the Courtyard Theatre before beginning the tour. Like *Little Sure Shot*, it was directed by Amy Leach, her first productions for the Playhouse. *Kes*, of course, was originally a Ken Loach film adaptation of the book *A Kestrel for a Knave*, by South Yorkshire-born Barry Hines. The production was a two-hander: Dan Parr played Billy and Jack Lord played all the other parts – from Billy's mother and brother through to his teachers and football coach. In a departure from the book and the film, Jack also played Billy's older self, effectively the narrator of the play. When *Kes* was on tour, the production was accompanied by a short piece devised and performed by young people from the First Floor project.

In the same year as *Kes*, the Playhouse co-produced, with Red Ladder Theatre, a played called *The Damned United*. Like *Kes*, this had previously been a book and a film. Adapted by Anders Lustgarten, it tells the story of Brian Clough's forty-four days as manager of Leeds United, contrasting this with his previous six years with Derby County. In 2016, the play was a huge success, attracting those who were not usually theatregoers. The production featured in The Guardian readers' favourite stage shows for that year. As Helen Cadbury wrote, "I took my son, who understood the football, while I marvelled at the storytelling and the movement of the performers. By the end, I was hooked by the football story and he was hooked by the drama".[489]

It was therefore decided to revive *The Damned United*, both at the Playhouse and for the 2018 community tour. At the time, James Brining said:

"When we talked about *The Damned United* coming back to Leeds for another run I knew we should take it out as our community tour. It's important to us that the work we make reflects and engages with our city and *The Damned United* is a story that really means something to people in Leeds. Clough is both a villain and hero, and to this day, the mention of his name still stirs up powerful feelings in local football fans. It's a story wrapped up in people's experiences of growing up in the city so to bring this popular title to audiences in our theatre – and then out on tour to our local area – is a fantastic thing."[490]

The 2016 production had a cast of five actors, but also eleven young people who formed an ensemble of masked footballers and press reporters. For the community tour, the production was 'stripped back and freshly imagined', with a cast of three actors. After playing for two weeks in the Courtyard the production toured to nine venues, including West Leeds Sports and Social Club and Hunslet Rugby League Football Club. As one critic said:

"Perhaps one of the best elements of this highly successful show at the West Yorkshire Playhouse is the fact that *The Damned United* is a local story, provoking a local attendance and response by people who are not necessarily theatregoers. At one point the depiction of United's infamous dirty tricks provoked an angry heckle from a man in front of me; apparently when the show is staged in local working men's clubs audience reaction and commentary is very much a part of the evening. But their enjoyment is beyond doubt, their engagement adding a powerful extra dynamic to this show. All in all the evening can be summed up by one word said by someone sitting just behind me: 'Quality'."[491]

Before the Playhouse closed for redevelopment in the summer of 2018, there was another revival: *Talking Heads*. This time, three more of Alan Bennett's monologues were added, playing on alternative dates in the Courtyard Theatre. The monologues were also performed in people's homes, 'Talking Heads in Your Living Room'. The householders chosen, through an online ballot, were able to invite their family and friends to the performance. There were performances throughout Leeds, from a flat in Seacroft to a living room in Boston Spa. The tour seemed appropriate because these would be the sorts of homes in which Alan Bennett set the plays, but it was also seen as a celebration of the Playhouse's relationship with communities and organisations across the city.

Interviewed in advance of the tour, Amy Leach, who directed two of the monologues, explained:

"As one of the country's best loved playwrights, and a famous son of Leeds, it's an honour to be staging this ambitious project based around six of Bennett's iconic monologues with a team of brilliant actors and creatives. His monologues celebrate the minutiae of the lives of people living in this city and feel a fitting tribute to close this chapter in the life of our Courtyard Theatre. As an organisation deeply rooted in our local community, I'm also so excited to share them city-wide when they tour to homes and living rooms across all twenty-nine postcodes of Leeds".[492]

Act III

Scenario

WHEN THEATRE CRITICS AND OTHER JOURNALISTS attend on the opening day of the West Yorkshire Playhouse in 1990, they inevitably end up reviewing the building itself as much as the production of *Wild Oats*. Of course, they welcome the very existence of a brand-new theatre: for example, Michael Billington, in the Guardian, concludes, "As Diana Rigg said, 'A new theatre is a miracle' and the rest of the country can only look on at Leeds in envy".[493]

About the exterior of the building the critics are less kind, many suggesting that it looks like a supermarket. Some nevertheless acknowledge the intent of the architects: "Built in neo-industrial style, in banded brick of red, buff and blue, its look echoes Yorkshire's great historical heritage".[494] The fiercest comments are made by the architecture critic Kenneth Powell who writes in the Weekend Telegraph, "As a piece of public architecture it is, frankly, a failure and is already being compared locally to an overgrown supermarket ... Ironically the Quarry Hill area, in which it stands, is now being developed as an 'office city'. The Playhouse ought to be the focal point – a role, alas, of which it is quite unworthy".[495]

In this article and another for Country Life magazine he partly blames Leeds City Council; specifically their inability to provide guidance on the other developments intended for Quarry Hill, and he criticises their insistence that new commercial buildings should "reflect the so-called 'Leeds look' – basically, a derivative Post-Modernist style using red brick and slate roofs".[496]

Only one critic, Jim Hiley, comments on access to the building, possibly because all the others arrived by taxi at the main entrance. This critic, however, arrived on foot from the city centre, and records that "to reach it, you cross an alarmingly busy road and a knackering succession of steps".[497]

What of the interior? Critics are kinder in their assessment of the public spaces and the two auditoria. They inevitably compare the design of the Quarry Theatre to the National Theatre's Olivier space, but acknowledge that the Quarry is based on the design of the original Leeds Playhouse – which preceded the National Theatre by six years. They also compare the Courtyard Theatre to the National's Cottesloe (now Dorfman) Theatre, and again acknowledge that both owe something to the Georgian Theatre Royal in Richmond, Yorkshire. Several praise the thinking behind the Courtyard Theatre: a smaller space but equal in importance and status to the Quarry Theatre. Claire Armitstead, in the Financial Times, sees this concept as "bravely reversing the current exigency of consigning the new, worthy or difficult to studio spaces which are as likely to dwarf the imagination as the budget",[498] while Michael concludes, "Leeds has gained a superlative playhouse that is friendly, spacious and free of the antiseptic coldness of much modern civic architecture".[499]

Billington's description of the Playhouse as "spacious" must be pleasing to the architects: this is the feeling that they were hoping to create in the public areas of the building. If it has been successfully achieved, one reason is the open-plan nature of these areas. On entering the building, immediately within sight are the box office and shop, the entrances to the two auditoriums, the coffee shop and the bar-restaurant area. Another reason is the amount of daylight in these areas, especially in the bar-restaurant where daylight enters through the roof as well as the windows. Additionally this space is intentionally spacious enough for it to be a third performance space, with a raised stage area. The relationship of this area to the two auditoria is made clear with the inscription on the frieze surrounding the space: Hamlet's instruction to the Players 'to hold, as 'twere, the mirror up to nature'.

David Nobbs, whose play *Second From Last in the Sack Race* opens in the first year of the West Yorkshire Playhouse, comments that "the whole building has a lovely feel about it. Externally you can have divided views, but inside it's a triumph as a working theatre … I love the fact that the Playhouse is dedicated to the belief that the theatre is not elitist".[500] This is what Jude Kelly has been wanting, and she argues that the external appearance of the building is a part of making the building welcoming to all: "They feel comfortable with it, and so they come in … The audience has a sense of freedom in the foyer spaces outside the auditoria".[501] She also sees meaning in the absence of a functioning stage door: actors enter and leave through the front door with the audience, and use the public spaces alongside them:

"There is no sense that the artist closets himself or herself in the auditorium … I'm not saying that every member of the audience has to rub shoulders with every artist, but there has got to be some sense of a meeting place … When you come out into the foyer spaces, you must be allowed to exchange and debate. The attractiveness of other spaces in the theatre is not about how to make money at the coffee bar, it is about how to get that sense of community."[502]

After all the excitement of the opening period there is one immediate problem, which relates to the auditorium of the Quarry Theatre. It was hinted at by Jim Hiley when he said, "After the exhausting ascent to the main entrance, you must now abseil to your seat".[503]

Back at the Leeds Playhouse the audience had entered from the centre, whereas at the West Yorkshire Playhouse the audience enters from the back, through a wrap-around sound lobby to a series of doors leading to six gangways. The intention is to create a way in which latecomers may be accommodated without disrupting the performance. However, it means that all audience members have to contend with aisles down the steep rake, potentially a cause of vertigo and other hazards. The design of the auditorium does allow for wheelchair access, via a lift, from the centre, but only with the help of theatre staff. The aisles are at least broken up, because the seating is divided into Y-shaped bi-sections, but handrails are only possible on the side walls. Concern about falling results in audience members being told to ask for assistance and use the wheelchair access points if necessary, but obviously this is not a long-term solution. For everyone, using the toilets during the interval means ascending the steep rake, only to descend more stairs to reach these facilities.

And there is a further issue (though a debatable one amongst architects) regarding the Quarry's steep rake. Iain Mackintosh, a theatre design director, believes that, concerning the relationship between actor and audience, actors feel more in control when the audience looks up to them. Conversely, when the audience looks down on them they can feel that they are acting at the bottom of a well. His reservation about the Quarry is, the seating being "too steeply raked" thus creating "a centre of audience gravity too far above the actor's head" which he sees as "a major fault in too many modern theatres. This inevitably makes it more difficult for the actor to move an audience to tears or laughter".[504]

Because of the stage in the Quarry being at the same level as the front row of seating, only the first three rows look up at the actors, meaning six hundred of the seven hundred and fifty audience members are looking down. Aware that the Olivier stage at the National Theatre was raised after the first five years, he observes, "It will be interesting to see whether raised stage platforms become the norm at the Quarry, or whether a permanent increase in stage height is introduced as it was at the Olivier".[505]

As well as these issues in respect of the theatre's interior, concern continues in respect of other developments on Quarry Hill. In 1990 as the Playhouse opens, the undeveloped land on Quarry Hill is a popular area for shoppers' parking. The hope has been that this will lead to passing trade and an awareness of the Playhouse's location and provision, but it is realised that other developments on Quarry Hill are going to make this less likely. At the end of 1992, Governors are presented with a report which details concerns about public awareness of the Playhouse's existence. A survey conducted in the market area opposite the theatre has revealed that only fifty-four percent of those questioned know where the Playhouse is. Of those who answered 'no' or 'not sure', the building was identified to them and their answers revealed that they thought it was either offices, part of the Department of Social Security, or a shopping centre. This issue is raised by the Arts Council in March 1992:

"The building benefits from a more prominent position than the previous one, but is let down by weak exterior signing. Theatres need bold signs and exterior displays to make them more attractive to non-theatregoers ..."[506]

The report does propose new signage, including an outdoor LED panel at street level on St. Peters Street. However, arguably more significantly, it raises concerns about the location itself:

"The Playhouse is not located in a city central position; it has not become a primary venue to visit in the eyes of the day to day city dweller or suburban visitor. It does not fall in the regular travels of the daily shopper or business man. Therefore, without specifically intending to visit the Playhouse, it is not a natural place to meet, unlike many of the city centre shopping malls. Consequently, it is not readily identifiable in people's minds."[507]

These concerns increase because of the continuing uncertainty about the future of Quarry Hill, and are exacerbated when St. Peter's Street becomes part of the inner ring road. The MAB proposal, which included a multi-storey car park, has not materialised, but work has begun on the construction of Quarry House, the Department of Social Security building (now the Department of Work and Pensions) which opens in 1993 (and is nicknamed 'the Kremlin'!) causing problems with vehicular access. The building works have effectively rendered non-existent the access loop road (which has always been confusing to access) outside the theatre. Consequently there is no facility for coach drop-off, and disabled access has become a problem.

In July 1994 the Governors are presented with another report which warns that the theatre "will become a remote island and inaccessible to the city centre with devastating consequences on the Playhouse's role in the City as well as financial income".[508] The theatre management proposed an underpass below St. Peter's Street, but only improved pedestrian crossings were seeming likely.

Besides these concerns about access, longer-term problems regarding the interior are now becoming apparent, partly due to the reworking of the Appletons' original design, described by some as 'value engineering' and others as 'cost-cutting'. One problem is the lack of office space for the ever-increasing staff team. Another is insufficient rehearsal space, meaning that the Playhouse has to rent rooms elsewhere in Leeds. A third is the lack of storage space for scenery, costumes and so on. The latter problem is initially resolved by using the St. Peter's Square building, bought by the Playhouse prior to 1990. However, since this is not the best use of this building, other possibilities are now explored. One is a space underneath the theatre, which starts to be referred to as the Rock Void – possible only if rock gets removed!

There is also no shortage of ideas as to how the St. Peter's building can be better used. Apart from the obvious conversion for office and rehearsal space, there is even talk of creating a third auditorium. All this speculation results in a National Lottery application, in August 1996, for £20,000 to fund a feasibility study "to identify possible remedies for the shortcomings of our existing building and to examine possible ways of expanding our cultural remit". A grant is awarded, and consequently several possibilities are considered, all dependent on clearing the St. Peter's building and/or some new building. A mezzanine level above the staff car park is considered, as is a stand-alone rehearsal building. In terms of expanding the work of the Playhouse, there is talk of a larger recording studio; a new writing laboratory; facilities for developing partnerships with other arts organisations in the region, and for professional theatre training; even a space for use by national and international arts practitioners. There is also talk of converting part of the St. Peter's building into flats and apartments for use by actors, performers and production staff; another idea is to create a café-bar and Jazz Club on the ground floor.

So in 1998, Ian Appleton returns to the Playhouse to carry out the feasibility study. Unfortunately, the completion of his report coincides with the Arts Council award from the Stabilisation Unit, and the need to eliminate the trading deficit. When the results are finally presented to the Finance and General Purposes Committee in late 1998, considerable reservations are expressed. Many of the new building developments and adaptations would necessitate a substantial bank loan, the granting of which is felt unlikely, given the existing cumulative deficit. New rehearsal space and flats/apartments are costed on full usage, which would depend on external hire by other organisations, making these ideas somewhat risky. New developments are also dependent on further Lottery funding, and at this time the Arts Council has 'frozen' such funding whilst conditions for grants are being reconsidered.

Hence it is decided just to improve the existing facilities. This includes equipment, in some cases brought from the Leeds Playhouse which will soon need replacing, given that higher production standards need new technologies. There is also talk of letting out or even selling the St. Peter's building. One change that does happen is the lease of the ground floor and basement, which open in 1999 as The Wardrobe café-bar, restaurant, and live events venue.

With the Playhouse's tenth anniversary approaching, it is recognised that the foyer and restaurant areas are looking tired and in need of refurbishment. This takes place in the summer of 2001, and the box office is also extended. The latter means closure of the shop – but it has been making a loss anyway. In the same year, the Playhouse takes another step in resolving the ever-present problem of storage by purchasing the nearby St. Patrick's Church, presbytery and social club. The church is kept for storage, but the other parts are sold – in the case of the social club to the Leeds community organisation East Street Arts.

With the sale of part of the staff car-park in 2008, parking once again becomes a problem. Alongside this sale has been a commitment to providing a multi-storey car park, to include provision for disabled parking. By 2009, the plan has been put on hold for five years, and like so many of the proposed developments on Quarry Hill, it never happens.

Upon the celebration of its twenty-first birthday in 2011, the West Yorkshire Playhouse looks back on what has been achieved over those years while taking a long look at the future. It recognises that in the coming decade the theatre will need to plan for refurbishment and redevelopment. Planning thus begins in 2013, and four main aims are identified which will resolve the problems with the building that have become apparent over the years.

First is the intention to 'turn the theatre round' to face the city centre. This is now considered particularly appropriate, given the developments on the opposite side of St. Peter's Street (the Victoria Gate development will open in 2016). Secondly, it is recognised that improved access is needed within the building, especially in respect of the Quarry Theatre. More generally, movement around the building needs to be improved, in particular in respect of disabled access. Third is the need, identified by all the Artistic Directors, for a studio-sized auditorium. The Birmingham Repertory Theatre and the Crucible Sheffield have studio theatres seating up to one hundred and thirty and two hundred people respectively. Realistically, plays such as those which form part of the Northern Exposure festivals are simply-staged productions, and never need the potential of the Courtyard. They are never going to fill the three hundred and fifty-seat capacity. It is for this reason that other spaces, particularly the Barber Studio, are used for performances. Fourthly, it is recognised that developments are needed to improve the resilience of the theatre. This is seen as both an environmental and economic need. Concerning the latter, it is intended that the redevelopment will lead to generating more income from daytime use of the new café and bar, as well as from the restaurant.

An initial application to the Arts Council for capital funding gets rejected, primarily because of concerns over the City Council's commitment to the project. However, when the Council agrees, as owner of the building, to act as lead in the management and delivery of the redevelopment, early in 2016 an Arts Council grant of £300,000 is made towards the cost of producing a Development Plan. The Council is then invited to make a further application for capital funding within eighteen months. In this period, certain changes are made to the original proposal. Most significant is a rethink about turning the theatre to face the city centre. As is reported to the Council's Executive Board, "the proposal contained in the feasibility study to re-orientate the building to face the city centre and for the theatre building to effectively turn its back onto Quarry Hill is not necessarily the best way forward. This is particularly in light of other proposed developments on the Quarry Hill site. The design proposals now seek to create a much more porous, permeable and accessible building for all".[509]

A new eye-catching entrance facing St. Peter's Street still gets proposed, but so does a mid-level entrance from the area which will become known as Playhouse Square. The existing main entrance is also to remain. Glasgow-based architectural practice Page / Park is selected as the design team to produce a Development Plan. They have previously worked on similar projects in Glasgow and Inverness. Their plan is developed during 2016 and in the first months of 2017.

In order to improve access, crucial to their design is a new route through the theatre at mid-level. This route is to be easily accessible through all entrances (from the new St. Peter's Street entrance, accessible by a large seventeen-person lift). From this level there will be access to the Quarry Theatre, and to new wheelchair spaces in the auditorium. Consequently, the original need for all audience members to enter the auditorium from the top will be eliminated: entry, as in the first Leeds Playhouse, is to mainly be at the sides, half-way up the rake. A reconfiguration of the seating will allow for an increase to eight hundred and fifty seats.

The Development Plan also includes changes to the Courtyard Theatre. Access is created directly at the mid-level; changes to the stalls area and a shallower rake allow an increase in capacity of more than fifty seats. As with the increase in the Quarry Theatre, this is also seen as economic resilience: increasing revenue and allowing for a wider range of touring productions.

In the summer of 2017, the City Council agrees to capital funding. By the end of the year, an Arts Council grant of £6.3 million is given, and planning permission is agreed. A contractor, BAM, is appointed to work with Page / Park on the detailed design. This, as happened when the West Yorkshire Playhouse was originally built, necessitates cost-cutting – 'value-engineering' – again. Mostly, this is work which can be carried out at a later stage when funds allow, including improvements to the Quarry Theatre lighting and replacing the existing roof of the building. Nevertheless, the final estimated cost exceeds the budget, so further funding from the City Council and from Playhouse funds is necessary. Ultimately the redevelopment of the Playhouse costs £16.5 million. Half of this amount is contributed by the Arts Council, and £5.1 million by Leeds City Council. The balance is met from Playhouse funds: fund-raising includes a £1 million grant from the Bramall Foundation, and £1.75 million from other organisations and trusts.

In July 2018 work begins on the redevelopment when the building is handed over to BAM. There is a slight hold-up in September when human remains are unearthed, thought to originate from a former burial ground. Nevertheless the work is completed in time for the Playhouse to reopen in October 2019. An Open Weekend is organised to encourage people back to the building.

For the general public the most obvious change is the new entrance facing St. Peter's Street. Gone are the loading bay and the staff car park. Instead there is a tall façade topped with the letters PLAYHOUSE, perhaps a tribute to the first Leeds Playhouse where the same word appeared at the top of the building. The new façade incorporates four panels of brightly-coloured ceramic tiles. Given the possible interpretations of the design – some people have seen the W and Y of West Yorkshire in it – it is best to refer to the explanation by the architects Page / Park:

"The use of ceramics externally roots the façade in the strong local tradition of ceramic and faience seen around Leeds. In our research on the historical context of the site we learnt about Burmantofts Pottery, with their colourful ceramics made locally but exported globally, and we discovered an appropriate synergy with Playhouse productions that are very frequently 'local' in content yet focus on universal themes that allow them to be toured nationally and internationally.

"Ceramic enabled us to exploit the plasticity of the material to create a three-dimensional façade that alters with the light conditions, with the trapezoidal form linking back to the geometries of the original building. As professional story tellers, Leeds Playhouse pushed us to develop a strong narrative behind the pattern of these panels and the idea emerged of the actor standing on the stage being represented into the patterning on each of the four panels, with each panel depicting one of the four main spaces (Quarry, Courtyard, Bramall Rock Void and Barber Studio). The black tiles represent the actor in the foot lights looking out at their audience, with the fading of the colours into darkness. Each panel is lit from the bottom (representing the stage foot lights) with the light fading out as you eye rises up the panels."[510]

The remainder of the façade consists of glass panels which reveal the four levels at this end of the building. Those who use this entrance to the Playhouse do so through a new café area; entrance to the rest of the building is via two staircases or a lift. Meanwhile the new mid-level entrance is reached from St. Peter's Street by steps through an attractive landscaped area. Entry is through the new bar area, leading on the same level to the relocated box office. Externally the Playhouse Square shares this space with the entrance to the Quarry Hill campus of Leeds City College, which also opens in September 2019.

For theatregoers the other most obvious change is the creation of a new auditorium, the Bramall Rock Void – named in recognition of the Liz and Terry Bramall Foundation's financial contribution. This is a very flexible space, utilizing the void underneath the previous theatre box office, with seating for up to one hundred and twenty people. It is to remain a 'found' space:

"...a cavernous series of spaces with unpainted brick walls and a sandy floor. Although it was always thought necessary to add acoustic panelling to some of the wall and ceiling surfaces, and to provide a flat floor for seating and staging, it was noted that it would nonetheless be desirable to preserve as much of the 'found' character of the space as possible, not least in the interests of creating an experience very different from the theatre's more formal auditoria."[511]

Of course, the other big change is the name of the theatre. The intended reversion to the Playhouse's old name is announced as the theatre closes for redevelopment. Interviewed by The Guardian at this time, James Brining explains that the name change is partly for practical reasons: "West Yorkshire Playhouse" often leads to the question "...but where are you?". But for James the chief issue is to name, promote and celebrate the city of Leeds:

"Leeds has brilliant cultural assets, but punches below its weight. The city is the home of major arts organisations including Opera North, Northern Ballet, Phoenix Dance Theatre and Red Ladder Theatre – none of which use the word Leeds. Leeds is the heart of Yorkshire, it is the biggest city in Yorkshire. We want to celebrate and promote Leeds around the world."[512]

ACT III

ACT THREE SCENE ONE

"Brining has installed in this [pop-up] theatre a repertory company. Outside of Scarborough's Stephen Joseph Theatre and a couple of theatres around the country, this once ubiquitous model of creating work has died out. 'I think it's great for the audiences, the actors, the productions. Audiences get to know the actors and get to see them playing in really different roles and different shows'."[513]

ROAD by Jim Cartwright
5ᵗʰ September 2018

THE REDEVELOPMENT OF THE PLAYHOUSE starting in the summer of 2018 meant closing the Quarry and the Courtyard Theatres for a year. However, a decision was made to create a temporary auditorium, the Pop-Up Theatre. This was located in one of the building's workshop spaces, with an entrance on the St. Peter's Square side of the building at street level. James Brining said at the time:

"While the main theatre building is being developed we have created a really special theatre in an entirely unique part of the building. We've had to knock down a wall and make a hole in an exterior wall to create a fire escape, but we think it's worth it."[514]

He hoped that the programme would encourage audiences to stay in the theatre-going habit.

A bar and a small seating area were created but there was no room for toilets: temporary ones had to be installed outside the building. With limited heating, it was very much a venue to attend for the play, rather than to socialise before or after the performance. In the auditorium the stage was a long thin strip with little backstage space. Seating for three hundred and fifty people was in long rows, but also with side-facing views at either end.

The stage was particularly suited to the first production, *Road* by Jim Cartwright, since the set represented a row of terraced houses, on two levels. The 'found space' nature of the auditorium was also appropriate given the run-down reality of the setting. As one reviewer commented, "Hayley Grindle's superb set design, which recreates a dilapidated terraced street, provides a generously sized space for the actors to play in. Moreover, the temporary nature of the Pop-Up Theatre enhances the rough and ready aesthetic of the production".[515]

Road was first produced in 1986 at London's Royal Court Theatre and was very much seen as a state-of-the-nation political play. A revival in Leeds was most appropriate given the northern setting of the play, and arguably its continuing relevance in terms of the consequences of poverty for many communities. One reviewer alluded to this, likening the Pop-Up Theatre's first play to the very first one at the Leeds Playhouse almost fifty years previously:

"The choice of Jim Cartwright's *Road* as the first play under the new/old name is inspired. For a start, the original Leeds Playhouse was famed for the brilliant agit-prop of Bill Hays who would have revelled in the energy and passionate political indignation of Cartwright's play, originally staged in the Thatcherite years, but sadly still appropriate today". [516]

The Pop-Up Theatre season had something else in common with the early years of the first Leeds Playhouse: it involved a company of actors – mostly from the north of England – employed for the whole season. Of the cast of nine in *Road*, six of them performed in four more plays, taking on highly contrasting parts. Some already had strong connections with the Playhouse: Tessa Parr and Dan Parr, for example, played the lead roles in the 2017 *Romeo and Juliet*. Like *Road*, that production was directed by Amy Leach, who went on to direct three more productions in the Pop-Up season.

The season was also innovative in introducing a live audio description, making the production more meaningful to visually impaired audience members. In *Road*, there was a red phone box on stage from which cast members, when not involved in the action would – whilst still in character – describe what was happening onstage.

As to the run of plays selected for this pop-up space: *Road* is a dark and bleak play, which some audience members would have found shocking. It was followed by a revival of another new play, this time from 1994: *Europe* by David Greig, written as a response to the civil war in the Balkans, but set near an unnamed border, probably in eastern Europe. Specifically it is set at a railway station where the trains no longer stop, but where two refugees arrive. Essentially the play focuses on the human effects of economic collapse, so this was another political play which, like *Road*, could be seen as topical and relevant twenty-five years after its first production, with the Guardian concluding it was "grimly compelling".[517] Directed by James Brining, another reviewer contrasted it with James' previous work:

"As a choice for the current political moment—and for the Leeds Playhouse's temporary space—this is fascinating; coming after outward-looking, celebratory works with which James Brining and co closed the Quarry, this feels grittier, more probing and urgent: more drizzle on the Danube than *Sunshine on Leith*."[518]

This reviewer also commented on the suitability of the Pop-Up Theatre's stage dimensions for the stretch of railway line where the play is set, as did another reviewer:

"The edgy nature of this play makes it perfect for the rebranded Leeds Playhouse's Pop-up Space; the bricks, concrete and girders of the temporary theatre seamlessly blending into the shabby doors and rusty tracks of Amanda Stoodley's set."[519]

After *Europe*, the mood lightened for both actors and audiences with the Christmas production: *A Christmas Carol* – a restaging by Amy Leach of her production at Hull Truck Theatre the previous year. It was chosen because of its appeal to adult audiences, revealing one of the limitations of the location of the Pop-Up Theatre: weekday matinees were not possible because of the noise and dust created by the construction workers in the rest of the building.   *A Christmas Carol* was the Pop-Up company's third production, and the consistency of actors was clearly proving beneficial, with one reviewer observing that "on the evidence of the work so far, they've bonded magnificently. I'm not the only audience member to have expressed the hope they keep the concept of a Leeds Playhouse Ensemble going once the construction project is completed".[520]

The production continued the recent development of including a dementia-friendly performance and a "relaxed" one as part of the run of the play. It also continued the practice of casting local young people in Christmas productions. The part of Tiny Tim was alternated between two boys, Lipalo Mokete and Seb Smallwood, cast after an open call-out resulting in over fifty young people auditioning.

Following *A Christmas Carol*, and whilst the company was rehearsing with director Amy Leach for their next production, *Hamlet*, two other plays were performed in repertory. One was a revival of the 2016 production of *Kes*, with Jack Lord reprising the role of 'Man'. This time Billy was played by Lucas Button; the original Billy, Dan Parr, was now in the Pop-Up company and rehearsing the role of Laertes. The other production was a one-woman play, *random*, by debbie tucker green.

When *Hamlet* opened in March 2019, the obvious talking point was the casting of a woman as Hamlet; Horatio and Polonius were also played by women. This was the most interesting aspect of rehearsals for Simona Bitmate, the actor playing Ophelia:

"It means every discovery Tess [Parr – playing Hamlet] makes is something I've never seen before. And then the knock-on effect that it has on other characters and the rest of the play. It informs absolutely everything and it's really very thrilling and exciting."

It was not the first time that Hamlet had been played by a woman. Maxine Peake had taken on the role in 2014 at the Royal Exchange Theatre in Manchester. However, in the Playhouse production, Hamlet was an actual woman: a Princess rather than a Prince. This obviously affects the relationships in the play; for example, Hamlet and Ophelia are same-sex lovers.

Without exception the reviews were full of praise. Critics totally approved of the casting, some even claiming that a female Hamlet makes more sense:

"It adds an extra layer of complexity while also imbuing elements of the text with more weight and significance. A young woman, whether we like it or not, would have far less agency at court than her male counterpart, so Hamlet's vacillation makes more sense. Male inaction becomes, in a way, frustrated female subjugation". [521]

They were full of praise for Tessa Parr's performance as Hamlet:

"...extraordinary ... embodying the vast range of emotions that make Hamlet the most chameleonic figure in world drama. In a wordless prologue (a delightful addition from Leach), we get a rare glimpse of the way she was before her father's murder, and her obvious affection for Ophelia ... makes her violent renunciation of their relationship later on even more heartbreaking. Crucially, Parr unequivocally captures Hamlet's overwhelming sense of grief." [522]

Critics praised all the other actors, once again highlighting the value of the season's ensemble company. Perhaps the most praise was given to Amy Leach, directing her fourth production in the Pop-Up season, one critic declaring her production "the finest *Hamlet* I've seen in the theatre". [523] Several commented on the fast pace, suggesting that "Leach's invention and energy could introduce it to a whole new audience". [524] The Yorkshire Post found it "a pacy, energetic and totally engaging production", [525] while The Culture Vulture described it as "a brilliant re-imagining of the tale for an audience with an open mind". [526]

After *Hamlet*, the last two plays in the Pop-Up season saw a split in the ensemble company: the men performed an adaptation of *Around the World in 80 Days*; the women performed *Be My Baby*, a play by Amanda Whittington from 1997.

Around the World in 80 Days continued the established practice of taking a Playhouse production on a community tour. After the run at the Pop-Up Theatre the play was performed at nine venues in the eight community partner areas within Leeds. In four of these, there were both matinee and evening performances, a reflection of the popularity of these community tours. At Rothwell Baptist Church Hall the matinee was a dementia-friendly performance, the Playhouse once again demonstrating its concern with inclusion and accessibility.

Be My Baby was a co-production with Mind the Gap, the Bradford-based theatre company founded to give professional performing opportunities to people with learning disabilities and autism. The cast included Anna Gray, from Harrogate, one of Mind the Gap's artists. The production saw another innovation which further demonstrated the priority given to inclusion. Integrated captioning featured in every performance, rather than just on one specific occasion. This followed the trial of captioning glasses during the previous two productions.

As well as the Playhouse productions in the Pop-Up theatre, there were other performances using this space. The Furnace Festival was held once again in October, which included further performances of *Blackthorn* by Charley Miles, following a four-week run at the Edinburgh Festival. The season also included *Salt*, performed by Selina Thompson, following her retracing of one of the routes of the Transatlantic Slave Triangle. In November, Nick Ahad's *Partition* was revived for six performances. The Playhouse also developed or supported productions elsewhere in 2018-19, including Red Ladder Theatre Company's production of Brecht's *Mother Courage and Her Children*, a promenade one at the Albion Electric Warehouse.

Then in October the Playhouse commissioned *Airplays* to celebrate the seventieth anniversary of the arrival of the Empire Windrush. These were four fifteen-minute radio dramas by Yorkshire writers which explored immigration. They were performed at Leeds College of Music (now Leeds Conservatoire) and broadcast live on BBC Radio Leeds. November saw the staging of *The Things We Wouldn't Otherwise Find*, an entertaining look at libraries both in the past and in the age of the internet search engine. Written by Emma Adams, this was a site-specific production, appropriately performed at the Leeds Library, celebrating their two hundred and fiftieth year. November also saw a co-production with Opera North, *Not*

Such Quiet Girls by Jessica Walker. Performed at the Howard Assembly Room within the Grand Theatre, it was the story of three women who volunteered as ambulance drivers on the front line during the First World War.

At around the same time as the theatre's temporary closure, recent Playhouse productions were successfully touring elsewhere. After the run of *Still Alice* in the Courtyard Theatre, a tour followed in the Autumn of 2018, playing for one week at each of ten theatres across England and Scotland. Immediately after performances in the Quarry Theatre, *Sunshine on Leith* played in Coventry. Then it could be seen in Dundee: most appropriate because this is where James Brining had directed the original production back in 2010.

Two of the Playhouse's Christmas productions were also having a life beyond Leeds. *Strictly Ballroom* was the 2016 Christmas production, which was remounted at London's Piccadilly Theatre for seven months in 2018. Even more successful has been the 2017 production of *The Lion, The Witch and The Wardrobe*. First of all, it played at the Bridge Theatre in London for three months from November 2019. A new version based on the Leeds production toured extensively for six months, including at the Lowry Theatre in Manchester over Christmas in 2021. This new version also played at the Gillian Lyne Theatre in London for six months the following year. Its performance life continues: it was the Christmas 2023 production at the Birmingham Repertory Theatre, with a return to the Playhouse for Christmas 2024.

Through the Pop-Up space and through its commissions and support of off-site productions, as well as through these touring productions, the Playhouse managed to maintain a presence and an influence – and, crucially, an audience – during its period of closure.

ACT III

ACT THREE SCENE TWO

"By designing a re-opening programme which is a rich mix of varied productions and activities, we hope to encourage both existing and new audiences to discover this incredible building. Whether that be through a workshop at the Open Weekend, a cup of tea and a cake in the new café or a family trip to 'The Wizard of Oz', we look forward to seeing the theatre alive and thriving again at the heart of the community with a theatre experience open to all."[527]

THERE ARE NO BEGINNINGS
By Charley Miles
11ᵗʰ October 2019

THE NEWLY NAMED LEEDS PLAYHOUSE'S special events for its re-opening in autumn 2019 included a visit from HRH The Princess Royal and a Civic Reception, plus an Open Weekend when tours of the building and free activities took place. However, a new name and a new auditorium did not mean a new direction for the theatre's work. Indeed, the first months after the re-opening saw a continuation of the developments shown in previous years.

It was appropriate that the first production following the redevelopment should be performed in the new space, the Bramall Rock Void. The choice of the play *There Are No Beginnings* by Charley Miles, set in Leeds' Chapeltown district, can be seen as a statement that the newly-named Playhouse was still committed to producing local stories by local writers. Charley Miles is from Kilburn in North Yorkshire and her first play, *Blackthorn*, was staged at the Playhouse in 2016, after which she became the theatre's Channel 4 Playwright-in-Residence. The idea for *There Are No Beginnings* came about during this time. In between, her second play, *Daughterhood*, was produced by Paines Plough and Theatre Clwyd, and like *Blackthorn* the previous year was performed at the Edinburgh Festival in 2019.

There Are No Beginnings can also be seen as developing the theatre's work from the West Yorkshire Playhouse and the Pop-Up Theatre, being directed by Amy Leach and one of the four actors being Tessa Parr. The publicity for *There Are No Beginnings* clearly stated that 'This is not a story about the Yorkshire Ripper'. What it is about is the impact of his attacks and murders on all women in Leeds, many living in fear – as shown through the lives of four women. June is a social worker, working with vulnerable young women like Helen, who has been pushed into prostitution. Helen is brought to June by Fiona, a young police officer. The fourth character is Sharon, June's daughter. The play spans a period of six years, from 1975 until 1981, and shows, in particular, how Sharon develops from an awkward fifteen year-old into a politically aware young woman. This is contrasted with Helen's life, and the play also explores the bond between them as they grow up together.

Reviews for *There Are No Beginnings* uniformly praised the four actors, including Julie Hesmondhalgh who played June: "Four powerhouse performances;"[528] also praising Amy Leach's direction: "subtly dynamic";[529] "another assured and compelling piece of direction".[530]

Inevitably, reviews also commented on the new auditorium. For this production the space was a traverse setting, with steeply-raked banks of seats on either side. The Guardian described it as "cosy but airy" and carrying a promise as "a place where new work can be tested. Its opening production comes through with flying colours".[531] BritishTheatre.com described it as a "simple and exciting space"[532] while the Northern Soul review argued that this simplicity benefited the production, having "no wing space, nowhere to hide and nowhere to change unless you leave the room. Amy Leach's excellent production uses this to advantage as the actors sit at the side, watch each other perform and change their outfits in view of the audience. It creates a claustrophobia that fits and enhances the storytelling".[533]

The British Theatre Guide similarly concluded that it was the perfect place for productions "which might take risks but which are, on this evidence, nonetheless skilfully crafted and polished. This inaugural production eases by with a sure-footedness which makes for an engaging drama and a confident opening to this promising new space".[534]

The value of this third space for new work was next demonstrated when the Rock Void was used for the annual Furnace Festival. As well as being a more appropriate space, it meant that the Courtyard Theatre could be used for visiting and co-productions. In the first months, this included the return of the *Barber Shop Chronicles* (October 2019), which the Playhouse had co-produced with the National Theatre before the temporary closure. Since its performances in Leeds and London the production had toured to eleven other cities in England and Scotland. However, the return of this play revealed a limitation following the redevelopment: the Courtyard could no longer be adapted for theatre-in-the-round, as for the original production prior to the renovations.

Meanwhile the Quarry Theatre's first production – and James Brining's first direction since the re-opening – was *The Wizard of Oz*, evidencing a continuing commitment to substantial all-age Christmas programming. Also seasonal, the Courtyard put on *The Night Before Christmas* by Robert Alan Evans, directed by Amy Leach, intended for three to seven year-olds, while the Rock Void was used for a touring production, *The Snow Mouse* – advertised as being for the "zero-plus" age-group.

The 'big' Christmas production in the Quarry had usually been well-received, and the last one in 2017, *The Lion, the Witch and the Wardrobe* was always going to be a hard act to follow. Fortunately, *The Wizard of Oz* did not disappoint:

"You'd expect something spectacular to be the first Christmas show at the restyled, renamed and reopened Leeds Playhouse and *The Wizard of Oz* certainly fits the bill. James Brining's production throws pretty much everything at the classic MGM film – and makes nearly all of it stick. There are over twenty cast members, nearly as many again in the splendid young ensemble, a fine eleven-piece band, some superb visual effects, plenty of flying, inspired choreography and much more". [535]

One of the unusual aspects of this production was the casting of Dorothy. Most often played by an adult actor, here the role was shared between Lucy Sherman from Leeds, and Agatha Meehan from York, aged fourteen and eleven respectively, but neither were new to theatre. Lucy had been in *Chitty Chitty Bang Bang* at the Playhouse and on tour, while Agatha had had two West End roles: in *School of Rock* – *the*

Musical and in *Annie*. Both would go on to perform in the 2021 Playhouse and Opera North production of A *Little Night Music*.

In addition to Lucy and Agatha, members of the Playhouse Youth Theatre also had roles. Separately, the Youth Theatre had, in late October 2019, presented *Influence* by Andy McGregor, commissioned by the Playhouse and five other UK-wide theatres. What was special about this production was the Youth Theatre's new partnership with Leeds City College. The play was performed in the college's new theatre space; their staff and students were involved with costumes, video projections, lighting and stage management.

The first productions at the Playhouse after the redevelopment all continued to reflect the theatre's aim of making its work as accessible as possible, which was of course also a major aim of the redevelopment work itself. Productions now regularly included sign language support, audio-described commentaries and captioned performances. As had happened during the run of *The Wizard of Oz*, for one matinee the production was adapted to meet the needs of people living with dementia. Another was a "relaxed" performance, for those with learning difficulties. And another first: a special performance of *There Are No Beginnings* was one where parents could attend the theatre with their babies. Like other accessible performances, small adaptations were made to the lighting and sound effects, and the auditorium lights were kept slightly raised.

Accessibility was taken a stage further with the first Quarry Theatre production in 2020. *Oliver Twist* opened on 28th February – a co-production with Ramps on the Moon which was set up in 2015 as a consortium of six regional theatres, including the Playhouse, to encourage these theatres to "enrich the stories they tell and the way they tell them by elevating the presences of deaf and disabled people on and off stage".[536] Three months earlier another Ramps on the Moon co-production, an adaptation of Winsom Pinnock's play *One Under* had toured to the Courtyard. Whereas other productions had included occasional signing, captions or audio descriptions, for *Oliver Twist* these were integrated into every performance, and issues around deafness formed part of the story. So in this version, adapted by Bryony Lavery, Oliver is deaf, as are Fagin and the Artful Dodger. This *Oliver Twist* is set at a time when signing was seen as less civilised, was banned in schools, and when deaf children were being forced to speak. All this gives a whole new dimension to the story. Thus for this production the language of Dickens needed to be stripped back. One reviewer commented, "the dialogue is more headline than subtlety: but the novelist painted in broad strokes, and nuance is there in those hands and the shrug of bodies".[537]

This was another production directed by Amy Leach, who saw it as being much more than an exercise in inclusion:

"[it's] the opposite of gender-blind or colour-blind or disability-blind casting: when you embrace people's actual identity, it just brings so much richness to things … When it's a creative thing then the possibilities are endless, aren't they? That's the whole point of theatre."[538]

She also felt that *Oliver Twist* had a contemporary relevance, so no doubt would have welcomed the assessment of one critic, that the production drove home "the fact that a lot of things Dickens describes are still with us, and have perhaps even more dismayingly, seen a resurgence, and it does this while populating the stage with deaf and disabled actors, insisting on visibility. Disabled people are still woefully under-represented in the arts, but Amy Leach's production offers an entertaining, embracive, necessary corrective".[539]

Sadly the run of *Oliver Twist* and the tour which should have followed was cut short when the Covid 19 lockdown closed the Playhouse and all other UK theatres. Fortunately it was possible to film the production, so in 2021 it was available to watch online.

A first for Leeds Playhouse and every theatre was the challenge of surviving a pandemic. The Covid 19 lockdown happened just five months after the theatre had re-opened, and just as the Playhouse was about to celebrate its fiftieth anniversary. Instead the theatre had to cancel hundreds of scheduled performances and furlough ninety percent of its staff. But the Arts Council's Emergency Relief Funding of £680,000 kept the theatre afloat, along with the subsequent grant of 2.3 million pounds from the government's Culture Recovery Fund.

But how could the Playhouse sustain its hard-won relationships with audience and community? A Playhouse Connect programme was organised for the duration of the lockdown. Youth Theatre members were offered online interactive drama sessions; other young people could access online video resources; older people were supported through befriending phone calls; similar support was given to people with learning difficulties and to refugees.

It was only in May 2021 that the theatre's fiftieth anniversary could in any way be celebrated. For three weeks the Courtyard re-opened for performances of *Decades: Stories from the City,* for which the Playhouse had commissioned six writers to contribute short monologues. Each writer was allocated one of the six decades since the 1970s in which to set their monologues. The first three decades were covered by writers who had already had their work produced at the Playhouse: Simon Armitage, Alice Nutter, and Maxine Peake. The plays set in the new millennium were by Leanna Benjamin, Kamal Kaan and Stan Owens. With Covid 19 restrictions still in place, theatregoers were tested on arrival, masks were required, and the auditorium seating was socially distanced. A reviewer for the Culture Vulture commented, "It's the applause the catches you by surprise. Even with the Courtyard Theatre auditorium two thirds empty to satisfy requirements to keep audiences safely segregated, the sound of maybe a hundred people showing their shared appreciation together feels very strange after fifteen months of enforced isolation".

The praise of the theatre's safety measures must have been moving for a staff who were surely feeling the strain:

"All credit to what felt like legions of Playhouse staff and volunteers who, on reopening night last night, made the relatively sparse number of visitors feel most welcome and, above all, safe".[540]

The review reminds us of all the challenges the theatre had had to overcome, and provides a cameo of those exceptional times – and one exceptional, doughty theatre's survival.

ACT III

Post-show Discussion

ONE CAN ONLY IMAGINE THE JOY felt by the original members of the theatre campaign group on the 17th September 1970. After many years of hard work and after many setbacks, the Playhouse building they had dreamed of became a reality. Now, over fifty years and five artistic directors later, to what extent have their dreams for the theatre come true? In 2024, is the building still in keeping with the kind of Playhouse they worked so hard to build? How much has financial necessity made the realisation of artistic hopes impossible?

Soon after the first Leeds Playhouse opened, it quickly became apparent that the building was not big enough to house all the staff, resources and activities of the theatre's work. Equally, the need for a second, smaller auditorium became apparent. It was, however, only a temporary home. Although it took ten years longer than planned, the 'permanent' West Yorkshire Playhouse opened its doors on the 8th March 1990. It was a very different building to the Leeds Playhouse; there was much more space: rehearsal rooms, scenery workshops, and office space in particular.

The campaign group always knew that the original location of their theatre was not ideal. It did indeed prove to be wrong both in respect of the distance from the city centre and the implications of its proximity to the university campus. When the possibility of a new playhouse on Quarry Hill arose, most saw this location as a far better one. However, whilst the location of the West Yorkshire Playhouse was much nearer to the city centre and visible from The Headrow, its location was not truly central to Leeds; as in, not somewhere that the general public would pass by, except if parking on the empty land of Quarry Hill. Furthermore, as the area began to be developed in the ensuing years, it became obvious that the theatre was facing in the wrong direction. With hindsight, the design competition entries that were orientated to St. Peter's Street would have been more appropriate. In recent years, as the Victoria Gate development became the most obvious place to park, so most theatregoers approached from St. Peter's Street, only to be greeted by solid brick walls – the back of the building.

The redevelopment of the Playhouse in 2018-19 could have been the opportunity to properly turn the building to face the city centre. Indeed this was the proposal of Nick Brown Architects who, fearing that the Playhouse might be dwarfed by other developments on Quarry Hill, proposed "a folding façade that captures additional space within, and provides a dramatic and dynamic 'billboard' from the outside. The scale and visual strength of the concept would also ensure that the WYP would be able to stand out amongst its existing, and future, context".[541]

Unfortunately, the compromise – creating three possible entries to the theatre – has done little to improve the situation. The new frontage does make the building more striking when viewed from The Headrow and St. Peter's Street; however, this new entrance leads into a café area, and the route to the box office and the auditoria is unclear and only accessible by stairs or a lift. Once the café is closed, or when evening performances begin, this street level area is a useless space. Posted on the Skyscraper City website, one comment about the new frontage was – "it just looks a bit tacked-on. It neither integrates with nor redefines the look of the building. There's nothing fundamentally wrong with the design, but in my humble opinion, they should have found a solution that created a new facade across the whole front rather than just a bit of the corner".[542]

Nevertheless, the redevelopment of the Playhouse has obviously been very successful in improving disabled access both to the auditoria and other public areas, and with better lift access. For everyone, access to the Quarry Theatre other than from the top of the seating is much better. These developments perhaps explain why the Playhouse won The Stage's 2020 Theatre Building of the Year Award. However, the open-plan feel to the public areas has been somewhat lost, and entrance to the auditoria is now confusing, necessitating colour coding. Sadly, a Times reader concluded he "used to go to the West Yorkshire (now Leeds) Playhouse regularly, but prices have risen and the theatre's been catastrophically 're-imagined' (polite way of saying they've moved its frontage and in the process buggered up the flow of the interior). Simply don't like the experience".[543]

Much is being made of Quarry Hill becoming the cultural quarter of the city. The marketing for the SOYO project describes this as 'a new mixed-use development in the heart of Leeds' cultural district'. The area now has the headquarters of BBC Yorkshire, Leeds Conservatoire, Phoenix Dance Theatre, Yorkshire Dance, and Northern Ballet. Unfortunately, the Skyline apartment block, built on the Playhouse staff car park, is something of a barrier between the theatre and the other organisations based on Quarry Hill. How many theatregoers arriving from the city centre or the Victoria Gate car-park are aware of what else is on Quarry Hill? In particular, are they aware of the Playhouse's work at First Floor, in the St. Peter's Square building?

Most people remember the first Leeds Playhouse as friendly and welcoming, and as a place where there was always a lot going on in addition to the stage productions. The bar and restaurant facilities were open all day. Despite limited space, art exhibitions were regularly organised; lunchtime plays were regularly produced. The Playhouse attracted not only theatregoers but people who loved music and cinema. Fifty years later, it seems almost unbelievable, for example, that hundreds of people would turn up for a film-showing just before midnight.

Continuing this principle, upon moving to its new site, the Playhouse – now West Yorkshire Playhouse – went on offering much more than the stage productions. Lots of daytime activities were organised for children and young people; the Heydays programme for older people was immediately a big success; at one stage there was a cyber café for public use. In the opinion of one expert, Nick Thompson (design architect for the Crucible Theatre in Sheffield), the public areas of a theatre have an essential function: "You need to build an audience before you let them into the auditorium. You've got to get their pulse up".[544] The West Yorkshire Playhouse did much to achieve this, with a bookstall, often live music in the bar-restaurant area, and 'Outloud' events regularly taking place prior to the evening performance: a talk by actors or directors; an event relating to issues raised by the play; a performance of another short play by the playwright.

Of course, the biggest difference between the first Leeds Playhouse and the West Yorkshire Playhouse was a second auditorium. It was intentionally not a small studio space, by then common in many regional producing theatres. The Courtyard Theatre was one equivalent in size, for example, to the Octagon Theatre in Bolton and the Stephen Joseph Theatre in Scarborough. It was, nevertheless, a 'black box' space in the sense that it could be configured in different ways or used for promenade productions.

Having two auditoria, the West Yorkshire Playhouse was now able to do what had mostly been impossible at the first theatre: receive productions by national touring companies. It could also host visits from other companies in the Leeds area. The theatre quickly became a home for productions by Phoenix Dance Company (now Phoenix Dance Theatre) and by RJC Dance, now considered the leading inclusive Black dance organisation in the north. Northern Ballet has also been a regular visitor, and in 2005, the Leeds Amateur Operatic Society became the first amateur society to perform at the Playhouse.

Neither auditorium, however, provided an appropriate space for small-scale productions, such as work by local writers. It took nearly fifty years to achieve, but the 2018-19 redevelopment included the creation of a studio theatre, the Rock Void. No longer is there a need to use other inappropriate spaces, including the Barber Studio, for these productions.

The small group of people who began the campaign for a repertory theatre in Leeds back in 1964 were clear about who this theatre would be for. They wanted a 'people's theatre'. This is a vague term, but it helps to know that those who started the campaign considered themselves politically very left-wing. Doreen Newlyn wanted the theatre to reach people from disadvantaged communities and attract working-class families, and in particular people who "didn't know a theatre, didn't know what it was".[545] The appointment of Bill Hays as the first Artistic Director was clearly appropriate for this kind of theatre. If he had been allowed to continue in post for more than just two years, perhaps a people's theatre might have been established. Or would financial constraints have resulted in him producing programmes of plays similar to those of his successor?

Whatever the financial and other factors that modified the theatre's founding ideology, was the 'people's theatre' ideal at least partly realised? Nearly fifty years later Michael Attenborough, looking back on his time as Associate Director, concludes:

"I think the blunt truth is that it wasn't. When people talk of a 'people's theatre' what they're actually saying is a classless theatre, for people whose education may not have encouraged them to go and visit live theatre but would actually want to come. Amassing, encouraging, and maintaining a working-class audience is something that a lot of people have aspired towards and failed. The Leeds Playhouse audience was a fairly solidly middle-class one. However, it was a very young audience; that made the theatre very vibrant and exciting to play to."[546]

Since the beginning, the question of who the Playhouse is *for* has often been asked. If it is, as its first name reflected, for the people of Leeds, are there particular communities within the city that are – as was expressed by the campaign group – target audiences? Did the eventual name-change imply a wider, West Yorkshire audience, and did the talk of the Playhouse as the 'National Theatre of the North' suggest an even wider reach?

The 1999 findings of a piece of research carried out by the theatre (in partnership with the Joseph Rowntree Foundation) would undoubtedly have disappointed those early campaigners. The project surveyed the Ebor Gardens estate which, at its closest point, is just three hundred yards away (though separated by the A64 inner ring road). Out of a population of three thousand, just seven addresses appeared on the Playhouse marketing database (which totalled one hundred and forty thousand entries); furthermore, of the seven hundred members of Heydays, none were from that estate. Just three tickets had been sold to residents in the previous two years.

The project found that residents "didn't really feel excluded from the Playhouse – they just didn't see it as relevant to their lives, and though it was there, they saw no need to engage with it". [547] As one resident commented, "I think people always thought of the Playhouse as very off limits, snobby, an over-priced place. They used to walk past saying 'That's not for me, you'd have to dress up".[548]

If the campaign group would have found this research disappointing, they'd have been especially upset by the proposal ten years later in the 2010 Business Plan, which recognised that the Playhouse needed to attract a wider demographic but suggested that priority be given to attracting regular attendance from the "more affluent areas on the outskirts of Leeds" – justifying this on the basis that 'influential' people live there, who generate good income.

Like any other theatre, the programming of productions has had considerable influence in respect of the audiences the Playhouse will attract. The theatre has, for example, been very successful in choosing Christmas productions with a broader appeal than do pantomimes. This has resulted in excellent attendances.

Nevertheless it is possible to achieve 'sold out' productions with a very different audience. Those who came to see Ian McKellen and the Courtyard Company productions were likely very different from those coming to see plays such as *The Damned United*. An example that perfectly reflects the challenges of programming was the decision to stage Irvine Welsh's *You'll Have Had Your Hole*. Perhaps the most perceptive critic of this production was Phil Gibby in The Stage, who concluded, "What Irvine Welsh's latest offering reveals is the gulf that now exists between the new generation of audiences and the older generation of critics. This show has been panned unanimously as being unfit, morally and dramatically, for presentation on the stage. Yet the audience at the West Yorkshire Playhouse, almost entirely aged under thirty, cheered it to the rafters".[549] In the same vein, Nick Curtis of the Evening Standard interviewed young people leaving the theatre, including a couple in their late twenties who had only been to the theatre once before, who had been drawn to the Playhouse by Welsh's name: "He makes it a lot less theatre-y and intimidating".[550]

Some will have applauded the Playhouse for a production which attracted such young audiences, but the play worried chair of the governors Bernard Atha, who was concerned that, in "attracting new, mainly young audiences by such plays, there is a danger of alienating the regular supporters".[551]

Obviously Bernard was worrying about ticket sales. Over the years, the Playhouse – like many other regional theatres – has introduced various season ticket schemes to attract regular attendance, such as 'The Big Deal' which offered substantial savings if people booked in advance for four plays during a season. By the start of the 2004-05 season, nine hundred people had signed up. Somewhat worrying therefore, was the research carried out ten years later, revealing that in the 2013-14 season, seventy-five percent of audiences attended only once during the year.

This research also revealed that, regarding the Community Network scheme, where preview tickets were sold for three pounds to groups and organisations, in 2014 the take-up was good for the two Christmas shows but not a single ticket was sold for *The Crucible*. All this suggests that people visit the Playhouse because there is a production they want to see, rather than because of a commitment to or an affinity with the theatre.

Before the first Leeds Playhouse even opened, the Playhouse Club, later called Friends of the Playhouse, was an organisation of supporters whose commitment was (alongside campaigning, volunteering and so on) to raise funds. When this was ultimately abolished in 2014, Doreen Newlyn wrote an obituary:

"1968–2014: I want to offer up both eulogy and lament for the gallant voluntary efforts made over fifty years by a large number of people who helped the Playhouse come into existence and then survive. Let us all never forget, but remember with deep affection and great pride the giving without getting of that volunteer dedication: and the friendships that were made, and the satisfaction and delight of being part of a noble voluntary effort."[552]

The task of fund-raising was taken over by theatre staff, and another scheme, 'My Playhouse', was introduced. The membership fee of twenty pounds gave members discounts on tickets, refreshments and programmes, as well as occasional newsletters. A 'Patron' scheme, involving making regular donations, was also introduced, promoted as a way to "become part of the Playhouse family".

Do such schemes really result in a family of supporters in the way that Friends of the Playhouse had clearly achieved? Undoubtedly, community programmes such as Heydays and the Youth Theatre elicited loyalties and affinities with the Playhouse, as did the work with refugees in recent years, but such work does not necessarily lead to, nor even have the aim of, increasing attendances in the Quarry or Courtyard theatres. In fact the 2015 'Audience Development Strategy' proposed to prioritise "work that sits outside the conventional theatrical experience" – not even referring to the fact that the Playhouse has two large conventional auditoria.

As part of the 2018-19 redevelopment, the capacity of both these auditoria was increased, unfortunately resulting in the Courtyard no longer being a flexible, adaptable space: the Playhouse now just has two end-on auditoria. Of course, when increasing the seating capacity of both spaces, nobody could have known how Covid-19 would affect the Playhouse. So far, since the theatre reopened after the pandemic, there has only been a limited number of weeks with simultaneous productions in both. Ian Brown's opinion when he was Artistic Director (2002-12) had been that there were not enough theatre-going people in Leeds to support two auditoria with a total of eleven hundred seats. In 2023, are there enough people to support three auditoria, having thirteen hundred and fifty seats (two thousand nine hundred seats if you include the Grand Theatre)? Perhaps the time has come to rethink how these spaces are used. It was arguably a mistake not to continue with film showings at the West Yorkshire Playhouse, especially since the city centre still doesn't have an art-house cinema (despite having a very successful film festival). Also the West Yorkshire Playhouse used to regularly host comedy nights. In the 2009-10 season for example, six comedians – Marcus Brigstock, Jason Manford, Stewart Lee, Andy Hamilton, Sean Lock and Michael McIntyre – all performed to full houses in the Quarry. Comedy nights at the West Yorkshire Playhouse usually took place on Sundays. Now, the Playhouse is rarely open on Sundays except for extra Christmas matinees.

Perhaps the Playhouse could also become more involved in citywide events. 2024 sees the sixth Leeds Lit Fest, at which in 2023 there were fifty-eight events in fourteen venues including, in the city centre, the Howard Assembly Rooms, the Leeds Library, the Carriageworks Theatre and the Central Library. If the Playhouse organised events, people who are not regular theatregoers might potentially visit the theatre for the first time. The conclusion of another piece of research carried out in 2014 by Morris Hargreaves McIntyre, commissioned by the Playhouse, is perhaps still the case:

"The Playhouse lacks a brand identity. For all of the segments – core and non-core – there lacks a clearly articulated brand that sets the Playhouse apart from all the other cultural offers, speaks of its vision or values, and fosters a connection or sense of belonging. In short, while the audiences think the Playhouse is friendly and important to culture in Leeds, or that it offers a special night out, they don't have a relationship with the brand."[553]

Members of the original theatre campaign group would probably be shocked by such terminology – that the theatre they created has now become a 'brand'. They were very clear about the ideal identity of the theatre they willed into being. However, over fifty years later, the question must be asked anew: what is the role today of the Leeds Playhouse – and other regional producing theatres? The question is especially urgent in a new era, post Covid-19, when National Theatre Live – with big budget productions and star casts – is available at a cinema near you.

Dave Stannard

NOTES

1   Leeds Theatre Committee Statement 1964
2   Theatre Planning Committee Progress Report, September 1964
3   University of Leeds Review, Vol. XI, No. 1, June 1968, p.57
4   *Stirring Up Sheffield*, Colin George and Ted George, p.38
5   The handbill distributed
6   Theatre Connections, Doreen Newlyn, p.157
7   Yorkshire Post 13/2/1968
8   Interview, 12/3/2020
9   Yorkshire Life, September 2022
10   Interview 12/3/2020
11   *Close the Coalhouse Door*, Alan Plater, p. 7
12   Alan Plater's notes to Bill Hayes, Hull History Centre, Ref: U DPR/2/10
13   Ibid
14   Plays and Players, December 1970
15   Yorkshire Evening Post 18/9/1970
16   *Simon Says!* script, Hull History Centre, Ref: U DPR/2/10
17   Yorkshire Post 18/9/1970
18   Daily Mail 18/9/1970
19   Sunday Times 20/9/1970
20   Yorkshire Post 19/9/1970
21   Ibid
22   Ibid
23   Friends of the Playhouse magazine, March 1971
24   Guardian 14/3/2006
25   Bradford Telegraph & Argus 31/12/1970
26   Guardian 14/3/2006
27   Yorkshire Evening Post 27/11/1970
28   Yorkshire Evening Post 10/12/1970
29   The Guardian 10/12/1970
30   Financial Times 11/12/1970
31   Daily Telegraph 11/12/1970
32   Financial Times 22/9/1970
33   Bradford Telegraph & Argus 31/12/1970
34   Yorkshire Post 16/ 9/1971
35   Leeds Skyrack Express 24/9/1971
36   Bradford Telegraph & Argus 16/9/1971
37   Yorkshire Evening Post 16/9/1971
38   Draft information sheet for the applicants for the post of Director of the Leeds Playhouse
39   The Report of the Arts council Theatre Enquiry 1970, The Theatre Today, p. 50
40   Ibid, p. 67
41   Yorkshire Post 30/11/1971
42   Ibid
43   Leeds Weekly Citizen 19/5/1972
44   Skyrack Express 2/6/1972
45   The Stage 8/6/1972
46   John Harrison, *Not Quite Famous*, p230
47   *Torpedoes in the Jacuzzi* programme, 1987
48   Report to the Governors' Meeting 13/5/1987
49   Leeds Other Paper 14/9/1984
50   *A Theatre for All Seasons*, John Bailey, p.42
51   *Nearly Famous,* John Harrison p. 152
52   Ibid, p. 210
53   Ibid, p. 237
54   Yorkshire Evening Post 28/9/73
55   Yorkshire Post 28/9/73
56   Leeds Student Review 4/10/1972

57   The Times 27/11/72
58   Yorkshire Evening Post
       28/9/73
59   Guardian 29/9/1972
60   Yorkshire Evening Post
       28/9/1972
61   Leeds Student 6/10/1972
62   Doreen Newlyn, *Theatre
       Connections*, pp.99-100
63   Guardian 1/2/1974
64   Yorkshire Evening Post
       1/3/1974
65   Yorkshire Evening Post
       28/3/1974
66   Yorkshire Post 2/3/1974
67   Article by Philip Wilde,
       21/8/2023
68   Ibid
69   Yorkshire Post 22/2/1975
70   Ibid
71   Arts Council Statement on
       Leeds Playhouse, March 1978
72   Letter to the Chairman of
       Leeds Theatre Trust Ltd., 13
       March 1978, reproduced in
       Leeds Needs The Playhouse
       Factsheet 1
73   Minutes of Governors'
       Meeting 23/2/1987
74   Minutes of Governors'
       Meeting 1/7/1987
75   *Not Quite Famous,* John
       Harrison p.244
76   Interview, 10/3/2023
77   Yorkshire Evening Post
       13/2/1975
78   Interview 11/8/2023
79   Sunday Times 23/1/1977
80   Interview, 10/3/2023
81   Ibid
82   Ibid
83   *Not Quite Famous*, John
       Harrison, p.244
84   Forward to *Not Quite Famous,*
       John Harrison, p. v
85   *Raj*, Leeds Theatre In
       Education Company, p. 7
86   A New Theatre, undated

87   *Theatre In Education in Britain,*
       Roger Wooster, pp. 49-50
88   Interview 24/08/2021
89   Ibid
90   Doreen Newlyn, *Theatre
       Connections*, pp. 99-100
91   Yorkshire Evening Post
       24/5/1971
92   quoted in *A Theatre for All
       Seasons*, by John Bailey p.25-6
93   Yorkshire Post 22/1/90
94   Ibid
95   *Twelfth Night* programme,
       1989
96   Doreen Newlyn, *Theatre
       Connections* p. 99 -1000
97   Bradford Telegraph & Argus,
       31/12/1970
98   Yorkshire Evening Post,
       17/9/1971
99   Guardian, 22/9/1972
100   Leeds Student, 26/10/1973
101   Leeds Student, 26/10/1973
102   Ibid
103   Leeds Weekly Citizen,
       18/2/1972
104   Guardian 30/11/1971
105   Leeds Student 21/5/1976
106   Interview, 10/3/2023
107   Yorkshire Post 9/5/1989
108   Leeds Student 05/1976
109   Bernard Atha, Variety, *The
       Spice of Life*, p.164
110   Board of Governors' Meeting
       minutes 6/6/1984
111   Competition Brief 9:19
112   Letter to Will Weston
       17/07/1984
113   John Harrison, *Not Quite
       Famous*, p. 243
114   Building Design 01/03/85
115   Assessors Report 15/3/1985
116   Ibid
117   Board of Governors' Meeting
       minutes 8/1/1986
118   *Twelfth Night* programme 1989
119   Yorkshire Evening Post
       9/3/1990
120   Financial Times 10/3/1990

121 Plays and Players May 1990
122 The Mail on Sunday
     11/3/1990
123 The Times 10/3/1990
124 Weekend Telegraph
     10/3/1990
125 Yorkshire Evening Post
     23/3/1990
126 Yorkshire Evening Post
     30/3/1990
127 Yorkshire Evening Post
     9/3/1990
128 Daily Telegraph 14/4/1990
129 Yorkshire Post 12/4/1990
130 Halifax Evening Courier
     11/4/1990
131 The Stage 8/3/1990
132 Daily telegraph 2/3/1990
133 Country Life 15/3/1990
134 Yorkshire Post 29/5/1990
135 Yorkshire Post 24/5/1990
136 *Lifelines* programmes 1991
137 *Back Street Mammy*
     programme 1991
138 Plays International April/May
     1991
139 The Guardian 29/7/1993
140 The Observer 1/8/1993
141 The Times 29/7/1993
142 Yorkshire Evening Post
     6/5/1993
143 The Stage 29/5/1997
144 The Guardian 24/5/1997
145 The Stage 26/6/1997
146 Ibid
147 Caribbean Times 8/7/1997
148 Yorkshire Post 3/7/1997
149 The Stage 12/6/1997
150 Yorkshire Evening Post
     30/5/1997
151 The Stage 12/6/1997
152 Yorkshire Evening Post
     19/9/1997
153 The Independent 30/9/1997
154 Yorkshire Post 28/2/2001
155 Yorkshire Post 13/2/2002
156 Daily Telegraph 23/10/1991
157 Leeds Student Independent
     Newspaper 25/10/1991

158 *Pratt of the Argus* programme
     1991
159 Report to Arts Council of
     Great Britain 20/7/1984
160 Minutes of Board of
     Governors Meeting
     17/12/1992
161 Finance Director's Report
     28/08/1996
162 *Popcorn* programme 1996
163 Yorkshire Evening Post
     07/02/1996
164 Yorkshire Evening Post
     16/02/1996
165 Yorkshire Evening Post
     17/12/1996
166 Roles and Functions of the
     English Regional Producing
     Theatres, 2.4.3
167 Northern Echo 01/12/1992
168 Yorkshire Post 04/06/1992
169 The Guardian 05/06/1992
170 The Independent 06/06/1992
171 Daily Telegraph 11/02/1994
172 Yorkshire Evening Press
     29/07/1992
173 The Scotsman 06/04/2004
174 Arts Council Appraisal 1992
     3:4:4
175 *Don't You Leave Me Here*
     programme 2008
176 Daily Telegraph 30/6/1995
177 Skyrack Express 23/6/1995
178 *Carnival Messiah* Programme
     1999
179 Yorkshire Post 11/7/2003
180 Yorkshire Post 18/11/2003
181 Wharfe Valley Times
     24/7/2003
182 Northern Echo 22/7/2005
183 The Guardian 22/7/2005
184 Yorkshire Evening Post
     14/7/2005
185 Times Educational
     Supplement 27/9/1991
186 Yorkshire Evening Post
     3/2/1993
187 *Peter Pan* programme 2008

188 Yorkshire Evening Post 20/6/2016
189 Ibid
190 The Culture Vulture 14/9/2017
191 Anniversary programme 2015
192 *Searching for the Heart of Leeds* programme note
193 Ibid
194 The Culture Vulture 23/6/2018
195 Yorkshire Post
196 Yorkshire Evening Press 29/10/2003
197 Yorkshire Post 29/9/2003
198 The Guardian 29/9/2003
199 The Metro 25/4/2008
200 Yorkshire Post 25/4/2008
201 The Independent 24/4/2008
202 Independent on Sunday 26/2/1995
203 Financial Times 2/3/1995
204 The Guardian 2/3/1995
205 Independent on Sunday 26/2/1995
206 Yorkshire Post 6/10/1998
207 Yorkshire Post 24/3/2006
208 Yorkshire Post 24/2/2006
209 Yorkshire Post 24/3/2006
210 The Sunday Times 9/4/2006
211 https://wexarts.org/ performing-arts/improbable-theatre-hanging-man
212 Independent on Sunday 24/10/2004
213 Yorkshire Post 02/11/2007
214 The Guardian 7/7/2020
215 Yorkshire Post 8/9/1994
216 The Stage 15/9/1994
217 *Martin Guerre* programme 1998
218 The Spectator 19/12/1998
219 The Times 10/12/1998
220 Financial Times 28/9/2004
221 The Mail on Sunday 12/6/2005
222 The Independent on Sunday 12/6/2005
223 The Guardian 9/6/2005
224 Yorkshire Post 1/7/2004
225 Daily Express 10/9/2004
226 The Independent 10/9/2004
227 Daily Mail 10/9/2004
228 Daily Telegraph 10/9/2004
229 The Guardian 1/7/2004
230 The Guardian 9/9/2004
231 Yorkshire Post 9/6/2006
232 Yorkshire Evening post 30/06/2005
233 Yorkshire Post 27/06/2005
234 What's On In London 14/6/2000
235 The Stage 16/12/1999
236 Daily Express 17/12/1999
237 The Independent 19/1/2000
238 Evening Standard 23/6/2000
239 Daily Telegraph 26/6/2000
240 Daily Express 6/6/1998
241 Mail on Sunday 14/6/1998
242 The Times 4/6/1998
243 Daily Express 6/6/1998
244 The Guardian 16/3/2002
245 Yorkshire Post 20/3/2002
246 The Guardian 22/12/2003
247 Morning Star 24/12/2003
248 Metro 16/12/2003
249 Chairman's Statement to 2003/2004 AGM
250 The Stage 27/1/2005
251 The Stage 16/12/2010
252 Yorkshire Evening Post 22/12/2005
253 The Stage 27/1/2005
254 Interview 21/8/2023
255 Wharfedale Observer 23/12/2004
256 Yorkshire Evening Post 17/12/2004
257 Yorkshire Post 13/12/2004
258 Yorkshire Post 14/12/2007
259 Yorkshire Post 9/12/2005
260 Independent on Sunday 25/6/2000
261 Daily Telegraph 13/9/1996
262 Daily Telegraph 3/11/1995
263 *The Crucible* programme 1996
264 Daily Telegraph 13/9/1996
265 Yorkshire Post 5/6/1998

266 The Independent 26/02/2004
267 Daily Mail 26/3/2004
268 Ibid
269 The Independent 25/3/2004
270 Ibid
271 Interview 21/8/2023
272 Quoted in Ian Appleton's
     obituary, The Times
     07/05/2020
273 *Balancing Acts* by Nicholas
     Hytner pp. 37-38
274 Shakespeare Memorial
     Committee. 1916. The
     Shakespeare Memorial
     National Theatre: Objects and
     Importance of the Movement.
     National Theatre Archive.
275 Consultative Green Paper on
     Drama in England, Arts
     Council, May 1995, 3:4:1
276 Arts Council appraisal of West
     Yorkshire Playhouse March
     1993, 3:2:2
277 Ibid 3:2:3
278 Ibid 3:2:6
279 Letter to Arts Council from
     Councillor Bernard Atha,
     25/06/1992
280 Tribune 02/07/1993
281 *The Gulf Between Us*, by Trevor
     Griffiths, pp. vii – viii.
282 Tribune 02/07/1993
283 Financial Times 20/10/1994
284 The Guardian 12/11/1994
285 Daily Telegraph 25/01/1995
286 The Guardian 25/01/1995
287 Yorkshire Post 25/01/1995
288 Minutes of Annual General
     Meeting 5/9/1990
289 Metro Yorkshire 28/08/2001
290 Yorkshire Post 14/08/2001
291 *Johnson Over Jordan*
     programme 2001
292 Sunday Times 23/09/2001
293 Independent on Sunday
     16/09/2001
294 Daily Mail 14/09/2001
295 Independent 19/09/2001
296 The Stage 5/12/2002

297 The Times 30/11/2002
298 Mail on Sunday 1/12/2002
299 Yorkshire Post 2/10/1998
300 The Guardian 24/9/1998
301 Sunday Telegraph 15/11/1998
302 Observer 15/11/1998
303 Mail on Sunday 15/11/1998
304 Financial Times 14/11/1998
305 Sunday Times 27/12/1998
306 Financial Times 18/12/1998
307 Sunday Times 27/12/1998
308 Yorkshire Post 17/12/1998
309 Sunday Times 14/2/1999
310 Sunday Times 27/12/1998
311 Country Life 21/1/1999
312 *Variety* by Bernard Atha p. 171
313 Ibid p. 171
314 Ibid p. 173
315 Daily Telegraph 26/02/1998
316 Sunday Express 01/03/1998
317 Sunday Times 01/03/1998
318 The Observer 01/03/1998
319 Interview 21/8/2023
320 The Stage 6/5/1993
321 Yorkshire Evening Post
     21/4/1993
322 Daily Telegraph 26/4/1993
323 Sunday Times 20/3/1994
324 Yorkshire Post 16/9/1995
325 The Times 30/9/1995
326 Observer 1/10/1995
327 Daily Telegraph 2/10/1995
328 Sunday Express 1/10/1995
329 Financial Times 3/10/1995
330 The Times 21/10/1999
331 Ibid
332 Wharfedale Observer
     21/10/1999
333 *Hamlet* programme 2002
334 The Metro 8/11/2002
335 The Guardian 8/11/2002
336 Mail on Sunday 10/11/2002
337 Country Life Magazine
     21/11/2002
338 Harrogate Observer
     25/10/2002
339 Ibid
340 Daily Telegraph 8/11/2002
341 The Guardian 26/9/2010

342 Yorkshire Evening Post 7/10/2010
343 Daily Telegraph 30/9/2011
344 The Stage 29/9/2011
345 Financial Times 16/5/1995
346 Independent 20/5/1995
347 Letter to J. Peters 22/5/1995
348 Yorkshire Evening Post 6/10/2011
349 BBC Northern Exposure advert, 2005
350 The Big Issue 5/4/2003
351 Yorkshire Post 24/05/2004
352 Yorkshire Post 14/4/2006
353 Yorkshire Press 15/6/2007
354 Yorkshire Post 22/6/2007
355 The Guardian 24/5/2007
356 Yorkshire Evening Post 30/5/2005
357 Playhouse Quarterly Issue 2 April – July 2006
358 Yorkshire Evening post 4/5/2006
359 Playhouse Quarterly Issue 2 April – July 2006
360 Yorkshire Post 14/4/2006
361 *Nine Lives* by Zodwa Nyoni, page 28
362 A Younger Theatre 1/6/2014
363 The Guardian 16/12/2016
364 The Observer 22/2/2015
365 British Theatre Guide (undated)
366 Yorkshire Post 15/6/2017
367 Yorkshire Evening Post 09/6/2003
368 Daily Telegraph 14/6/2003
369 Metro 4/4/2003
370 Daily Telegraph 16/4/2003
371 The Stage 17/4/2003
372 Chairman's Statement for the year ending 31/3/2004
373 Interview 21/8/2023
374 Yorkshire Post 27/10/2006
375 Yorkshire Post 3/10/2008
376 Yorkshire Evening Post 25/9/2008
377 Minutes of the Extraordinary General Meeting 17/11/2008
378 Yorkshire Evening Post 17/6/2010
379 Yorkshire Post 18/6/2010
380 Interview 21/8/2023
381 Daily Telegraph 8/12/2011
382 The Independent 6/12/2011
383 The Stage 2/12/2011
384 Yorkshire Evening Post 15/12/2011
385 *Animal Farm* programme 2008
386 The York Press 30/10/2008
387 Interview 29/08/2023
388 Ibid
389 Ibid
390 Yorkshire Post 14/5/2010
391 Yorkshire Evening Post 6/5/2010
392 Yorkshire Post 7/5/2010
393 Ibid.
394 Yorkshire Evening Post 6/5/2010
395 Interview 29/8/2023
396 Ibid
397 Leeds Guide 28/2/2011
398 The Times 25/2/2011
399 Yorkshire Evening Post 24/2/2011
400 Daily Telegraph 10/10/2012
401 The Arts Desk.com 15/10/2012
402 Interview 29/8/2023
403 Programme for *Sweeney Todd* 2013
404 The Stage 07/10/2013
405 Daily Telegraph 04/10/2013
406 Yorkshire Post 04/10/2013
407 The Observer 15/12/2013
408 The York Press 14/12/2013
409 What's On Stage 8/12/2013
410 Programme for *Of Mice and Men* 2014
411 *The Lion, the Witch and the Wardrobe* programme 2017
412 The Observer 10/12/2017
413 Northern Soul 9/12/2017
414 Theatre in Crisis: the Plight of Regional Theatre, a National Campaign for the Arts briefing, July 1998

415 Connect Magazine (Arts Development Report) 2002-2003

416 Minute 652, Annual General Meeting 1/10/2002

417 The Guardian 4/10/2008

418 Ibid

419 Yorkshire Post 6/10/2008

420 Country Life 25/2/2009

421 Daily Telegraph 19/2/2009

422 The Metro 20/2/2009

423 The Observer 22/2/2009

424 Interview, 21/8/2003

425 Minutes of Finance Committee Meeting 20/1/2009

426 Business Plan 2010 page 4

427 Transform Business Plan page 1

428 Business Plan 2010 page 10

429 Minutes of Finance Committee Meeting 26/1/2010

430 Metro 14/6/2011

431 Leeds Confidential 10/6/2011

432 Leeds Confidential 20/6/2011

433 Culture Vulture 24/6/2011

434 Yorkshire Post 13/4/2012

435 Yorkshire Evening Post 26/4/2012

436 Yorkshire Post 27/4/2012

437 BBC Website 23/4/2012

438 Yorkshire Post 7/10/2011

439 Transform Business Plan page 11

440 Colin Chambers, *Black and Asian Theatre in Britain*, p.190

441 The (York) Press 24/2/2012

442 Ibid

443 The Arts Desk 7/2/2012

444 The Big Issue in the North 30/1/2012

445 Yorkshire Evening Post 12/3/1990

446 West Yorkshire Playhouse and Black Expressive Theatre Enterprises Three Year Plan, undated

447 Minutes of Arts Development Unit Sub-Committee, 6/7/1999

448 Yorkshire Post 25/6/1999

449 The Times 23/6/1999

450 Yorkshire Evening Post 24/6/1999

451 Leeds Student 28/11/2003

452 Yorkshire Post 11/10/2003

453 Leeds Playhouse: Plan for Change (circulated July 2021)

454 Yorkshire Post 01/10/2012

455 Season brochure 2012-2013

456 A Younger Theatre 22/7/2013

457 Yorkshire Post 27/7/2013

458 A Younger Theatre 17/3/2014

459 National Association of Youth Theatre website: Zoetrope by Rebecca Manley – National Association of Youth Theatres (nayt.org.uk)

460 The British Theatre Guide (undated)

461 *The Crucible* programme

462 A Younger Theatre 21/3/2016

463 *Romeo and Juliet* programme

464 Ibid

465 Yorkshire Post 3/3/2017

466 Yorkshire Post 9/3/2017

467 Theatre in Crisis: the Plight of Regional Theatre, a National Campaign for the Arts briefing, July 1998

468 York Press 11/7/2014

469 The Guardian 16/10/2013

470 *My Generation* programme 2013

471 Yorkshire Life 10/5/2012

472 Yorkshire Evening Post 24/02/2003

473 The Guardian 22/9/2015

474 York Press 11/7/2014

475 Analysis of theatre in England, Arts Council England, September 2016 p. 9

476 Refugee Council website 03/04/2013

477 The Guardian 24/11/2015

478 Ibid

479 Playhouse Quarterly, Issue 1, 2006

480 Connect (Arts Development Report) 2004/2005
481 Times Educational Supplement, 5/12/2003
482 *To Kill a Mockingbird* programme, 2006
483 The Stage, 29/7/2004
484 *Untold Stories* programme 2014
485 Artistic Director Report to Governors, 16/01/2015
486 Dementia Friendly Performance Information (YouTube video)
487 West Yorkshire Playhouse Guide to Dementia Friendly Performances, May 2016
488 Every Third Minute: a festival of theatre, dementia and hope, YouTube video
489 The Guardian 16/2/2016
490 South Leeds Life 9/4/2018
491 British Theatre.com 1/4/2018
492 The Arts Shelf 4/5/2018
493 The Guardian 10/3/1990
494 Daily Mail 10/3/1990
495 Weekend Telegraph 10/3/1990
496 Country Life 8/3/1990
497 The Listener 22/3/1990
498 Financial Times 10/3/1990
499 The Guardian 10/3/1990
500 *Second From Last in the Sack Race* programme, 1990
501 *Making Space for Theatre*, Mulryne and Shewring, p. 76
502 Ibid pp. 76,79
503 The Listener 22/3/1990
504 *Architecture, Actor and Audience*, by Iain Mackintosh p.137
505 Ibid, p.138
506 5:1:7 page 30
507 Page 2
508 Report of the Administrative Director to Board Meeting, 6/7/1994
509 Report of the Director of City Development to Leeds City Council Executive Board 17/7/1017
510 Page / Park website
511 *Play On* by Alistair Fair, p. 177
512 The Guardian, 22/6/2018
513 Yorkshire Post 3/9/2018
514 Yorkshire Post 3/9/2018
515 British Theatre Guide, undated
516 What's On Stage 10/9/2018
517 The Guardian 19/10/2018
518 British Theatre Guide, undated
519 BritishTheatre.com 18/10/2018
520 The Culture Vulture 27/11/2018
521 Yorkshire Post 12/3/2019
522 British Theatre Guide, undated
523 Ibid
524 The Stage 16/3/2019
525 Yorkshire Post 12/3/2019
526 The Culture Vulture 7/3/2019
527 Yorkshire Times 16/5/ 2019
528 The Wharfdale Observer
529 The Guardian 17/10/2019
530 British Theatre Guide, undated
531 The Guardian 19/10/2019
532 BritishTheatre.com 20/10/2019
533 Northern Soul 22/10/2019
534 British Theatre Guide, undated
535 What's On Stage 27/11/2019
536 Ramps on the Moon website
537 The Observer 8/3/2020
536 The Stage 5/3/2020
538 The Guardian 26/2/2020
539 The Stage 5/3/2020
540 The Culture Vulture 20/5/2021
541 Nick Brown: Architects website
542 Skyscraper City website, 3/6/2019
543 The Times 16/12/2022

544   *Stirring up Sheffield*, by Colin George **and** Ted George, p. 131
545   Interview, 12/3/2020
546   Interview, 10/3/2023
547   *In Our Neighbourhood*, by Dick Downing, p. 20
548   Ibid p. 20
549   The Stage 05/03/1998
550   Evening Standard 05/03/1998
551   Chairman's Statement to the 1997/1998 Annual General Meeting
552   Obituary – Leeds Playhouse/Friends of the Playhouse: 1968-2014, undated.
553   Quoted in *Engage, Reengage and Grow*, Audience Development Strategy 2015-2018, p. 6

Bibliography

Arts Council England / BOP Consulting, *Analysis of Theatre in England*, Arts Council England, 2016

Arts Council of England, *Consultative Green Paper on Drama in England*, The Arts Council of England, 1995

Arts Council of England, *The Next Stage: Towards a National Policy for Theatre in England*, The Arts Council of England, 2000

Arts Council of Great Britain, *The Theatre Today in England and Wales*, The Arts Council of Great Britain, 1970

Atha, Bernard Peter, *Variety, the Spice of Life*, Novum Publishing, 2019

Bailey, John, *A Theatre for All Seasons: Nottingham Playhouse, the First Thirty Years 1948-1978*, Alan Sutton Publishing Ltd., 1994

Bradwell, Mike, *The Reluctant Escapologist: Adventures in Alternative Theatre*, Nick Hern Books, 2010

Chambers, Colin, *Black and Asian Theatre in Britain: a History*, Routledge, 2011

Downing, Dick, *In Our Neighbourhood: a regional theatre and its local community*, Joseph Rowntree Foundation, 2001

Fair, Alistair, *Play On; Contemporary Theatre Architecture in Britian*, Lund Humphries, 2019

Fair, Alistair, *Modern Playhouses: An Architectural History of Britain's New Theatres, 1945-1985*, Oxford University Press, 2018

George, Colin & Tedd George, *Stirring Up Sheffield*, Wordville, 2021

Griffiths, Trevor, *The Gulf Between Us*, Faber, 1992,

Harrison, John, *Not Quite Famous: A Life in the Theatre*, Birmingham Stage Company Publishing, 2004

Hutton, Dan, *Towards a Civic Theatre*, Salamander Street, 2021

Hytner, Nicholas, *Balancing Acts: Behind the Scenes at the National Theatre*, Vintage, 2017

Leeds Theatre in Education Company, *Raj*, Amber Lane, 1984

Mackintosh, Iain, *Theatre Spaces 1920 — 2020, Finding the Fun in Functionalism*, Methuen Drama, 2023

Mackintosh, Iain, *Architecture, Actor & Audience*, Routledge, 1993

Mulryne, Ronnie & Margaret Shewring, *Making Space for Theatre: British Architecture and Theatre since 1958*, Mulryne and Shewring Ltd., 1995

National Campaign for the Arts, *Theatre in Crisis; the plight of regional theatre*, National Campaign for the Arts, 1998

Newlyn, Doreen, *Theatre Connections: a very personal story*, Walter Newlyn, 1995

Nyoni, Zodwa, *Nine Lives*, Methuen Drama, 2015

Peter Boyden Associates, *Roles and Functions of the English Regional Producing Theatres*, Peter Boyden Associates, 2000

Plater, Alan, *Close the Coalhouse Door*, Methuen Drama, 1969

Rowell, George & Anthony Jackson, *The Repertory Movement: A History of Regional Theatre in Britain*, Cambridge University Press, 1984

Turnbull, Olivia, *Bringing Down the House: The Crisis in Britain's Regional Theatres*, Intellect Books, 2008

Wilson, Colin, *Strindberg*, Random House, New York, 1972

Wooster, Roger, *Theatre In Education In Britain: Origins, Development and Influence*, Bloomsbury Methuen Drama, 2016

Programme Notes

Alphabetical Indices of Actors, Directors, Other Players and Productions

Naked Eye Publishing

A fresh approach

Naked Eye Publishing is an independent not-for-profit micro-press intent on publishing quality poetry and literature, including in translation which is a particular focus.

Our potted thesis series publishes well researched and interesting non-fiction titles. These are written in an engaging style for the general reader.

Each of us at Naked Eye is a volunteer, competent and professional in our work practice, and not intending to make a profit for the press. We see ourselves as part of the revolution in book publishing, embodying the newly levelled playing field, sidestepping the publishing establishment to produce beautiful books at an affordable price with writers gaining maximum benefit from sales.

nakedeyepublishing.co.uk

9 781910 981306